the tank man's son

the tank man's son

A MEMOIR

MARK BOUMAN

WITH D. R. JACOBSEN

Tyndale House Publishers, Inc., Carol Stream, Illinois

Visit Tyndale online at www.tyndale.com.

TYNDALE and Tyndale's quill logo are registered trademarks of Tyndale House Publishers, Inc.

The Tank Man's Son: A Memoir

Copyright © 2015 by Mark Bouman. All rights reserved.

Cover typography created by Raymedamiedo. Used with permission.

Cover texture copyright © Lost & Taken. All rights reserved.

Cover photograph of soldier copyright © Kletr/Shutterstock. All rights reserved.

Cover photograph of tank tracks copyright © Regien Paassen/Shutterstock. All rights reserved.

Cover photograph of child copyright © DOF-PHOTO by Fulvio/Getty Images. All rights reserved.

Designed by Ron Kaufmann

Edited by Jonathan Schindler

Published in association with the literary agency of D. C. Jacobson & Associates LLC, an Author Management Company. www.dcjacobson.com.

Scripture taken from the Holy Bible, *New International Version*,® *NIV*.® Copyright © 1973, 1978, 1984, 2011 by Biblica, Inc.® (Some quotations may be from the earlier NIV edition, copyright © 1984.) Used by permission. All rights reserved worldwide.

Library of Congress Cataloging-in-Publication Data
Bouman, Mark.
   The tank man's son : a memoir / Mark Bouman with D.R. Jacobsen.
      pages cm
      ISBN 978-1-4143-9027-7 (sc)
   1. Bouman, Mark. 2. Bouman, Mark—Childhood and youth. 3. Families—Michigan—Biography. 4. Fathers and sons—Michigan—Biography. I. Jacobsen, D. R. II. Title.
   CT275.B58516A3 2015
   306.8742—dc23   2015004794

Printed in the United States of America

21   20   19   18   17   16   15
 7   6   5   4   3   2   1

To my sons,

Andrew and Nik

CONTENTS

PUBLISHER'S NOTE

Dear Reader:

The story you are about to read is true. The events depicted include vulgar language of a kind that typically doesn't appear in books we publish. But after careful consideration, we decided to include some dialogue that, though potentially offensive, is accurate, helps to capture the intensity of the events in an authentic way, and gives a truthful illustration of the human condition.

AUTHOR'S NOTE

THIS MEMOIR IS based on events that happened across nearly five decades, including events that occurred before I was born. I have tried to tell my story truthfully. For the sake of clarity, in some places I have chosen to use composite events, dialogue, and chronology, and I have changed some names and details to protect the privacy of individuals. As with any memoir, this version of my story is uniquely mine.

PROLOGUE

WHAT DID IT MEAN to be the Tank Man's son? It was as if Mark Bouman didn't exist—as if I were simply another object for my father to crush.

When I was a boy, I dreamed about freedom. I imagined fleeing my home in Michigan and escaping to the wide-open spaces of Montana, hunting and fishing to my heart's content. Montana was wild and unspoiled. In my dreams I always lived alone.

Yet I could not run away. My entire life was controlled and dominated by my father. I scarcely knew what to do when I had a few hours to myself. Being outdoors was my only joy—sometimes with my brother, more often alone with my dog—and a thin joy it was. It was less like joy and more like the temporary absence of fear and pain. There were fleeting moments in which fear didn't cling to my back, whispering to me in my father's voice. There were minutes and occasional hours when I forgot to remain alert for an openhanded slap. But always, real life returned full force.

The indelible image of my childhood is the brutal silhouette of my father's tank. His tank was a machine made for a single purpose: power. So it was with Dad. Whatever the end on which he happened to fix his attention, his family became nothing more than a means.

The story of my father's brutality is, perhaps, unusual enough to warrant a book. He was not entirely sane, and his particular brand of insanity was both conspicuous and cruel.

And the story of my suffering—and the suffering of my brother, my sister, and my mother—may be universal enough to warrant a book. We suffered greatly. We emerged on the other side of Dad's wrath as changed people, some more broken than others. But as I've written these stories, marveling anew at their nearly unbelievable strangeness and their casual viciousness, I've sensed something bigger hiding in the margins.

There lurks within these stories hints of something even stronger than my father—something not just stronger than a tank, but stronger than the human heart. Stronger even than the past.

How did I not simply *die* on those eleven acres of Michigan sand and scrub? How did the cowering, belt-whipped boy I was become the man I am today? How did I, the child of an abusive father, become a father myself—one who would gladly die for his boys and who loves them more than life itself?

Looking back, the plot of my life seems too incredible *not* to be true. But if I could tell my childhood self that one day he'd thank God for his father—well, that boy would laugh in my face. Or curse me.

Back in Michigan, my life resembled one of the trees on our land. I could grow in fits and starts, but no matter how high I reached, one day I would be crushed beneath my father's tank. Resistance was impossible. A broken trunk couldn't be resilient. And no matter what happened to me, I was, and always would be, the Tank Man's son.

PART ONE
A HOME

1

THE OAK TREE STOOD a dozen feet taller than the top of my father's tank. From where I was watching, I could feel the vibration rumbling up through the ground. Our eleven acres were peppered with trees, big and small, but ever since Dad had fired up his army tank for the first time, the number was steadily decreasing. Dad motored toward the oak at a walking pace. I could see the outline of his head sticking up through the driver's hatch. He was making subtle course corrections to keep his right-hand tread lined up with the tree. The tank halted several feet from the trunk, and the noise of the engine lowered for a moment.

Then a roar as the tank lurched forward. The tread hit the tree trunk dead center, and the tank climbed slowly upward. Foot by foot, with the engine snarling in time, the machine rose into the air. The tree strained against the increasing weight. It leaned backward, bending and shaking, and even above the noise of the tank I could hear groans and staccato pops from inside the oak. The tank pointed toward the clouds as if launching from a ramp, and then, with a sudden crack, the oak died, its trunk shattering even as its roots were torn from the earth. The tank slammed down and rolled forward, pulverizing the branches into splinters and grinding the now-useless roots into the ground.

I imagined taking my father's place at the controls, lifting the tank up and over a mighty tree and forcing it to the ground just like he did. It would feel exhilarating. It would terrify me. But I would win. I would be the one in charge, the one with the power. Nothing could stand up to that kind of power.

The tank turned toward me, continuing to roll. Ten feet before it reached me, its treads jerked to a halt. My father looked down at me from the hatch. I watched his lips move, scarcely able to hear him over the engine's growl. It took me a moment to realize what he'd shouted to me.

"Hey! Mark! Want to drive?"

•　　•　　•

Long before he became the Tank Man, Dad had been a kid, just like me. He had two parents and a little home in Grand Rapids, Michigan, with a finished basement and lace curtains and a set of Sunday china. He learned to ride a bike and write book reports and sweep the sidewalk. He grew taller and stronger and learned to swear and throw a punch. He taught himself to drive when he was still in middle school, pushing his dad's '39 Ford van out of the driveway and then starting it once he was a block down the road.

By the time he was thirteen, he was shuttling his mom to town so she could pick up groceries or supplies for the beauty parlor she ran in a small shop attached to the house. By the time he was fourteen and his parents sat him down to tell him that a divorce didn't mean they loved him any less, he had already turned his gaze out to the world—past Grand Rapids, past Michigan, out toward the horizon where there might be something better, just waiting for him to discover it and make it his own.

When he was fifteen, he joined his father on a trip to "see the world"—or at least the world between Michigan and the Grand Canyon. It took them three days, sharing the driving along the way. On the second day, when his father was snoring in the passenger seat, Dad slammed into the back of another car. By the time the highway patrol officer left with his report, Grandpa Bouman had everyone convinced that he'd been the one driving while Dad rode shotgun. Whether they hiked down into the canyon or took pictures or just sat quietly at the edge, Dad never chose to relate. The only parts of the story he cared to tell were the long drive and the sudden crash.

By the time he was sixteen, Dad talked his mother into signing a waiver that let him join the United States Navy. He said good-bye to her, didn't bother saying good-bye to his dad or his dad's new wife, Ginn, and hitched a ride to the Greyhound station. With his duffel bag slung over the chip on his shoulder, he stepped off the bus at the Great Lakes Naval Training Center outside Chicago, determined to make a name for himself. Next came Jacksonville, Florida, where he spent eighteen months discovering his knack for repairing engines on carrier planes like the T-34 and the F3D. That was the year the pilot of a twin-engine Beechcraft, a lieutenant, stuck his head in the maintenance hangar and asked for a volunteer to join him on a short flight to an air base up the coast. On the return trip to Jacksonville, the pilot asked if Dad knew how to fly.

"Yep, you bet!" came the instant answer. Dad flew most of the way back before the pilot realized Dad was improvising. That was how Dad lived: ready to try anything, supremely confident—often with no reason to be so—and always able to let consequences slide off his shoulders like water off a duck.

While waiting to turn eighteen, Dad struck up a friendship with Stew. Stew was Dad's kind of guy: independent, bold, and unafraid to tell everyone, including his superiors, what he really thought. They talked about guns and fast motorcycles and made lists of the know-nothing officers they'd like to teach lessons to. They spent their base leave in Jacksonville together, cutting up and causing trouble in the bars and pool halls. And it was sometime during their time together that Stew clued Dad in to the *real* cause of all the world's troubles.

The three of us Bouman kids—me, my older brother, Jerry, and my younger sister, Sheri—grew up knowing who Stew was. Dad would flip right to the picture of him in the photo album and tap his finger, and we would pretend to study the snapshot we'd already seen dozens of times. Stew sat ramrod straight in a wooden chair, wearing a crisply pressed Nazi uniform with swastika bands on each sleeve. His daughter stood behind him, one hand on her father's shoulder. She wore a Hitler Youth uniform, and behind the two of them was draped a Nazi flag.

"You kids know not to ask questions," Dad would say and then close the album.

Shortly after meeting Stew, Dad persuaded a squad of cadets to goose-step around the base, a stunt that earned him a trip to the psych ward for evaluation. In the early 1950s, so close to the end of the Second World War, the naval brass figured no one would be crazy enough to ape the Nazis unless he was *actually* crazy. My mother later told me that Dad was given a Section 8—that was how they discharged people judged unfit for military service, like homosexuals and the mentally ill. Dad's version of the story was different: his naval career ended when he punched some know-nothing officer who had it coming. Still, an honorable discharge arrived in Grandma Jean's mailbox, owing to the intervention of a family friend who happened to be a congressman from the great state of Michigan.

Maybe Dad would have left the Navy on his own, even if he'd never met Stew. It wouldn't have taken Nazi ideology to persuade my father to punch an officer—he would have done that on a dare. Either way, by age eighteen, Dad found himself out of the Navy, officially a man, and with no idea what to do next. If he'd been more driven and hard-working, perhaps he would have struck out on his own and moved to

Detroit or Chicago. He could have done what other young men did: find a job, make friends, date a local girl, and begin a new life. Maybe save up for a new sedan or a starter home. Join a bowling league or the local chapter of the Elks. Instead, he moved into his mother's basement, avoided work, smoked two packs a day, and filled out his six-foot-two frame with another forty pounds of muscle.

At the same time that Dad was lounging on his mother's couch and reading anti-Semitic books and military manuals about how to assemble land mines, Mom was making a name for herself at Unity Christian High School. She played first-chair French horn in the school orchestra and edited the school newspaper. She represented Unity at the state debate championship and placed second. Her unfailingly honest and responsible parents were no-nonsense workers—her father a carpenter, her mother a nurse's aid—who expected their children, Mom and her older sister, Janie, to take care of themselves and keep their heads down. They had moved the family from Arkansas to Michigan years before so the girls could attend a good Christian school. They never gave the girls birthday presents or celebrated holidays. Surviving the Great Depression had taught them that having fun was simply too expensive.

One summer afternoon, Mom drove Janie to Holland Beach on the shore of Lake Michigan. They planned on spending the afternoon swimming and lying in the sun. It was a popular place to see and be seen, and it also happened to be free. That same summer afternoon, Dad took his mother's car and drove to Holland Beach as well. Cruising the parking lot, he spotted two ponytailed teenagers sitting inside a Buick sedan. He eased his own car to a stop beside theirs. The girl in the passenger seat was cuter, but the girl in the driver's seat was closer, and her wide smile revealed her perfect teeth, so my father decided to simply go with what was right in front of him.

"Would you like to go see a movie?" he asked Mom.

That was that. From then on they were a couple. At least that was the way Dad remembered it: simple and to the point.

Mom's version was a bit different. They met at the beach, but it was Janie who first met Dad while they were swimming. She invited him back to shore to share their picnic, and Dad took the opportunity to suggest that the three of them see a movie together. Once they had eaten, Janie drove, with Mom in the middle and Dad on the outside. It thrilled Mom to sit next to Dad since it was Janie who always attracted the attention from boys.

On the drive home, the warm summer air whipped through the open windows, swirling Dad's thick black hair.

"What did you think of the movie?" Mom ventured.

"It was okay," he quickly answered, "but I really prefer war movies. And Westerns. I try to catch a movie at least once a week."

"Really?" Mom was incredulous. "You must have a great job!"

Dad hedged. "Actually I'm between jobs right now. I just got out of the Navy, so . . ."

Mom found herself looking sideways, not for the first time, her eyes tracing his strong arm draped along the edge of the rolled-down window. "What did you do in the Navy?"

"Aircraft mechanic," he replied smartly. "I haven't decided yet what to do for a job. I'm taking my time. Since I just got home, I'm not in any big hurry."

He grinned. Mom couldn't believe it. No big hurry to work? Movies once a week? Free to do whatever he wanted—maybe even to put one of those arms around her shoulders while they drove through the back roads together?

Dad looked at the sisters. He wanted to ask Janie out, since she was prettier, but that would have been awkward with Mom sitting between them. And here is where their memories come together, with Dad asking Mom if she'd like to go out to a movie again. Mom knew it was wrong to date, wrong to have fun, wrong for a high school student to cut loose with an ex-Navy man. And Mom knew just as surely that she wouldn't—couldn't—say no to the excitement Dad offered.

"Sure," she said, hoping he couldn't see the color rising to her cheeks. However it happened, the results were the same. As the summer ended and the school year began, Dad and Mom began dating in secret. To a girl who never went off script, Dad's fearlessness and disregard for convention seemed like a godsend. Maybe life didn't have to be as safe and boring as it had always been. Maybe her parents had been wrong about duty being the most important thing in life. Dad wanted to have all the fun he could at every moment he could, and that answered nearly every longing Mom had ever felt. She was newspaper, and Dad was a lit match.

Mom's decision to date Dad was the first crack in the facade of her exemplary life, and soon nearly everything crumbled. Dad stole money from his mother's beauty parlor so he could show Mom the kind of good time they both deserved. They drove too fast and snuck into dance halls. They saw the latest movies and kissed by the lake. She was a sixteen-year-old kid who lived miles from town—a kid with parents whose idea of a fun Saturday was to go fishing and then return home to clean and salt the fish. It's no wonder she felt free the moment she hopped into Dad's front seat and roared down the country roads toward anywhere but home.

Dad became Mom's only friend. More than that, he became her world. Her homework sat untouched for days at a time, and she dropped out of the school play. Her French horn gathered dust beneath her bed. When she heard about a job answering phones and filing documents for an insurance company, she dropped out of school, because what was the point in pretending? All she wanted was to be with Dad, and he'd take care of her as long as they stayed together. He picked her up from work every evening, and every morning she counted the hours until she could see him again. Her father was angry, but her mother was more than happy to save the school tuition every month. Mom overheard her mother telling her father, "If she wants to ruin her life, at least it won't cost us anything."

Mom smiled to herself. The only thing her mother seemed to care about was saving money, but Mom had found a way to make money and have fun at the same time. There was so much more to life than what her parents had allowed her to experience, and if she had to leave them behind, she would. She'd found her future in my father.

Several months later, Mom walked out of the bathroom she shared with her sister and blurted out, "Janie, I'm *sick*."

"What do you mean? Sick how?"

"*Pregnant* sick," Mom groaned, feeling the urge to vomit again.

Her parents knew Mom had a secret life, but they didn't know the half of it. Mom's questions spilled out as tears streamed down her cheeks. "*Now* what am I going to do? What will Mom and Dad say? What's going to happen?"

"You'll need to tell them soon," Janie said. "It won't help any if you wait."

A few hours later, her father arrived home from his construction job. He sat down at the kitchen table, reading the paper while he waited for his wife to finish making dinner. Janie and Mom entered the kitchen.

"She needs to talk to both of you," Janie announced, then stepped out of the way.

Her father lowered his paper and peered at his younger daughter over his thick, black reading glasses. Her mother stopped midturn on the linoleum, holding a plate of pickled beets.

"What's wrong?" she asked in a low tone.

Mom couldn't speak, so her sister spoke for her. "She thinks she might be pregnant."

Mom burst into tears, her head bobbing up and down from the great heaving sobs that swelled inside and threatened to overwhelm her.

"Well," pronounced her father, "that's a fine mess you've got yourself into."

"I'm *so* sorry," Mom managed, finding her father's eyes.

"Sorry doesn't solve the problem, now does it?" he said.

Janie moved to put her arms around Mom, hoping to console her.

"You'll have to marry that boy," her mother said as she resumed her dinner preparations. "If you're pregnant, then you're on your own. You know that. You've brought this on yourself. Don't expect us to help."

A child choosing to ruin her life was nothing an upstanding parent should stand in the way of. Mom stared at the floor, hearing the newspaper crinkle as her father went back to reading, hearing her mother at the chopping board, feeling her sister's arms. That's when Mom realized two things: that she'd have to marry Dad, and that it was the last thing she wanted to do.

Not that she had a choice. Ending her pregnancy wasn't an option for her, and her parents were kicking her out, so keeping the baby at home wasn't an option either. In 1958, in rural Michigan, independent single mothers simply didn't exist, especially ones without a high school diploma. Over the years, her parents had made sure Mom knew that good and honest people never became pregnant out of wedlock—and if they did, God forbid, they got married immediately.

That advice would have been easier to follow if her parents hadn't made such a point of convincing her that Dad would never make a good husband.

Mom was trapped between truths, and the only way forward was a wedding. Except a wedding was impossible. None of the parents would attend or help pay for it. Mom didn't have the emotional strength to organize even a civil marriage ceremony, so Janie took it upon herself to arrange things. She was the only one present when Dad and Mom stood in front of a justice of the peace at the courthouse in Grand Rapids and promised to love each other for better or worse, in sickness and in health, until death parted them.

Dad's mother couldn't bear the thought of the couple starting their married life living in a car, which is exactly what Mom and Dad would have been forced to do, so she bought them a trailer—a steal at $250 because it had been damaged in a flood and the previous owners had moved out. After the ceremony at the courthouse, Dad's stepmom, Grandma Ginn, hosted a reception at her place: a simple cake, some photos, and an hour of awkward small talk. Then the happy couple drove back to their water-stained trailer to begin life together as man and wife.

That was late winter 1958. Dad was nineteen, and Mom was seventeen. Jerry was born just over six months later. I was born two years after that, and Sheri two years after me. We were the Boumans, a clan of five crammed into a trailer in Cannon, Michigan, trying to make our way in the world.

2

THERE WASN'T A SINGLE DAY when Mom and Dad didn't loathe their moldy trailer, but it was their only option, year after year. It was already a pit when Grandma Jean bought it for them—it had electricity at least, but no running water—and adding one, two, and then three children didn't improve it. Neither did Dad's habit of burning through whatever meager pay he earned. Dad was working a string of dead-end, nonunion jobs, then cashing his checks so he could treat himself to dinner and a movie. When he got fired from one job—for lying about his qualifications, for insulting his boss, for bringing a pistol to work and threatening someone—he'd just move on to the next.

Mom, meanwhile, was in survival mode. Besides scrounging food, lugging water, washing diapers by hand, and trying to keep track of us kids, she had her husband to care for. Since he was out winning bread, he expected Mom to keep him clothed and fed. He made rules on the fly, which she was expected to follow—no matter how unreasonable—or face the consequences.

Early on there was often little or no food at the trailer, so Dad and Mom would drive to Grandma Jean's house for dinner. Dad would usually disappear into the basement by himself while Mom helped prepare the meal.

"I bought you some food," Grandma Jean said once. "It's in the entryway near the door, and you can take it with you tonight after dinner."

"I don't understand him," Mom said, struggling not to cry. "He won't get a job. I work all day, and he just sits around and plays. He's either eating out or running around with his friends."

"Well, I thought he might have some trouble being a good husband. He never learned to work hard. When he was living here, after the Navy, I told him to save money for a rainy day, but he wouldn't listen. And now it's pouring."

"I wish I knew what to do. He won't listen to me."

"Well," Grandma Jean said, "he didn't listen to *me* much either."

•   •   •

Despite his habit of spending his time and money however and wherever he wanted, Dad must have sensed that he needed to get his family out of that trailer—or at least get himself out. He hated it every bit as much as the rest of us did, and so he schemed his way toward a real house.

His plan started with empty land, which was all my parents could afford on his typical fifty-dollars-a-week pay. After asking around for a few months, Dad was able to get eleven acres outside town in Belmont, nearly every square foot of which was covered in sand. Other than growing oak trees and a type of weed with heavy, barbed burs, the sand was useless for almost everything else. It couldn't be cultivated, it made a poor foundation for building, and it was crisscrossed by constantly shifting ruts, dunes, and ridges. Still, land was land, and by the time Sheri was toddling around and Jerry was starting school, Mom and Dad owned eleven acres of it. Dad paid a man to jack the family trailer off the ground and tow it the fifteen miles to their new homestead. Same old trailer, same young family, both in a brand-new setting.

At first, it was an even worse setting for Mom. Not only was she farther from town, but the land had no running water, and she was immediately forced to ask the closest neighbors for help. Apparently water wasn't something Dad had considered before relocating the trailer, or else it was something he simply assumed Mom would take care of.

And she did. Dressed in slacks and a light blouse, her long, dark hair swaying behind her, she marched down one sandy hill, up another, and through a collection of cars in need of repair, until she found herself at the front door of a typical Michigan split-level home.

"Come on in," said the woman who answered. "Name's Emmy. Emmy Dietz. Sit down for a minute and have a cup of tea."

"That's okay, I just came over to see if I can get a jug of water from your spigot. We don't have water yet."

Emmy gave Mom an evaluating once-over. "Of course you can use our spigot, sweetie, but first come in for a spell."

Emmy held open the door until Mom entered, then gestured toward the kitchen table. "Just pull up a chair there and push that stuff out of the way until you can sit down."

Mom moved a pile of magazines and some dish towels, clearing a place for herself, and Mrs. Dietz set a mug in front of her with a tea bag in it.

"The water will heat up in just a minute," Emmy said as she cleared another place at the table, causing a few of the magazines to tumble to the floor. "So how's things going, living out here in the boonies? It's a bit too far from town for most people, but we like it that way. Nice and quiet." She smiled.

"It's quiet all right," Mom agreed. "It'd be a whole lot easier if we had water and a phone. My husband says he's going to get a well drilled, but we don't have the money yet."

"Aren't you building a house? How do you build a house without water?" Emmy chuckled. "I thought you're supposed to put in a well and *then* a house. What's that husband of yours thinking?"

"I don't know," Mom admitted. She stared at her cup.

"Ah, he'll figure it out!" Emmy added, rising to take the hissing kettle off the stove. She poured hot water into Mom's cup, returned the kettle to the stove, and took a framed family photo off a shelf, placing it in front of Mom. Everyone in the picture was dressed in plaid.

"Take some sugar," she said, plopping two cubes in the hot tea. Then she pointed with her fingertip at the children in the picture. "This is Darwin, our oldest. Then this is our daughter, Judy. Here's Tim, and then Mike. Want a cookie?"

Mom shook her head and took a sip of her sweet tea. "You have a wonderful family," she ventured. "Your youngest looks about the age of my boys."

"We're not rich, that's for sure, but we're a good family! We're just trying to pay the bills like everyone else." Emmy leaned back in her chair. "Les never finished school, so he can't read, but my kids are going to learn and stay in school, or I'll let them have it." She shook her fist for emphasis.

When Mom's tea was gone, she stood up to leave. "Thank you, but I need to get back to the house with the water."

"No problem at all. Our well is only sixty-five feet down, but it has lots of water."

Mrs. Dietz walked Mom to the door, then watched as she carried her plastic jug to the spigot and filled it. "You come over *any* time you need water, honey," she called.

Mom offered a grateful smile and then turned to the task of carrying her sloshing, forty-pound load back to the trailer.

While Mom didn't care for this new arrangement, Jerry and I loved our new land. It was a vast, sandy playground, and our favorite thing to play was army. Dad had given us a large bucket brimming with green plastic army men, and the sand made the perfect battlefield. Before each battle, we'd divvy up the soldiers. Some tossed grenades, some crouched behind machine guns or aimed rifles, and some held pistols, but my favorite was the grunt with the bazooka on his shoulder.

Once, as we dug walls and pits in the sand to protect our armies, Sheri announced that she was going to play with us. I stopped digging and looked up at her. A doll dangled from one hand, and she was scratching her hair with the other.

"You can't play," I informed her, returning to my important work. "You're a girl."

"I'm telling Mom!"

Jerry and I looked at each other and shrugged, then resumed our battle preparations. Once our fortifications were complete, combat consisted of lobbing rocks, one at a time, toward the other person's army. Any soldier knocked over or buried by a rock was considered dead, and the battle continued until one side was completely out of commission. We had learned that it was best to spread our armies out across a wide swath of sand, thus eliminating the chance that a single well-placed rock could end the battle.

Minutes later, Mom arrived. Hands on her hips, she declared, "You boys need to include your sister when you play! She has no one else to play with out here."

Sheri stood defiantly by Mom's side, glaring at us. Jerry and I both sighed.

"Oh, all *right*," I relented, motioning her over. "Come on."

Mom left as Sheri skipped over to our battlefield. "What do I do?"

Jerry explained the game to Sheri, step by step, all the while redividing the plastic soldiers into three piles. I ground my teeth in frustration— how could he be so patient? She stared at the little green men, turning them over in her hands until Jerry reached the end of his explanation.

"So what's *this* guy?"

"He has a grenade," Jerry answered.

"What's *that*?"

I couldn't take it anymore. "Don't you know anything?"

She threw a question back at me. "What does he *do*?"

"He *throws* it, *duh*," I said, as if every preschool girl should know about grenades. Was she going to ask about every single weapon? "Just put them in the sand so we can start our war!"

Sheri knelt down, and after scooping out some low depressions in the sand, she placed her men in neat little rows, shoulder to shoulder.

I snorted, and she looked up at me. "Just a *minute*—they all gotta stand up *straight!*"

When she was finished, Jerry announced that he would take the first turn. He grabbed one of our stockpiled rocks, took a step back, and pitched toward my base. His opening salvo took two of my riflemen out of action.

Sheri went next. She could hardly lift her stone, and her first throw landed harmlessly in the sand, well short of either opposing base. She stamped her foot.

"My turn," I said, choosing my favorite rock. It was smooth and had the ability to roll after it landed, causing collateral damage. I took careful aim, wound up, and lobbed a perfect bomb into the heart of Sheri's base. Her entire army fell like dominoes.

"Aaand . . . they're dead," I announced.

She stamped her foot again. "Not fair! You knocked 'em down all at once!"

"I guess you shouldn't have put them so close together," I said.

"But I didn't know!"

"Well, now you do."

"I don't want to play your dumb army game anyway!" Sheri stormed off. I was glad to see her go, and Jerry didn't seem to mind either. Without a word, we drafted her fallen soldiers back into our armies, preparing for the coming fight.

•   •   •

All three of us were united in our hatred of the sandburs, however. No matter what we did outside and how careful we were, they were like evil Velcro, attaching themselves to our shoelaces, socks, shorts, and even the backs of our shirts and our hair. Once latched on, they'd worm their minuscule hooks deeper and deeper, irritating our skin. Our shoelaces became so intertwined with clumps of burs that we could no longer untie our shoes. Removing the burs with our fingers was painful and usually pointless. Few came out, and more would quickly take their place.

While Jerry and Sheri and I were dealing with the burs, and Mom was lugging water up and down the sandy hills, Dad plunked down a good-sized chunk of his paycheck for private flying lessons.

When his desire for a real house became strong enough, though, it overpowered many of his lazier instincts. Dad already had plenty of land, and he struck gold at a county auction when he was able to purchase two entire houses for a grand total of two dollars. They were being torn down to make room for a new highway that the state was punching through a section of Grand Rapids. Dad picked those houses clean like a crow on roadkill: lengths of lumber, partial sheets of plywood, cinder blocks, cabinets, bathroom fixtures, pipes, and even the occasional straight nail.

Soon, atop one of our sandy hills nearest the road, there was a pile of building material bigger than our trailer. Over the days, weeks, and months that followed, we watched Dad slowly transform that pile into a new house. It was a simple rectangle built from cinder block, twenty feet by forty feet, set lengthwise where the driveway ended. He mapped out a kitchen, a living room, a laundry room, one bathroom, and three small bedrooms, all of which he framed with the scavenged wood. While we continued to live in the cramped trailer, the Bouman residence steadily took shape, and with each completed step came a bit more of the feeling that better things were in store for us.

•   •   •

"Dad, is our new house ready yet?"

I was trying to keep still so as not to bother Dad while he was working, but the sand and burs in my shoes made me shift from foot to foot.

Our new house wouldn't have sand in it like the trailer did, and now that the construction was almost done, I was starting to think about it more and more. I'd never lived in a house, but I could imagine what it would be like to live somewhere without mold growing on the walls, somewhere with a room big enough that I wouldn't bump into my family whenever I moved. I could also imagine my own bed. Jerry and Sheri and I were all crammed onto a single mattress, and between Jerry elbowing and kicking me and Sheri wetting the sheets, there weren't many nights when I got enough sleep.

"About a week," Dad answered.

Dressed as always in black leather shoes, white socks, khaki pants, and an untucked white shirt, he was working in front of a cinder block wall, just below one of the square window openings. I'd watched him use a trowel to smear wet cement in a line around the edge of the opening, and now he was holding a pane of glass in a thin frame. He lined up the glass with the opening and then pressed it against the wet cement, which oozed out around the edges like jelly from between two slices of Wonder Bread.

"There's another one done. I gotta finish a few things before we can move."

Dad turned to look at me. He seemed like a giant, building a house by hand and carrying windows as if they were one of our plastic dinner plates. Then he turned back to his work, lowering himself to one knee and pulling off his elastic silver watch with a single motion and slotting it in his pocket. His hands worked down in the cement bucket, kneading, then returned to the water bucket. When he drew them out, I watched water run down through the black hair on his powerful forearms. His wrists and hands were huge. Dirt and grime marked the creases of his fingers and the lines of his hands, and the edges of his fingernails were wide, black arcs.

More cement, another window, and no further conversation. I thought about the room behind the window Dad had just finished. It would be dry and warm and full of space. Dad continued to work in silence, and I watched. As he worked, his arms swung heavy and slow, slightly away from his body, as if they were too muscled to swing where everyone else's did. He walked differently than others did too—he'd pick a point ahead of him and march toward it without slowing. Tagging along in his wake at a store or a gun shop or a swap meet, I had watched people step aside for him, parting like grass in a strong wind. When I walked behind him, when I watched him work, his smell was a mixture of machine oil, sour sweat, and sunshine.

The gusting breezes ruffled Dad's hair, up and down and up again, like a bird's wing. When Mom called from the trailer behind us, it didn't seem like Dad heard. He switched on the outside light he had recently wired up and continued to work. I waited a minute longer, feeling the wind pick up speed. I could hear grains of sand spattering against the wall of the house and on the new windows. Then I turned my back on the house and walked home to the trailer.

•   •   •

When Dad came back from building, he yelled at Mom. "Potatoes? Again? Why can't you cook some real food?"

"Because you spent your paycheck on movies in town!" she yelled back.

Jerry and I were sitting on our bed, playing army men in the mountains and valleys of the blanket, and Sheri was lying beside us, sucking her thumb. I thought about how cool it would be to go to a war movie in town with Dad, but he always went to movies alone. When Mom stuck her head in and told us to get our jackets on, we knew all of us would be eating dinner at Grandma Jean's. Dad's mom had pointy eyeglasses and a house full of curtains and carpet. On the drive over, we rode in silence, and I saw lightning flash in the distance.

By the time dinner was over, rain was beating down on Grandma's roof so loudly that we had trouble hearing one another talk. By the time Dad had polished off the apple pie and decided it was time to brave the storm, rain was pelting sideways against the windows. Our car swerved and shook as we drove back to the trailer.

We turned off the gravel road. "I hope you can make it up," Mom said.

Deep ruts cut back and forth across the sand driveway as if a giant crayon had scribbled them. The torrential rain had gouged them even deeper, and the car lurched back and forth as Dad tried to steer around the worst of them. The headlights, when they were pointed at the ground, showed us a driveway that looked more like a muddy river than a road. An occasional flash of lightning revealed oaks waving and bending all around us. One of Mom's hands was pressed to the ceiling, and in the backseat we bounced crazily into one another. It might have been fun if it hadn't been so frightening.

There was a sudden pitch forward and the engine died, and in the second or two of relative silence that followed, I could hear gasoline sloshing in the tank. Dad opened the door and stuck a leg out, announcing as he did that we'd just walk the rest of the way and get the car out in the morning. But his instructions were interrupted by Mom's near-hysterical voice.

"Wait, the light! Why can't we see the light up at the house yet?"

As rain poured in the open door, Dad squinted through the windshield into the darkness. The car headlights were aimed too low to help. The only thing we could see ahead of us, up the driveway, were raindrops and blackness. Dad turned to face Mom. "Don't worry. The house is still there."

Dad stepped out into the night, leaving the driver's door open. He trudged up the driveway, spanning the ruts without breaking stride. Lit by the headlights, he turned back to the car, cupped one hand around his mouth and shouted, "The power is probably out! Stay here while I get a flashlight!" Then he disappeared into the storm, and we were alone in the car. Mom's breath came faster and faster.

Several minutes later Dad's white shirt floated down toward us out of the darkness. He climbed into the driver's seat and slammed the door.

Raindrops ran out of his hair and down the back of his neck. He put both hands on the steering wheel.

"We're going back to Grandma's," he announced.

He cranked the engine once, twice, and when it caught the third time, he yanked the gearshift into reverse and floored it. There was a moment when nothing happened, and then the wheels found just enough traction to propel us backward down the hill. Dad spun the wheel hard right, and Jerry, Sheri, and I were smashed into one another in a pile against the door. Then we were bouncing down the driveway, sliding out onto the road, accelerating.

Mom stared at Dad. In a voice barely loud enough to hear, Dad answered her silent question. "It's gone."

Mom began to cry into her hands. I grabbed the back of the front seat and levered myself to my feet, ready to shout one of the dozen questions I'd just thought of. Jerry did the same. Dad killed our questions before they could begin with a single gesture, his right hand coming up into a fist below the rearview mirror. We plopped down and closed our mouths.

We drove back to Grandma Jean's through the black night. The drone of the car was interrupted only by Mom's sobs in the front seat. When Grandma opened the door, wearing her nightgown and holding a flashlight, she didn't seem surprised to see us.

The next morning, Grandma's voice woke us, calling us to the kitchen for oatmeal.

"Where's Mom?" Jerry asked.

"She and your father went to look at the house," Grandma answered, setting three steaming bowls in front of us and handing us silver spoons.

"But is Mom okay?" Sheri worried.

"She'll be fine," Grandma answered. "And you'll be fine if I get you some milk, hmm?" She poured it from a tall porcelain pitcher that matched our bowls.

Jerry lifted his bowl slightly off the table, examining the delicate designs traced around its rim. "Where'd you get these, anyway?"

"From England," Grandma replied. "Aren't they nice?"

"They look like they could break."

"Yes, they could," she agreed. "So we'll be careful, won't we?"

We nodded, Grandma nodded, and we ate the rest of our oatmeal in silence. It wasn't until lunchtime that Mom returned. Her face was still puffy and streaked with red. Sheri ran to her.

"Mom, are we going home now?"

"Yes, we're going back. The trailer is okay."

Jerry frowned. "The trailer! But what about the house?"

"It will . . ." Mom tried to answer, but stopped speaking until she could battle back a fresh round of sobs. Eventually she was able to finish. "It will be a while before we can move into the house, kids. There was a tornado."

Grandma walked us to the front door, and while we sat to tug on our shoes, she pressed a wad of money into Mom's hand.

"It'll be okay," she offered.

Mom nodded, but didn't speak. Grandma watched from the front door as we climbed back into the car and pulled away.

Back at home, we managed to inch our way up the driveway. There was the trailer, right where it always was, looking no worse than it always did. And there, at the top of the hill, perched jumbled piles of cinder blocks, topped with splintered wood. The walls had all been blown out, as if scattered like one of the sand castles Jerry and I liked to build and then destroy. The roof was lying in the valley behind the house.

Dad was still too stunned to say much. He kept walking around the pile of rubble, stopping now and then to touch a cinder block or a length of pipe.

"Mostly intact," he said more than once. "Mostly intact."

We kept living in our trailer. Dad had a deep well drilled near the top of the hill. And three months later, Dad announced that he was finished rebuilding the house and we could move in. The trailer stayed where it was. Dad tried to get rid of it, but no one would take it, even for free.

3

IN ONE WAY, moving into our new home drew a sharp line—on one side were our cramped, primitive trailer days, while on the other stretched a future filled with luxuries like our own beds, running water, and a living room where we could lie on the floor and play games of Monopoly by the woodstove. In other ways, however, life went on much the same as always. A different dinner table, maybe, but the same chronic shortage of food—and the same wandering days filled with exploration and battles and boredom and sand.

When Jerry started school, I didn't think much of it. While he was gone, I played by myself—except when Mom forced me to play with my sister—but since I slept late and the bus brought him back early, my routine remained much the same.

I had a vague sense of the year passing by and summer arriving—then Jerry and I *both* slept in—and suddenly it was time for me to start school as well. From what Jerry had told me, school wasn't anything much: just somewhere you had to go, and when the bell rang, you had to come back home again. Lunchtime sounded like one of the only bright spots. You could get a hot meal with fish sticks and Jell-O in a little cup and mashed potatoes that they slopped onto your tray with an ice cream scoop—for free. Recess didn't sound bad either, since you could play on a field of grass so big that it took a whole minute to run across it, with not a sandbur to be found.

Our refrigerator at home never had more than a few things in it: milk, a tub of leftovers from the night before—nearly always potatoes and some dry, flavorless meat—maybe some eggs, and a stick or two of butter. When Mom wanted to make us a treat, she'd use a boxed mix to bake a cake in a low, wide pan. She'd slide it, unfrosted, onto the bottom shelf of the fridge, and we'd use forks to scoop out however much we wanted to eat. I couldn't wait to try the cafeteria Jell-O.

On that first day, Dad didn't send me down the driveway to wait for the bus with Jerry. Instead, after I dressed in the same thing I always wore—brown corduroys, brown leather lace-up shoes, and a dirty T-shirt—I climbed into Dad's pickup truck. When we arrived at school, Dad led the way to my classroom, never turning to see if I was following. He walked directly to the front and interrupted the teacher, who was talking with another parent.

"If you have any problems with him, let me know. I'll take care of him when he gets home."

The teacher stammered that nothing like that would be necessary.

"Well, if you need to slap him upside the head, that'll be fine too. You won't hear any complaining from me."

The teacher looked past Dad and found me. Then a quick glance back to my dad. "No, no, that won't be needed, Mr. Bouman," she managed. "Ah, thank you anyway, but . . ."

Dad, without saying good-bye, was already out the door, forcing the incoming kids to step aside. I found my desk and sat down with my arms crossed. Then I found the wall clock and tried to count the minutes until lunch.

•   •   •

Despite starting school, though, the eleven acres of sand on Blakely Drive remained my world. Apart from school, we rarely left home, and if I wasn't doing a chore, and if there wasn't a blizzard or an ice storm, I spent almost all my time outside, usually with Jerry and sometimes with Sheri tagging along. Mom had a stock response to our complaints of boredom—complaints that only increased as we grew older and the shine of living alone in the boonies faded.

"Go outside and *play*," she'd always say, looking up from her laundry or her pressure cooker or her dustpan. "And take your sister with you!"

Jerry and I would slouch out the door, and nearly every time Sheri would ambush us.

"Where ya going?"

"Nowhere."

"Well, can I come?"

"We're just gonna walk around."

"But I wanna come too!"

Jerry and I would stand there, hoping she'd disappear. It wasn't that we didn't like our kid sister—it was that she ruined our fun just by tagging along.

"You know," I'd say, "we aren't even *going* anywhere."

"Yes you are! You already said so!"

"Fine. *Fine*. We're going to walk up that hill, through those thick, scratchy bushes."

We'd set off at a fast walk, and Sheri would have to pump her shorter legs to keep up. It didn't take long for the whining to start.

"Wait!" we'd hear from behind us. "*Wait!*"

"We're going exploring, Sheri, and if you want to explore, you have to keep up!"

"But where? I'll meet you!"

"We don't *know* where—we're exploring! Come on!"

"Forget it!" she'd yell and tromp back toward the house. Jerry and I would shrug, watch her go, and return to our exploration.

It didn't always happen like that, of course. Sometimes she managed to keep up with us for hours. She was a tough little kid, and she knew better than to try for sympathy from Jerry or me when she acquired a new scrape or bruise. Other times we managed to leave her at home by just sitting around outside until she became so bored that she wandered back inside, at which point we'd race into the woods without her. If she suggested a game, we'd ignore her, even if it was what we already wanted to play, like hide-and-seek. And when Jerry or I suggested a game, we tried to pick one she wouldn't want to play, like exploring or staging yet another skirmish in the sand with our army men.

Sheri's face was covered in freckles that stood out against her red cheeks whenever she worked hard or stuck her tongue out at us. Her toes had always pointed inward, which didn't so much slow her down as make her look like she was about to fall over when she raced ahead of us across the dirt or through the oak trees. She usually wore plaid pants—dirt-and-sand-colored plaid—and Mary Jane shoes, along with a white shirt, also stained.

Mom sometimes brought home toys Sheri could play with by herself, like an Easy-Bake Oven or small pieces of plastic furniture for her dolls, but Jerry and I made most of our own toys out of whatever grew and whatever we could scavenge from the junk Dad was always bringing home.

Jerry and I knew our property by heart, as if we'd built it for one of our miniature battles. From the street, our driveway lanced directly uphill for about a hundred yards, and at the top of that first hill sat our house. On one side of the house was the well pit, and on the other side was Dad's shed—which he had covered with a generous supply of tar paper. Leaning up against the shed were piles of hoses, pipes, and unfinished projects. Next to that, a broken generator perched atop its trailer, the trailer's tires long since empty of air. Wedged between the generator and the shed were large piles of rusted steel that had been lying there long enough that weeds grew up around them.

Next to the house was a level area where we parked Mom's Ford Custom and Dad's Ford pickup. There were two small valleys behind the house, both of which Dad figured out uses for. The first was our personal garbage dump, while the second was where he tossed or dragged his ever-growing collection of discarded vehicles. One, a rusting VW minibus, was filled with old tires, as well as what seemed like a million dead leaves that had blown in through the open windows. Beyond that rusted a motley collection of other equipment he'd acquired at swap meets, auctions, and estate sales.

The rest of the eleven acres was mostly rolling hills covered in trees and scrub, although there was also one noteworthy hill, a short jog past the edge of our property, that was covered in a thick grove of oak and maple trees. At the foot of the hill was a pond. Years before, whoever owned the land had attempted to dig a basement for a home, but it had filled with water, so he abandoned the whole project. It was deep enough that we had our own private swimming pool, as long as we didn't mind trespassing, swimming in cold, dirty water, and then hoofing it the half mile or so back home.

Even better, someone had tied a rope to one of the highest branches of the biggest oak atop the hill. We would grab the rope and walk backward until we stood on tiptoe with our arms stretched above our heads. Then we would race forward and leap, white-knuckled when the rope took our weight, watching the ground drop away below our windmilling legs as we swung, laughing, far into the air.

•   •   •

We couldn't spend all our time outside, of course, and although we had officially moved into the house soon after the tornado, Dad never properly finished it. The list of what was broken, unfinished, or ram-shackle was nearly endless. Maybe he'd been building things more care-fully at first, but after the tornado, he cut corners with a will. He even had a go-to response when an issue came up. It didn't matter whether the trouble was a missing chunk of drywall, an electric outlet that didn't work, or a door that wouldn't shut all the way—when a concern was brought to Dad's attention, he would fire back, "You know good and well I'm no finish carpenter!"

One night after Mom complained about something and Dad fed her his line, Jerry asked Dad exactly what he meant by the finish carpenter part. I was on my stomach in the living room, drawing with Sheri, and I looked up in time to see Dad slap Jerry across the face.

"I mean what I said, you imbecile!"

Jerry ran to his room and Mom raced after him while Dad went outside, slamming the door behind him. When Mom came back to the living room, I went to check on Jerry. He was on his bunk in the bedroom we shared, staring at the wall.

"Hey," I said. "You okay?"

"Yeah. Forget it."

"All right."

With nothing else to do, I lay in my bunk and looked around the room. The ceiling was bare Sheetrock, with the brand name and dimen-sions still stenciled on its peeling, yellow surface. When I was bored enough, I counted the hammer marks on it. Our closet was a single length of steel pipe held parallel to the wall with two brackets, and our dresser drawers fell onto the floor if we pulled them out past halfway. The window, like all the others I'd seen Dad install before the tornado, was a single pane of glass set against the cinder block wall with a flimsy frame and no insulation. When a really strong wind howled up, flakes of snow would eddy through the gaps around the window and float down to our floor, where they would slowly melt on the flower-patterned linoleum. In other words, our new room was a million times better than the trailer.

With Dad already outside, I hoped it would be a night we wouldn't be called upon to fix the pump in the well. Dad had cut a rectangular hole into the dirt around the well and installed an old pump and a reservoir tank. It was insulated so poorly, however, that the pump often seized, and Dad liked to say that Jerry and I were "just the right size" to climb down into the well and bash an old hammer against the side of the pump until it began running again.

When the well was first drilled, we were all grateful to have running water. However, the water contained so much iron and other metals and minerals that we could almost feel the grit between our teeth. Mom spit out the first sip she took, declaring it unfit for humans.

Dad must have tasted it too, because he didn't seem surprised when a salesman came a few days later to tell us about the latest in water-softening technology. We watched with interest as he collected water from our well in a small vial, then added drips and drops of various chemicals, periodically checking tables of colors and numbers in a three-ring binder. Then he announced that we had some of the hardest water he'd ever tested and that we'd need two complete filtration and injection systems, along with double the normal amount of salt.

We bought a single system. Jerry and I were supposed to add salt to the machine each week, but that lasted only until the initial supply of salt ran out, because when we told Dad it was time to buy more, he shrugged. From then on our softening system simply served as a conduit for our freakishly hard water. Mom still had to walk to the Dietzes' for drinking and cooking water every few days, taking Jerry with her to help lug it back. Dad had found an orange five-gallon plastic cooler, and it lived on the kitchen counter next to the sink. For the washing machine, however, Mom was forced to use the well water, and everything she washed turned yellow. T-shirts and underwear were the color of lemons after one wash, the color of urine after two, and a ruined, rusty orange not long after that. Evidence of the hard water collected all over the house: an orange stripe ringed the toilet, the water that came out of the showerhead turned two of the bathroom walls orange, and beneath each faucet that dripped—which was every faucet—there was a dark spot the size and color of a penny.

Dad looked at his honey-do list, looked at the condition of the house, and decided the next logical step would be to obtain a luxurious bathtub. One day he marched into the bathroom with a saw and cut a rectangular hole in the floor. He sawed right through the floor joists as well, and soon we could see clear down to the sand beneath the house, several feet below.

"I got a deal" was all he'd tell us.

When Mom got wind, she crossed her arms and declared, "This is going to look absolutely ridiculous—a *sunken* tub, in *this* house?"

Dad grinned like she'd walked into a trap. "You know, lots of the finest homes have sunken tubs."

The following day a man drove up in a truck and helped Dad unload the tub and muscle it into the bathroom. Dad took over from there, sliding it into place with pry bars and lowering it into the hole he'd cut. The top of the tub stuck up about six inches above the floor, creating a serious tripping hazard. The length, however, was an even bigger problem. The hole Dad had cut was about a foot too long.

"Not my fault," Dad grumbled. "They gave me the wrong dimensions! *Jumbo* tub, my ass."

There really wasn't a good way to cover the hole back up, given that Dad had removed all the joists, so he simply gave up on the entire project, leaving us with a semisunken tub and a one-foot gap.

•   •   •

The hole in the bathroom floor wasn't a problem for us kids. We loved it. One of our never-ending chores was to sweep up the sand that seemed to multiply in the house, and the hole made a perfect place to dump it without going outside.

The sand bothered Mom the most, and she got it in her head that a cement front porch would make a good place to kick off our sandy shoes, thus keeping the floors clean. Dad refused to pour one.

"Why don't you do it yourself if you're so fired up about it?" he griped.

The next day Mom called a cement truck. She scrounged some old pieces of wood from the yard and nailed them into rough forms around the front door. When the driver arrived, he took one look at the forms and refused to pour. He knew Mom's handiwork would simply buckle and allow the wet cement to ooze across the sand. After he and Mom just stood there for a minute, the driver asked Mom for Dad's toolbox and rebuilt the forms himself so that he could pour the cement. Since Mom didn't have any cash, she raided Dad's stash of ammunition and gave the man a few boxes of shotgun shells.

Two days later, when it dried, we had a real porch sure enough— although if it made any difference in the amount of sand inside, I couldn't tell.

The constant sand invasion was the reason for our excitement when a traveling salesman stopped by to demonstrate a Kirby vacuum. We actually dared to dream that our sweeping days would be over, since the vacuum, we were all assured, could run on both carpet and hard floors. We gathered in the living room, Dad in his armchair and Mom on the couch with the three of us. The salesman stood in the center of the room, talking about its wind-tunnel design and lifting capacity and precise manufacturing tolerances, after which he made eye contact with Mom and asked, "Ma'am, would you like to see a demonstration?"

He unwound the power cord with a practiced flourish and plugged it into the wall. On the way back to his machine, he made a show of walking slowly over our carpet, studying its gold, scarlet, and green designs. Then he clicked on the vacuum and ran it over a particular spot, back and forth, back and forth. By the third pass, the vacuum was leaving a thin but clearly visible line of sand in its wake. When the salesman ran the vacuum back across the trail of sand, the vacuum sucked it right up—and then deposited a fresh line of sand in a slightly different spot.

Jerry and I elbowed each other and counted our lucky stars—this was one time someone *else* would get the blame for not cleaning up all that sand! The salesman was visibly withering. With each pass of the vacuum across the carpet, his shoulders slumped a bit lower. His forehead wrinkled. He pushed and pulled the vacuum more and more frantically, and I could see his lips moving silently.

Suddenly, he turned off the vacuum. For several seconds he stared at it, and we stared at him. Then he crouched down and plucked some sand from one of the long lines marking the carpet. He rubbed his fingers and the sand fell back to the carpet.

"Well," he said, "what in the *heck*?"

"I'm sure—" began Mom, but the salesman interrupted her with a quickly raised hand.

Without speaking, he flipped the vacuum upside down on the carpet, unplugged it, and began taking it apart, all the while muttering about what might be ailing his incredible machine. As soon as he had it all put back together, he turned it back on and tried again. The vacuum traced the same lines of sand across the carpet with each pass. In desperation, the salesman pulled the collection bag off the back of his machine. He unfastened the clasp, unrolled the top of the bag, and reached his hand in. When his hand came back out, it was full of white sand, which ran through his fingers and down onto the carpet. The bag looked like it was already more than half full.

Mom started to laugh, her hands floating up to the sides of her mouth, and her laugh was like the first rock in an avalanche. Soon all of us were laughing, even Dad and the vacuum salesman—laughing so hard our sides hurt.

"You know," chortled Dad, "that fancy vacuum of yours actually works pretty good. Just *look* at all the sand it picked up!"

And so as the laughter died away, we resigned ourselves to ongoing sand duty—part of what Dad called "policing the place," though we had no clear idea of what that meant—each time carefully pouring the collected sand into the hole beside our sunken bathtub.

• • •

Our house was too far out in the country to have garbage pickup. There was a municipal dump, of course, but Dad decided that driving our trash to the dump would be a waste of effort when we had a perfectly empty valley right behind the house. Each time a trash can in the house filled up, one of us would dump it outside—which meant that every so often Dad would notice the trash pile was getting out of control.

"You boys go out back and get some burning done."

We always tried not to smile when Dad handed down that particular task, fearing he'd decide to do it himself or even give the job to Sheri. Compared to sweeping the never-ending sand in the house and our newest chore—filling the ruts in the driveway—burning the trash pile was nearly a treat.

We had a routine. On the way to the garbage pile, Jerry and I would each grab a long, sturdy stick. Then as soon as we reached the pile, we'd look for something like a frayed tarp or a garbage bag, which we'd divvy up and wrap tightly around the ends of our sticks. A flick from one of the Zippos we both carried and—*fwoosh*—we were explorers, holding aloft our torches. Flames ready, we'd clamber to the center of the pile, holding the torches well away from our bodies, since more than once a blob of molten plastic had dripped onto our exposed skin, searing us for an instant before sputtering out. Once we were in the center, we worked our way outward, touching our torches to anything that looked flammable: phone books, shredded shirts, the odd scrap of lumber. All the while, our plastic-fueled torches burned a bright, nearly neon blue, even in the sunlight, and the sound of their flames—*ship ship shiiiip*—became a private language, telling where to step and what to burn.

After we set fire to everything that wasn't wet, metallic, or made of glass, we would retreat to the edge of the pile. Still holding our torches,

we'd stand and watch the flames spread in fits and starts across the discarded landscape, sometimes stepping back into the pile to prod or
relight some object. I could imagine I was a giant, watching an entire
countryside burning, from the rotting valleys all the way to the peaks
of rusty iron.

Dad's chore was pointless. The flames never consumed the pile—
there was far too much that couldn't burn—and over time it grew and
grew. The valley was glutted with garbage, trash so damp and compacted
that no burning short of an explosion could have altered its shape. Dad
must have understood that. He knew the trash pile as well as anyone
in the family, and he knew the shape of fire even better. Yet every few
weeks he sent Jerry and me back to burn. And so my brother and I would
stand, shoulder to shoulder, and watch flames become embers become
smoke and ashes, and then we'd walk back up the sandy hill to the house,
content for a moment that we'd done exactly what our father required.

• • •

Once, when Jerry and I were trudging back from the trash pile at dusk,
Dad barked at us to get some two-by-fours from behind the shed because
he had something to unload from his truck. We knew the drill. Dad
came home with strange objects all the time, and more often than not
we had to help him transfer whatever it was—nearly always something
mechanical and too heavy for one man and two boys to move safely—
from the truck to the yard. We had no idea what this particular item
was, but we could tell Dad was excited about it.

"This baby was on a destroyer in dubya-dubya-two, boys," he said.
"Got 'er off a guy near Detroit for a song, and I'm about to get 'er working."

"But . . . what *is* it?" I asked.

"A searchlight, Mark," he answered, motioning us to come closer.
He unbolted something on the back of the thing and pulled off a hatch,
pointing to a deeply concave mirror.

"This reflects the light and concentrates it." He stopped to look at us, savoring the moment before adding, "Concentrates it enough to see things *two miles* away."

He nodded happily as we gaped at the mirror. "Yep, two miles. Don't look into it or it'll blind you. It gives out as much light as one hundred twenty *thousand* candles."

Jerry and I both blurted the obvious. "When are you gonna turn it on?"

"I'll hook it up and we can try it out," he answered. I'd never heard him happier. As he began to fiddle with the searchlight, Sheri wandered out to watch.

"What is that?"

"It's a searchlight from a destroyer!" I bragged.

"What's a destroyer?"

"A *ship*," I said impatiently. "Now let Dad work."

It took Dad a while to get everything ready. He never seemed in doubt about what to do but moved around the searchlight quickly and purposefully, adjusting and tightening and lubricating, ignoring our questions until we stopped asking.

Finally it was time. Dad had run a thick cable from the searchlight to a nearby generator.

"This'd be useful on a ship—it's what it was made for, after all."

He looked at his audience, winked at Mom, and flicked a switch on the back of the searchlight.

"And . . . There. It. Goes."

We stared, stunned. It was brighter than the sun—the brightest thing I had seen in my life. The beam of light was like a solid thing, like a bridge of brightness you might be able to walk on wherever it pointed. No object was too far away for Dad to touch: the bottom of the driveway, the stop sign down Blakely Drive, the radio tower on the far hill.

"Don't get in front of it," he warned. "You *will* get burned."

He spun a small wheel with a handle attached to it, and the eye of the searchlight narrowed to a small hole. Then he spun the wheel the other way, and the light expanded.

"Amazing," I sighed, pulling the word out across the seconds while I followed the beam.

I heard Mom snort behind me, and then I heard the door open and close. Dad knew he still had an audience, however, and he pointed the searchlight at the ground, then suddenly flicked it up toward the sky. The beam lanced through the night, up and up until it lit the underside of a cloud.

A *cloud*. I could scarcely understand what I was seeing.

That night, as I curled beneath my blanket in bed, I remembered what I'd seen. The searchlight seemed part of my father, as if he were really the one illuminating the distant trees. Tall and proud—taller than nearly every other man I knew—Dad could force the world to bend with his bare hands and wide shoulders.

•   •   •

That was how time passed. Week in, week out, month in, month out. We panted through the summers and shivered through the winters. When the weather was bad enough, we drew or played board games or stared at the fireplace, and we always did whatever chores Dad assigned us: taking out the garbage, watering whichever plants were currently surviving near the house, sweeping, washing and drying dishes, washing and folding laundry, and shoveling ruts in the driveway. He assigned jobs that even we, inexperienced schoolkids, could tell were baloney. More than once he looked at Jerry and me and growled, "Get outside, and whatever's out of place, put it back!" Since almost everything outside was either broken, messy, or out of place, and nothing we did could change that, we interpreted his instructions to mean that we should look busy until he stopped noticing us. Dad noticing us wasn't something we particularly wanted. Better for him to do his stuff and for us to do ours.

We bused to school and bused home, too, caring very little about what happened between the two trips. But apart from those minor interruptions, we wandered wild and free—with an emphasis on *free*. Mom was always working at home or trying to work in town. She talked about making ends meet and scraping by. Dad seemed like he was always playing with guns and old vehicles at home, or working in town and then staying in town to play by himself. Almost none of the Bouman family's meager resources of time and money trickled down to us kids.

We lived hour by hour, not thinking about what might come next, doing as we liked and liking a decent amount of what we did. Somehow whole seasons passed that way, and I had little inkling that folks lived other ways, or that my own way of life was soon to change.

4

ONCE THEY CLEARED the hurdle of raising three responsible, school-age kids, Mom and Dad began to leave us home alone more often. Mom would set out three bowls of food on the table—usually plain oatmeal— and tell us we needed to be good while they were gone. She'd say that she and Dad were going out to eat dinner in town or see a movie or play cards. Mom would always leave us with the same advice.

"We're going to be out late, so be sure to get everything just the way your father likes it before we get home."

The first few times it felt fun to stay home alone at night, but we soon changed our tune. There wasn't really anything to do that couldn't be done during the day, and at night we had the unwanted responsibility of predicting what counted as "perfect" in Dad's mind. We might do nothing to clean up while Dad was away, only to have him come home and go straight to bed without a word, while other times Jerry might force Sheri and me to clean and straighten for more than an hour, only to have Dad notice the smallest little thing out of place, like a single sock on the laundry room floor. Once Dad woke me up to yell about a plastic army man I'd left on the table in the living room, and he stood hulking over me in my bed, looking daggers, until it finally occurred to me to go clean it up.

Another time, we woke in the morning and went into the kitchen to eat breakfast before school, only to find Dad cleaning a disassembled pistol on the table, glaring at us. He waited until Jerry opened the cupboard to grab the container of oatmeal, and then, quick as a snake, Dad reached out and slammed the door closed.

"You kids left food out on the counter last night, so it looks like your food will be staying *in* the cupboard this morning."

We trudged back to our bedrooms, put on our school clothes, and went to wait for the bus, earlier and hungrier than usual. What was there to say? We were learning that when Dad said and did things like that, they weren't up for discussion. Certainly not with him. He'd glare or shout or clench his fists, letting us know with certainty that his significant weight advantage gave him the final word. Not with Mom, either, who kindly and gently told us not to question our father. And not even with each other. None of us had any answers, so we didn't waste time asking questions. Life happened the way life happened. Most days were okay, but when you ran into a bad one, the best thing to do was keep your head down and wait for the next one. At least that morning there were fish sticks to look forward to in the cafeteria.

Staying home alone forced us to act older than our ages. With so much freedom and such sporadic supervision, we Bouman kids tended to get hurt quite a bit. Fortunately for us, there was a man named Doc Kramer who ran a clinic in the basement of his nearby home. He looked like a real-life version of Herman Munster, and we were on a first-name basis with him. Between all the junk around the yard and the condition of the house, Jerry and I already had a serious scar collection. Sheri hadn't escaped the carnage either. Besides getting special shoes from

Doc Kramer that helped her walk more like a regular kid, she'd had a tetanus shot after puncturing her foot on a rusty nail, a burned leg from when she bumped into a hot motorcycle muffler, and stitches for a gash that opened her palm nearly clean through. While Jerry and I deserved our wounds—because we liked to do things like jump out of trees and scramble around inside the carcass of an old steam engine—Sheri usually didn't.

The time she sliced her palm open, she was simply opening her dresser, and the ancient glass handle shattered in her grip. Mom and Dad were both in town, separately, and Jerry was off by himself outside.

"Mark. Mark. *Mark!*"

I dashed from the living room to Sheri's room, yanking open her door to find her clutching her hand and whimpering in pain. I could tell it was serious with a glance: blood was spurting from between her clenched fingers, covering her hands and dripping *pit-pit-pat* onto the floor. She was staring at the blood and shivering.

"It . . . it . . . it hurts."

"Hang on!" I said, swallowing bile in my throat. "I'm going for a Band-Aid!"

I raced to the bathroom and banged around in the cupboard, eventually locating a Band-Aid. I could hear Sheri in her room, pleading for me to hurry. Back in her room, I told her to hold out her hand.

"Hold still, hold still!" I begged. "Lemme get it on!"

I opened the Band-Aid and pressed it down on her palm, crosswise to the cut. A fresh wave of blood pumped out of the cut, completely covering the Band-Aid. Sheri was left holding a palm full of her own blood, and it *pit-pit-patted* over the brim and onto the floor.

"Call Mom!"

"I don't have her number," I managed. "We've got to go somewhere. The Dietzes'!"

I returned to the bathroom and grabbed a hand towel. I wrapped it around Sheri's palm and told her to hold it tight with her other hand.

Sheri whimpered the whole way to the Dietzes', and because both of her hands were occupied, streaks of tears and snot ran unchecked across her lips and down her chin. When we neared our neighbors' house, I sprinted ahead and banged on their front door.

"Anybody home? Please! Who's home?"

Emmy opened the door.

"Sheri cut herself bad and no one's home and it's still bleeding and I don't know what to do!" My sister arrived behind me, still whimpering.

Emmy stepped over to her and unwrapped the towel with a quick motion, then just as quickly rewrapped it.

"Yep, Doc Kramer's it is," she said. "Judy! I need a clean hand towel, sweetie!"

Emmy brought Sheri up to the entryway. While Judy placed a clean towel around Sheri's hand, Emmy picked up her purse and fished out her keys.

"Come on, Sheri. Let's get you fixed up. Ride with us, Judy."

And then they were gone, leaving me alone inside the Dietzes' house. I heard the car doors close outside, then the sound of the car pulling away. Not knowing what to do, I walked home, went inside, and sat on the couch, staring at the wall.

It seemed like hours later when I heard the knock on our front door. I found Judy there, with Sheri in tow. I managed to thank Judy, who turned away with a swirl of her ponytail, and then I found myself helping Sheri to her room. She could barely walk, and she leaned her weight against me as we shuffled down the hall.

"Twelve stitches," she mumbled, then lay down in her bed.

I went back to sitting on the couch.

Mom returned from town a few hours later. When I told her what had happened, she didn't say anything. She simply disappeared into Sheri's room and didn't come out.

Dad returned from town a few hours after that. Mom heard his truck rumble up, and she was waiting for him at the front door.

"What are we having for—" was all he managed before Mom read him his marching orders. He went right back out the door, returning a minute later with his toolbox. Sheri's jagged dresser handle was soon replaced by a jerry-rigged bolt, and nothing more was said about the accident.

Mom began to cook dinner while Dad read a book on the couch. I wondered what had happened to our hand towel—the blood-soaked one we'd left at the Dietzes'—and hoped its loss wouldn't be counted against me.

• • •

Dad wanted everything in the house to be shipshape, all the time, but shipshape wasn't easy for three young kids to pull off, no matter how hard we tried. It could be a messy table, a light left burning, or a doll forgotten on the couch. Dad almost always found something if he looked hard enough.

One night, after being left alone again, Jerry and I were woken by the noise of Mom and Dad's return. This wasn't the kind of noise we could ignore, either, like the noise they made in their bedroom many nights, after they'd sat on the couch, listening to records and whispering with their heads close together. This was the noise of screams, and those could have consequences. Jerry was in the bunk above me. Both of us were lying motionless, waiting, hoping we wouldn't hear Dad's footsteps coming toward our door. I pulled my covers over my head and tried not to breathe. Out in the living room the argument stalled. Then a long silence. Maybe everything was over.

Suddenly our bedroom door flung open. I saw the overhead light flash on through my blanket.

"You kids get out of bed!" Dad barked. "Didn't I tell you to clean up the house? Why didn't you wipe the counter off?"

I leaped out of bed. My brother swung from the top bunk and landed on the floor beside me. Both of us stood at attention in our underwear. "We did!" both of us said together. It was true. We had taken Mom's parting instruction to heart and spent an hour putting things away, sweeping, and doing dishes before bed.

"Like hell you did! Why are there crumbs all over the counter?"

Dad stared us down, menacing and powerful. His shoulders bulged beneath his white T-shirt. "Get in there and look. Now!"

Jerry and I padded to the kitchen, still wearing only our underwear. We squinted in the bright light. The kitchen looked clean, but sure enough, over by the toaster, we could see a small collection of crumbs. We had made toast for ourselves that night after we cleaned up. At least there weren't many crumbs, and we could be back to bed in a few minutes.

But Dad no longer cared about the crumbs. They had been bait, and he was after a bigger catch.

"And which one of you did the dishes?" he demanded.

"We all did," Jerry replied.

Dad walked to the nearest cupboard, crouched down, and opened it. He reached inside and pulled out a dinner plate. He held it up to the light at arm's length. Most of our plates were made of clear blue glass—even a fingerprint was visible on them if you held the plate at a certain angle. Dad looked through the plate at the light, then back at Jerry and me.

"This isn't good enough. These plates are dirty." He stared at us for a moment longer. "Go get your sister."

I walked down the hall to Sheri's room to wake her up. I could hear Jerry and Dad in the kitchen, Jerry still fending off Dad's accusations. It wouldn't make any difference. I shook Sheri awake. I didn't tell her anything, and she didn't ask any questions. All we could do was see what Dad had planned for us.

Back in the kitchen, we stood in a line, shoulder to shoulder, facing our father. It was hard not to shiver as he looked us up and down. "I want you to get dressed and come back here. And then you will wash every single dish in this house. Go through the cupboards and take out every dish and wash them *perfectly*."

Jerry couldn't help speaking what we were all thinking. "Now?"

"Yes, *now!*" Dad glared at Jerry and then said, with perfect calm, "I don't care if it takes you the entire f—ing night." With that he left the room.

It was past midnight when we began our task. Our cupboards contained a lot more than stacks of blue dishes, and we took everything out and made piles on the counters and the table. There were mismatched coffee mugs, drinking glasses, bowls, silverware, and a collection of pots and pans that were scarred and charred black from years of use.

"I'll wash," Jerry said. "You and Sheri can dry."

He filled the sink with hot water, set a shaker of Comet on the edge of the sink, and began to wash. It was impossible for soap bubbles to form in the hard water, so the water simply turned a sickly blue color.

"This is going to take forever," Sheri whispered.

"I know," I agreed.

We pulled every spoon, knife, and fork, every pot and pan, every plate and cup and bowl from the cupboards and drawers, one by one, as quietly as we could. We piled, Jerry washed. We dried, Jerry washed. And we did that over and over.

"Mark," my sister whispered, "do you have a new towel? This one's getting too wet!"

"Keep using it," I implored her. "If we don't use it until it's soaked, we'll run out of towels and have to do laundry, too!"

"Mark," my brother whispered, "do you think this is clean enough?"

He held up a pan and I frowned. It was caked with what looked like years of blackness.

"Try scraping it with a knife?"

Jerry tried, his scritch-scratching drowning out the soft squeak of our towel drying. He gave up ten minutes later.

"It won't come off!" My brother's voice was thin and desperate. "It just won't get any better!"

I sighed. "We should just throw some of these dishes on the trash heap."

"This is the first time I've seen some of them," Jerry agreed, "and now we have to wash them *all*."

Sheri moaned softly.

We had been working like that for what seemed like hours, getting through almost everything we owned, when Dad strolled into the kitchen. Without a word, he walked to the cupboard and took out a glass plate. He held it up to the light, just as he'd done earlier, and he detected some of Sheri's fresh fingerprints. She'd put the dish back without cradling it in a towel.

"This is dirty," he said. "Start over."

We hated it, but we had no choice. Sheri and I lifted everything we'd cleaned back onto the counters. Jerry added more hot water and Comet to the sink and scrounged up some dry towels. We washed in silence—rewashed every single glass, mug, plate, dish, and piece of silverware we'd already cleaned.

We finished sometime after three in the morning. The pots and pans were still stained, but the dishes and silverware were glistening. Jerry held up the top few blue plates against the light and made sure they were spotless, and we prayed Dad would forget about the pots and pans by the morning. Sheri walked back to her room, and Jerry and I walked back to ours. We knew that we needed to get back to sleep, since only a few hours later Dad would wake us up to get ready for school.

5

WE KIDS DIDN'T UNDERSTAND why, but Dad was changing. He was moodier and less predictable. He was starting to slap Jerry and me, and sometimes Mom—though rarely Sheri. And he was growing obsessed with all things military. The shelves in our living room were filled with dozens and dozens of books: illustrated histories of various wars, guides to the weapons and vehicles of various countries, codes of conduct, manuals on how to make and deploy booby traps, political theory, German dictionaries, biographies of famous generals, infantry tactics. He seemed to have books on every conceivable military subject, and he scoured swap meets and auctions for more. Mounted on two walls of the room were several of his favorite guns and bayonets, one of which had been used, he told us, "to gut a man clean up the middle." There was a German army helmet and a grenade Dad said was almost certainly inert, and if we pulled open the second drawer of the end table, perhaps hunting for a pencil to use on a Yahtzee score sheet, we'd see the gleaming metal of a pistol.

The compulsion even prompted Dad to start his own business. One afternoon he rummaged around the shed and found a can of black paint and a small brush. Then he strolled down the driveway to the mailbox, opened the can of paint, and got to work. An hour later, Dad completed the final stroke in the words *Boumar Custom Gun Company*—and that was as official as things were going to get. The "mar" at the end of "Boumar" was actually the first part of Terry Marion's last name, a friend of Dad's who lived down the road and helped with gun projects, although for some reason the fifty-fifty split between their two names was lost on most people. At least it wasn't the only odd sign on Blakely Drive. Just down the way, the initial *R* had fallen off our neighbor's mailbox, which from then on proclaimed that "ay Guy" lived there.

As word of the gun company spread, Dad became a sort of clearinghouse for people looking to sell or buy weapons that Dad liked to call "collector's items" and "guns from when they still knew how to make guns." If you wanted a standard rifle, you'd be better off visiting the local shop in Grand Rapids. But if you wanted something a bit more exotic, you simply needed to grab some cash and drive out to the Bouman place.

As more and more people did exactly that, Dad kicked things up a notch. His first improvement was to construct a gun range. He used a borrowed bulldozer to carve out a flat, level rectangle into the side of one of the hills behind the trash valley, leaving a high wall of dirt as a backstop. He pushed the extra dirt into mounds on the sides, forming a large area where he could place various targets. With the help of some gun buddies, he dragged an old, broken-down washing machine to the center of the range. It made the perfect backstop for most bullets, although some of the largest-caliber slugs were capable of punching a hole in both the thin metal at the front of the machine and the thicker steel at the back of it. While the front of the machine looked like the surface of a sponge with its countless smooth holes, the back looked like the claws and teeth of some mechanical nightmare. We kids—especially Jerry and me, who began to spend more time helping Dad with his guns, while Sheri spent her energy avoiding Dad—quickly learned to walk a wide berth around the back of the machine, since its jagged edges could slice open skin and clothing like a scalpel.

Once the gun range was up and running, it was guaranteed that on Saturdays and Sundays, Jerry and I would be in constant demand as reloaders and spotters. From somewhere he wouldn't reveal, Dad had acquired a World War II–era antitank gun, which was basically a gigantic rifle capable of penetrating—through sheer, brute force—the armor of a tank. Once Dad found a guy who could sell him shells for it, he began to charge people to fire the weapon. Jerry and I helped him set up targets made of plate steel, and then whichever guys happened to be hanging around could buy ammo from Dad for three bucks per shot. Each shell was an inch across and nearly as long as my forearm, and there was so much recoil that the gun needed to be fired from a prone position. The shells loaded through a curved magazine on the top, and the gun's long barrel rested on a short tripod. Since each shot was so precious, the guys would take their sweet time: loading, sighting, standing up and discussing what might happen, checking the wind, resighting, and so on. It was almost like a religious ritual for them, the climax of which came when their shot punched a hole through a couple inches of solid steel. Dad would preside over the shooters, hands on his hips, smirking as if he'd built the gun with his own hands.

After building the range, there was the problem of where to put everyone who wanted to shoot. During the busiest times, there might be six or eight of Dad's friends out behind the house, each with a weapon or three, so Dad built a two-story gun tower off to one side of the house, next to the shed, about two hundred yards from the range. The first story was all braces and pilings, along with a ladder, and the second story was a flat platform—about the size of a large bedroom—accessed by a hatch in the floor. From the second level, the guys could shoot and brag and cuss and swap guns to their hearts' content.

Mom hated the gun range, but not because she hated the guns.

When she and Dad were dating, they had gone rat shooting at the dump with .22s, and they had even driven all the way to Montana once to hunt bear. No, what galled Mom was that Dad considered it part of his business—that blowing up a bunch of junk with his buddies counted the same as her cooking and cleaning and mending or the same as one of her part-time jobs as a receptionist or clerk in town. But what could she say? The proof was right there on the mailbox: it said Dad was running a gun *company*, not a hobby.

"Your father likes his playtime," she would sometimes say, "but it's not playtime you boys need to be part of."

That was her opinion, but Dad had a different one. We *did* have to be part of his playtime, whether we liked it or not. At least when he was inside with his buddies, he forgot about giving us jobs. He would invite guys over, and when they knocked, he would open the front door with his left hand. Then he'd bang his heels together and stick his right arm out in front of him, like he was pointing at the sun.

"*Sieg heil!*"

His friends would do the same thing back, and often they were dressed in tan or camouflage uniforms. If the weather wasn't good for shooting, they would sit around the living room, playing records with German songs and talking about guns and Jews and wars. Their favorite leader was Hitler, and they all agreed he should have won the war. He was trying to keep his country safe and strong, but his other generals and communists and Jews lied to him and caused him to lose. But Hitler's ideas were still alive, Dad said—they were just waiting for the right time to rise again.

Guns began to take up increasingly more space in our lives. The gun range and the gun tower were obvious to anyone, but more subtle signs of the Bouman weaponizing were everywhere: oil stains on towels Dad used to clean gun barrels, large drums of gunpowder in the laundry room, and shell casings littered all over the property, winking up from the ground. Jerry and I got used to answering Dad's call, expecting to be given some chore or a tongue-lashing, only to have Dad show us a weapon that was inside a crate.

"You kids don't tell *anyone* you saw this," he'd say. "If someone asks, you don't know a thing!"

We quickly lost track of which guns we were allowed to talk about and which ones were hush-hush, but it scarcely mattered. Most kids in elementary school had no understanding of weapons, so they wouldn't have cared about our secrets, and most adults wouldn't have believed that kids our age knew the difference between a legal M1 carbine and an illegal German broomhandle Mauser that could fire on full auto.

A police officer once came to my classroom to give a talk about neighborhood safety. When he asked if anyone had any questions, I piped up. "Do you guys ever have to deal with gas bombs?" He gave my teacher a strange look, then asked if there were any *other* questions.

•   •   •

I never had any big plans. Most days all I wanted to do was play, eat, stay out of trouble, and get a good night of sleep. I didn't like my chores, and I didn't like school, but what could a guy do? They were just part of life.

Dad's behavior, though, caused me to change the way I lived. Jerry, Sheri, and I started to pay more attention to him, specifically so we could avoid him. If we were at home and Dad wasn't, we kept our senses on constant alert, ready to scatter at the sound of his truck.

"Dad's home!" one of us would yell. It was like yelling *Fire!* in a movie theater. If we were inside, perhaps playing cards, we'd toss the cards back in the drawer and either race outside, assuming we could get out and away before Dad parked, or else race to our rooms and try to look busy. If we were outside, we'd head for the hills, getting far away as fast as possible. Who knew what job we might be given? One weekend he forced us to shovel sand and dirt into the driveway ruts for two backbreaking days, and then Monday morning he kept us home from school to finish the job.

Sometimes Dad snuck past our radar, though. One afternoon, when Jerry and I were lounging on the living room floor drawing, Dad suddenly appeared in the doorway. "I need you boys to come help on the range."

We knew better than to dawdle, so we tugged on our shoes and jogged around to the back of the house toward the gun tower. Four of Dad's buddies were already there, hanging around the bottom of the ladder, packing guns that looked big enough to bring down an elephant. They nodded, then went back to ignoring us. Dad showed up a minute later and shoved a stack of paper targets at Jerry, then tossed a roll of masking tape to me. We knew the drill by heart. While Dad and his friends climbed into the tower with their rifles and cases of ammunition, we ran the two hundred yards across the field to get everything ready for them. Jerry and I taped the first target to the front of the washing machine, and then we clambered up the mound on the left and took cover behind the dirt.

The first shot rang out: a sharp, staccato crack, followed by an echo that rolled up and down the hills.

Jerry took the first turn spotting. He ran back to the target, leaned over to look at it, then straightened and screamed back toward the tower, "Inch high, two inches left!" Five seconds later, he was leaping over the dirt berm and sliding down toward me. *Crack!* Then it was my turn to check the target and scream back the information. Every few trips, one of us would tape a new target to the front of the washing machine to ensure we didn't mix up which bullet hole was which.

Twenty minutes later, we were both sweaty, covered in dirt, and desperate for a chance to rest our aching legs. One of the guns was having trouble sighting in, and a job that usually took us ten minutes or less was stretching on and on.

Crack. Run, check, holler, run. *Crack.* Run, check, holler, run.

As the minutes wore on, we stopped hiding our entire bodies behind the dirt and began crouching at the top of the rise. When my next turn came and I ran back from the washing machine, I couldn't face climbing all the way up the slippery berm for what seemed like the hundredth time. I simply scrambled up partway, then turned to watch the next shot come in.

Each time a bullet hit, the entire washing machine shuddered and the dirt behind it kicked up. Whatever rifle they were firing was powerful enough to shoot clear through the target, ripping it apart in the process.

Crack. Another shot—and my right leg buckled beneath me. I collapsed in a heap and rolled down the hill, stopping in the weeds at the bottom.

"Jerry!" I screamed. My right ankle felt like it was on fire. Panicked, I tried to stand up but immediately collapsed again. I couldn't put any weight on my foot, which felt like a piece of dead meat that someone had attached to my body.

I dared to look down. Blood, and a lot of it. "Jerry!" I screamed again. My mind raced to comprehend what had happened to me. I tried to stand again but collapsed. Why couldn't I feel my ankle anymore?

My hands shook and my breath came in gasps. I could feel my right foot again, but for some reason it was growing warmer and warmer. I sat up and grabbed my ankle, trying to relieve the pain, but it hurt worse than ever. I pulled away hands covered in blood.

Jerry sprinted to my side. "Stay down and don't move—Dad's coming!"

I squinted up at my brother. He was cradling his right arm, and blood was oozing through the fingers of his left hand. Before I could say anything, he asked, "Did you get shot too?"

Suddenly I realized why my leg didn't work—I *had* been shot. It was a realization that caused a fresh wave of panic. We were just kids—what in the world was happening to us?

I turned and saw that Dad was already halfway across the field. He must have seen me hit the ground right after the shot was fired and assumed the worst. He was in a full-out sprint, his arms swinging up near his head and his thighs pumping like pistons with every stride. I'd never seen him move so fast. He skidded to a stop at my side, sliding to one knee and putting one hand down for balance. He took one look at me, then scooped me into his arms. "Let's go," he said.

Then we were speed walking back across the field. I could hear every breath exploding out of his mouth. From below, Dad's face was foreign. I couldn't remember him ever carrying me before. I could see the lump in his throat bobbing, see up his nostrils. I could see his eyelashes. His smell was the same as always, sour and ripe. When we reached the bottom of the hill below the house, Dad began to run, straight up the hill with me in his grip.

At the car, Dad balanced me with one arm and one raised knee while he opened the rear door with his other hand. He leaned forward and laid me across the backseat, headfirst. From my back, I raised my chin to my chest and watched him pull off my shoe. I saw blood slosh out of it. Dad held the shoe at arm's length away from the car and turned the shoe over, like he was pouring out the dregs from a thermos. The sight of my own blood poured out in the sand made my stomach clench, and I gritted my teeth against the bile I could taste in the back of my throat. Dad reached back into the car, set my shoe on the floor, and unrolled my sock. Then he disappeared. I could see Jerry, who had been standing just behind Dad outside the car. He was still calmly cradling his right arm, and the blood that had leaked out over his fingers was drying and darkening. Dad returned with an old towel and told Jerry to get in the front. Then Dad leaned over me again and, as if he were tying my shoelace, knotted the towel around my ankle. The door slammed, Dad hopped into the front seat, and then the engine roared to life and we were bouncing down the driveway.

I expected Dad's furious lecture to begin at any moment, but the fifteen-minute drive passed in complete silence. My ankle felt like an ocean was raging inside it, with waves of pain crashing loudly enough that I could feel them in my ears. I watched upside-down trees whip past the window—*flick flick flick*—and I tried to see how many I could count between blinks.

Dad screeched to a stop in front of Doc Kramer's clinic. He yanked open the car door and lifted me out, carrying me down the outside stairs to the basement entrance. Jerry opened it and stood back, and Dad marched in. Doc Kramer didn't have a receptionist, but from Dad's arms I could see four other patients waiting in the room. There was an old woman with gray hair and large glasses, and beside her were two middle-aged women, frozen in midconversation. An elderly man nearly fumbled the magazine he'd been reading. I saw them at a crazy angle, my head resting in the crook of Dad's arm. I wondered why they had all come. Arthritis? A sore throat? I wondered if any of them had ever been shot.

Then I was inside the examination room. Doc Kramer looked as tall and tired as he always did. The sight of two young boys with bleeding wounds didn't faze him—or at least not when they were the Bouman boys.

"Put him on that table," he said to my father. Then he stepped out of the room for a minute, and from where I lay on the table I could hear him apologizing to his other patients. Jerry sat nearby on another table. When Doc Kramer came back, he ignored Jerry and me, walking to stand nose to nose with my father. "What happened?" he asked, peering over his wire-rim glasses.

"Well, the boys were tending targets . . ." His speech was hesitant, sheepish. I'd never heard him speak that way. Doc didn't blink, and Dad was forced to continue. "And they . . . got a little too close." Dad closed his mouth and floated to the edge of the room, where he stood alone with his arms crossed.

Doc Kramer didn't say anything at the close of Dad's explanation—just shook his head as if Dad had invented a whole new type of stupid. "Get me a sewing kit, please," Doc Kramer said quietly to his nurse, and the two of them moved over to my brother. The nurse laid out the kit on a tray, and Doc went to work on Jerry's arm. When he lifted the flapped skin to see what had caused the damage, he found several pieces of metal, silver atop the pink of Jerry's bicep muscle.

"Well, look at that," he said, and with a large pair of tweezers he removed the shards, dropping them one by one onto a metal tray. *Plunk. Plunk. Plunk.* Jerry barely blinked.

"And I told the boys to stay behind the berm, but . . ." Dad's voice trailed off as quickly as it had started.

Doc Kramer pulled the largest piece from Jerry's arm. It was twisted, and red blood coated it. He looked at my brother. "I want to make sure I get all the pieces," he said, and Jerry nodded. As Doc probed the wound, Jerry observed stoically, as if he were watching Mom clean a spot of dirt from his sleeve.

"I'm done with you," Doc Kramer said as he finished stitching. "Now let's take a look at your brother's ankle." Doc Kramer leaned over me and frowned, then reached up and pulled the overhead light closer, inspecting my ankle under the bright glare. Lying on my back, I couldn't see my leg. Instead, I watched his face go in and out of focus as it moved back and forth in the bright glare. When I could see it, his eyebrows were even lower than usual. His lips pinched into a thin line and he shook his head. Then he flicked off the light and straightened.

"I'm afraid I'll do more damage than good if I try to remove that shrapnel—too many nerves in that part of your ankle. I don't want to dig around in there and tear it up worse. Let's just leave it and see what happens. Who knows—it might eventually work its way out on its own."

That didn't sound comforting, but the thought of Doc Kramer digging around in my ankle—whatever that meant—was even worse. I shuddered. Doc bandaged my ankle, all the while giving Dad a lecture on how the wound needed to be cared for.

"Now see if you can sit up," he told me, taking my hand and pulling me up. He crossed the room to a cupboard and then returned with a pair of crutches. "You'll figure out how to use these real quick—but they're not toys, so bring 'em back when you're done."

Doc walked toward the sink, pausing to look back across his shoulder at my father and say, "I'm finished."

Dad left without a word. Jerry helped me to the floor and made sure

I had each crutch snug under my armpits. It took me several minutes to navigate the doors and reach the top of the stairs. Dad was already in the car, engine running. *What's Mom going to think?* I wondered as we drove. *I'm not even ten years old, and I have a shrapnel wound.*

Just after we parked in front of the house, I found out exactly what Mom thought.

The tips of my crutches sank into the sand, slowing me down, so Jerry entered the house first. I saw him displaying his bandaged arm as if he were a war hero returning from the front lines.

"What happened?" I heard Mom ask.

Dad arrived at the door, and I was right behind him. "Just had a little accident," he answered, "on the gun range."

That's when I came into the house, banging my crutches on the door as I negotiated the narrow entryway. Not to be outdone by my brother, I piped up. "And *I* got hit in the foot!"

Mom took a second look at Jerry, a first look at me, and then rounded on Dad. "*Hit?* Have you lost your mind? Don't you know *anything?*"

Jerry and I gaped at each other. We'd never seen Mom so mad. She was raging.

"They're all right," Dad said, trying to calm things down. "They just got a little too close."

"Too *close?*" Spittle was flying out of Mom's mouth now. "You're their *father*, for crying out loud! Why didn't you say something? It's a wonder you didn't kill them!"

From the way Dad backed down, we guessed even he had never seen Mom like that. "Okay, okay. I should have paid more attention to where they were standing."

As he talked, Jerry and I headed to our room. Our curiosity to see the fight was overpowered by our desire to stay out of it. So far neither of us had gotten in any trouble over the incident, and we wanted to keep it that way. We closed the door behind us. Jerry sat down at our desk, and I lay on my bunk. We could still hear Mom yelling at Dad in the other room.

The fight tapered off a minute later, and as soon as it did, Mom opened our door and came in.

"Are you two all right?"

"Yeah, it was just a couple of small pieces," Jerry answered.

"And are you all right?" she asked, coming to kneel beside me.

"I'm okay. Doc didn't take any of the metal out—said it would be better to leave it in and let it heal."

Mom frowned, then shook her head. She seemed to stand up slow, like she was lifting something. "You boys need to be careful," she said, and then she left us alone.

6

DURING THE YEAR that Boumar Custom Gun Company was going gang-busters, Dad found himself with more and more admirers of a certain sort: men who viewed Dad as a hero and father figure and commander and cool kid all rolled into one.

One night, when I should have already been in bed, there was a sharp rap at the front door. When Dad opened it, a man I'd never seen before stood in the frame. Younger than Dad, the man wore a black beret, dark green military fatigues, and black leather boots that nearly reached his knees. Dad nodded, and the man stepped forward, taking off his hat and folding it into his hand. Then another man entered, dressed like the first, followed by another, and soon there were six men standing in a loose line in front of Dad, hats in hand. One of the men held a long tube of white paper, rolled up like a telescope. Dad looked them up and down, nodded again, and said, "Let's get to work."

Dad strode to the kitchen and the men followed. I could no longer see them from the living room, so I padded into the kitchen and ducked below the counter. I could hear wooden chairs being dragged out and then scraped back in, paper being spread out and smoothed on the table, and the thunk of metal objects being set down—knives or lighters, I guessed—to keep the rolled paper in place.

"Here it is," Dad said, and I could hear his finger tapping on the table. "Our proving ground. Eleven acres just *made* for this kind of thing."

"Oh *hell* yes," said one voice.

Another asked, "So, how do you figure it?"

Dad's answer and the subsequent discussion lasted the better part of an hour and included a lot of things I didn't fully understand. They talked about trenching techniques, reinforcements, firepower, booby traps, and command and control. They grunted agreement, asked questions, slapped backs, and finally—my legs were cramped after my long crouch—stood up, their wooden chairs again scraping the linoleum.

"Saturday, then, oh-eight-hundred," Dad said by way of dismissal. "Don't be late."

Everyone filed back to the door, with me trailing behind, and one by one the men left.

"What are you planning now?" Mom snapped as soon as the door closed.

"We're moving our war games over here," Dad said dismissively.

"Don't you think you should have asked me first? And what will the neighbors think—you should ask them, too!"

"It'll be at night, and the Dietzes sure won't care."

"Then what about all the shooting?" Mom continued, unwilling to give up the issue. "We already had someone call the sheriff on us because of bullets flying over their house."

"That was from the anti*tank* gun—and we're not using *that* gun for the war games." Dad was getting annoyed, and he let it show. His voice took on the lecturing tone he usually saved for the idiots and numskulls of the world. "Besides, we'll be shooting *blanks*."

Mom shook her head and left the room. Dad flopped down on the couch and began picking his nails with a knife.

•   •   •

Early Saturday morning, Jerry and I woke to the noise of idling engines and slamming car doors, followed by the rough, shouting voices of men. Since none of the shouting seemed directed at us, we pulled our blankets over our heads and went back to sleep.

Several hours later, I walked into the kitchen to find breakfast. Mom stood at the table, and what looked like several loaves of bread were spread across it, along with a jar of mayonnaise, two packages of Velveeta cheese, and a stack of bologna. I blinked in surprise at the assembly line as Mom ignored me and worked. It was more food than we usually had in our house, and it was all spread out at once. Whenever she finished with two of the sandwiches—dip, spread, slap, slap, stack—she'd take them in one hand and set them inside a large paper bag. She touched the ingredients with quick, almost disdainful fingers, like the task was hurting her.

When she'd filled one paper bag and started on a second, there came a knock at the door. Leaving the current sandwich open and without cheese, Mom rolled the top of the paper bag closed and carried it to the door, which she opened. One of the strange men was standing there, his face streaked with dirt and sweat. He stared at the ground and started to say something, but before he could, Mom shoved the bag of sandwiches at his chest. He caught it, cleared his throat, and then left. As Mom turned back to the kitchen, she kicked the door closed with her heel.

"Mom, who was that?"

"One of the men helping your dad."

"Helping Dad with war games?"

"It's just something your father is doing."

"Mom?"

"*What*, Mark?"

"Can I have breakfast now?"

Mom handed me one of the sandwiches and turned back to the assembly line. Taking a bite, I jogged out the door to look for the man.

I caught up with him near the gun range. He had just tossed the paper bag full of sandwiches down into some sort of hole in the ground—and before I could figure out what that meant, a small geyser of sand briefly spouted up from what I assumed was the same hole. What on earth was happening? A minute later I stood with my hands on my knees, panting—eating a sandwich while running really took the wind out of me—and the picture of what Dad was doing came into focus.

In the sand in front of me was a hole the size of a house. And in the house-sized hole were a dozen men in a flurry of activity. Shovels, sweat stains, wood being braced against the walls, bright sand flying every which way—it was like the earth had erupted. The men looked like they were working under strict orders, and even when the bag of sandwiches arrived, no one took a break. Unable to comprehend what exactly I was seeing, I pulled my eyes away from the project and looked for Dad. I found him, dressed in blue work pants and a filthy T-shirt, standing at one edge of the pit, his arms crossed.

"Dad, Dad," I called, running to his side, "what in the world is everyone *doing*?"

Silence. I didn't exist—not when he had an army to command.

After a few minutes of listening to Dad bark orders to the men, I wandered around to the other side of the pit. One of the men had just scrambled out of it, and I recognized him as Dad's friend Dale. Dad called him the "ammo man" sometimes, and they liked to go to swap meets together. I asked him what was happening. He glanced at my father, who wasn't looking, and said, "Underground command center for next week."

That explained everything, and also nothing.

From down in the hole, a shout that was nearly a scream jolted me. One of the men was rocking back and forth on his heels, his hands pressed to the side of his head. At his feet was a bucket full of dirt that must have fallen back onto him. Bright blood was leaking down his face and across his bare chest. I couldn't take my eyes off the contrast of red on white, even as other hands lowered the man bodily to the ground and began to fashion a sling out of shirts and rope. Once the man was rolled onto the sling and lifted back to ground level, my father barked orders.

"You, you, and you—help him outta here! The rest of you, take a break. Food's here."

Two of the men who had helped with the sling jumped back into the pit, while one stayed to help the wounded man back toward the house. I followed.

When they knocked on the door, Mom answered with another paper bag in her arms, presumably full of bologna sandwiches. When she saw the wounded man, however, she set the bag on the sand outside the door and nodded toward her car, then disappeared back inside. The men waited in the backseat. Mom reappeared carrying her purse and climbed into the driver's seat, firing up the engine without even glancing at me. The car bounced down the driveway, no doubt on the way to Doc Kramer's.

Alone again, I wandered back toward the wooded hills, hoping to discover more about the war games.

●   ●   ●

The next Saturday evening, men seemed to materialize out of nowhere, like clouds. Cars parked helter-skelter across the driveway and the surrounding sand, wherever there was an empty piece of ground, and when the men climbed out, they drifted together toward a point behind the shed. The uniforms and black berets were familiar by now, and all were carrying guns, along with pistols strapped to their hips and homemade hand grenades slung from harnesses worn across their chests.

At the center of the storm of activity stood Dad. An air of excitement and anticipation crackled around him. He wore his scuffed work boots and plain camouflage, so faded and stained it looked as if it had come from the Salvation Army. His trusty 8mm Mauser, the standard rifle of the German army in World War II, rested in the crook of his arm, and a .45 pistol was strapped to his side with a simple holster. He stood out among the younger men, all of whom were dressed in expensive and painstakingly customized uniforms, complete with insignia and patches and loops for extra gear. Most of them had cropped their hair in military fashion, while Dad was almost bald on top. But there was no mistaking who was in charge.

Jerry and I watched from the sidelines, awestruck, as the impressive array of hardware and men marched past. We sidled closer and closer to Dad, but no matter how close we stood, he chose not to acknowledge our presence. No one else did either. We were two skinny boys drowning in an ocean of men, guns, and egos. Each new arrival strutted, displaying his weapons, looking for approval from those already gathered.

The sun set behind the ridge on the other side of the road, and the oaks faded from dark green to gray to black. All at once, a serious mood descended on the group. The men sorted themselves into two teams— red and blue—and passed around armbands. Dad, standing at the front of the blue team, seemed to notice us for the first time.

"You boys stay out of the way."

With that we were dismissed. It was time for the men to get on with their serious business.

"Come on, Mark," Jerry said. "Dad doesn't want us out here. Let's get back."

But I had no intention of going inside. Over the previous few days, we had found bunkers, trenches, and traps scattered everywhere, and now they were actually going to be used for battle. I'd discovered one that had been almost completely hidden, carved into the side of a hill.

"Check this *out!*" I'd hollered to Jerry. "This thing is huge!" The opening was so small, we'd been forced to crawl through it, but the main room of the bunker opened up so we could stand upright.

"And check *this* out," Jerry had said, extending his arms as if holding a rifle. "You can shoot through this opening without being seen!"

The inside walls had even been lined with sections cut from felled trees to guard against collapse. There was no going back to green plastic army men and sand castles. This was the big time, and it was all ours. Or at least it would be when Dad and his buddies weren't using it. The bunker was one of half a dozen the men had carved out. Our minds boggled at the possibilities. And the night of the battle was when I'd first see all of these preparations actually used.

As if sensing my thoughts, Mom called from the house. "Mar-ark! *Mar*-ark!" Her voice stretched like taffy, calling me back for dinner and bed. She had warned me to stay inside during the war games, but that wasn't something I was prepared to do. I needed to see what happened that night—to see what all the fuss was about.

"Let's go watch TV," Jerry said.

I shook my head. "You go back. I've gotta see this, and see it up close."

The gunfire began at dark. The first shot startled me—even though I *knew* they were firing specially made blanks—and I immediately cursed myself for being a coward. As the pace of firing picked up—three shots here, five shots there—I crept toward the bunker I'd seen the men working on, hoping it would be part of the main battle. In the black of night, everything looked different to me. I'd spent countless hours outside around the house, of course, but never had I tried to remain unseen and safe in quite the same way. Familiar shapes felt otherworldly, changed somehow, even though my mind still recognized them. Just as I neared my target, the noise of what seemed like a hundred shots exploded up ahead. *Pop! Poppoppop! Poppoppop!* I could see orange flames leaping from the ends of rifle barrels, seemingly on every side of me.

Suddenly terrified of being caught in a battle—even a battle I knew was a game—I dropped to the ground and rolled onto my back. In panic

I looked for something familiar. And there it was: a familiar shape outlined against the sky, black on nearly black. It was one of the few tall
oaks that dotted the area, and I'd climbed into its highest branches many
times. Trying to stay low to the ground, leaning forward but keeping my
head up like Dad had showed us, I raced across the empty sand toward
the tree. As soon as I reached it, I stood with my back against its rough
bark, safe in the knowledge that I blended perfectly into its dark silhouette. I tried to control my breathing, but my heart was pounding hard
enough that I expected a sniper to hear it and pick me off at any second.

As soon as the next round of gunfire opened up, I began to climb.
Branch by branch, trying to time my ascent with the bursts of noise, I made
my way to a familiar perch, nearly thirty feet from the ground.

It was only then, as my breathing slowed, that I began to take in
the scene below me. Lit by a fingernail moon and a thousand bright
stars, all reflecting off the white sand, the battlefield lay before me like a
school diorama. Dark shapes darted back and forth across it, the flashes
of muzzle fire showing the outlines of heads and shoulders for fractions
of a second. The shots came from one direction, then shifted the opposite way, back and forth and then back and forth again. The gunfire
was punctuated by shouts, by the occasional scream, and twice by what
sounded like real explosions. It was a marvel of terror, spread below my
dangling legs.

Eventually—minutes? hours?—the fighting moved past my perch.
Rapid staccato slowed to an occasional pop, and after a time I realized
the battle was finished. Dazed and exhilarated, I climbed down the oak
and walked toward the house. Halfway home, I heard laughter from
the direction of Dad's gun shed, and I followed my ears. Light leaked
through the cracks and out onto the sand, along with the sound of men
being men. Without thinking, I walked straight to the door and pulled
it open.

In the sudden shine I saw my father, standing among his troops,
except that he was not my father. His face was striped, green and brown,

and from the jungle backdrop of his skin, his eyes and teeth gleamed like white fire.

"Come in, Mark!" he said, motioning.

It seemed the whole room stopped to look at me. Needing to break the silence before it overwhelmed me, I blurted out, "Is it over? Who won?"

"Your dad got his ass shot off!" one of them yelled, and the whole room erupted in laughter.

"Well, I got a few of them first," he countered. "And I—"

Suddenly the sound of gunfire filled the room. I screamed in pain and leaped into the air. Beneath me loomed the dark shape of a gun barrel, firing, firing, sending gouts of orange flame into my shoes and pants as I landed. The shooting stopped as I fell to the floor—just as one of the men yanked open the shed door to reveal the shooter, who had shoved his weapon beneath the door and unloaded a full clip of blanks.

I clutched my legs. The blasts had burned holes in my pants below my knees and burned my skin besides. I was the only one in the room without a weapon, and I'd just been shot, even if only by blanks.

Raucous laughter drowned out my cries of pain. The shooter stood to backslaps and congratulations for his bravery. I tried to laugh along but gave up when it became clear I'd been forgotten. I was, once again, a nonperson—a boy whimpering unheard at the feet of men.

In a triumphal crown to the war games, Dad raised his pistol over his head, and any thoughts I might have had were blown away by the tumult of shouts and cheers that poured from the throats of his men.

7

MOM REFUSED TO SURRENDER. She was saddled with a husband who spent most of his time shooting guns and reading up on the Third Reich. She owned a house that was barely a house and each day seemed one step closer to being reclaimed by the shifting sands that surrounded it. Her children were a wild, ragtag bunch. But she hadn't survived as long as she had by giving up when things got tough. Middle-class respectability—okay, *lower* middle-class—remained within her reach. That was one of the reasons she married Dad in the first place, at an age when she should have been in high school, rather than trying to raise us on her own.

Mom was waging guerrilla warfare against our family becoming white trash, and one of her preferred tactics was to make sure her kids went to church. One Sunday each month—two, if she was lucky—Mom would marshal us kids out of bed and spiff us up, checking our hair, teeth, faces, and fingernails.

"We're going to church," she'd bark like a drill sergeant. "Get *up!*"

Jerry and I slept in every chance we got. "Mom, do we *have* to? I *hate* going to church."

"Get up and into your Sunday clothes, now!"

"But Mom, my pants don't even fit!" Jerry tried.

"Wear them anyway," Mom retorted, bustling down the hall to check on Sheri. We moaned and dragged ourselves out of bed.

"I hate church," I groused to Jerry. "We don't know anybody, and we have to wear weird clothes."

"At least your weird clothes fit—my pants are up to my ankles."

"At least I don't have big dorky glasses," I shot back. Jerry shrugged. He knew I was mad at my dress clothes, not him.

Sheri met us in the kitchen, and we started eating our cereal. She always wore a black dress and black shoes to church, and not only did her outfit seem far more comfortable than our too-tight wool pants, stiff leather shoes, and button-up shirts, but she actually *enjoyed* dressing up. It was incomprehensible.

Mom came into the kitchen to check up on us while we ate.

"Change your shirt—that one's dirty," she snapped at me.

"Dirty?" I asked innocently, looking down at my shirt.

"You haven't washed it since the last time you wore it, Mark. Look at how dirty the collar is!"

That wasn't a news flash. Everything I owned was dirty. Heck, everything I owned looked dirty even directly after being washed—that's what happened when you bought the cheapest possible clothes and washed them in the worst possible water. And when you lived in the middle of acres of dirt.

I didn't say any of that to Mom, of course, but left my cereal to sog and slithered off to change my shirt. When I returned, Mom had turned her attention to Dad, who had wandered past on his way to the living room.

"Aren't you ready yet?"

"*I'm* not going," he stated proudly.

"What? Why not?"

"All those people want is your money."

"We need to go as a family!" Her voice had taken on a pleading tone. "It's important."

"They're just a bunch of hypocrites," Dad said. "They dress up and act holier-than-thou, then live like hell the rest of the week. Crooks and criminals, that's what they are."

Mom crossed her arms. "Don't you think it's important for our *kids* that we go as a family?"

His answer was brutally efficient. "No."

Mom stood there, staring venom, but he flopped onto the couch and cracked open a manual on the inner workings of an assault rifle. Mom caught us looking longingly at Dad.

"Let's *go*," she said in disgust. There was nothing for it, so we headed out the door, limping in our stiff shoes and itchy pants.

The church was a large, white building, set back from the road on a swath of neatly mowed grass. Its steeple came to a precise point, high above the largest trees on the church grounds, and wide steps led up to the double front doors. In the sanctuary, dim light from the yellow windows drifted down over brown carpet and row after row of long, wooden pews that had been polished to a gleam by generations of sliding dresses and slacks.

Since Mom always made sure we arrived in time for Sunday school, however, we entered the building through the parking lot and headed down the stairs to what was called "the education level," which in reality was a cold basement that smelled like damp paint. Jerry and Sheri and I would find our separate classrooms, and then I would be alone. I always chose one of the metal folding chairs close to the back of the room. I came to church just often enough that no one had to treat me like a visitor, but no one was my friend, either. Mostly I stared at the floor and waited for time to pass.

"Who wants to play a game?" the teacher liked to ask. His chipper voice was too loud for the small classroom. "Are you ready? Where is John 3:16? Whoever can find it in their Bible first will win a prize!"

We were all made to hold our Bibles over our heads with two hands until the teacher was satisfied that everyone was ready. He would look around dramatically, playing up the moment, and then punch his fist into the air and shout, "Go!"

All around me I could hear the sounds of Bibles hitting laps, covers being tossed open, and impossibly thin pages turning and turning like the spokes on a bicycle wheel. I no sooner opened my Bible at random and began saying to myself *Matthew, Mark, Luke, John* than a small blonde girl jumped out of her seat, yelling, "I've got it! I've got it!" She read the verse aloud to verify her claim, but to me it sounded like she had already known the words before looking it up. "ForGodsolovedtheworld, thathegavehisonlybegottenSon, thatwhosoeverbelievethinhim, shouldnotperishbuthaveeverlastinglife."

"Correct!" announced the teacher, and he reached across several children to hand the girl a piece of candy.

I closed my Bible and returned to thinking about how uncomfortable my pants were and how my leather shoes were starting to rub a raw spot on my left ankle. It was obvious I wasn't one of the good kids. While the teacher walked back to the front and the rest of the kids bantered about who would win the prize during the next "sword drill," I wondered for the hundredth time why Mom dragged us to church at all.

• • •

Even before I opened the door at home after church, I could hear one of Dad's German marching songs blaring from the record player. I'd barely entered the living room when he looked up from his book and barked, "Why'd you leave your breakfast dish on the table?"

I stood there, uncomfortable as ever in my church clothes, wondering what to do. Many times when Dad upbraided me for something, I felt I deserved it—even if I was innocent in that particular instance, I'd probably been guilty some other time.

That day, however, I was feeling just a pinch of self-righteousness.

I had just endured three hours of church on a sunny Sunday, after all, while Dad had lounged on the couch with his shirt off.

I piped into his expectant silence, "I *didn't* leave it, Dad, honest to *God*!"

He crossed the space between the couch and me in the blink of an eye. His slap to the side of my head stunned me, but I didn't move. I was rooted to the floor. "What did I tell you about using the Lord's name like that?" he shouted at me. "Who the f— do you think you are? You're *nothing*!"

He marched into the kitchen and returned with a bar of Zest soap. I opened wide—what was the point of resisting?—and watched down my nose as Dad's brawny fingers forced the soap into my mouth.

"Now bite down, dammit!"

My teeth sank into the waxy bar. The gag reflex was hard to suppress, but spitting the bar out would only reset my punishment. I squeezed my eyes shut and tried to flare my nostrils, desperate to pull air into my lungs that wasn't soap flavored. My cheek and ear were still ringing from Dad's slap. I knew Jerry and Sheri had already fled to their rooms. We hated watching one another get punished, partly because Dad had a way of spreading punishment around, but mostly because watching one another suffer was its own kind of suffering. Why suffer when you didn't have to?

"Now get out."

Dad's pronouncement came minutes later, and I ran for the bathroom. I vomited the bar of soap into the sink, my stomach heaving as the soap bounced around and settled near the drain. When I calmed down, I set it on the counter so I could carry it back to the kitchen later.

I grimaced at myself in the mirror. Some of the chunks of soap stuck between my teeth were obvious, and I picked them out with my finger and flicked them into the sink. Other bits, however, hid between my molars, and no amount of picking could dislodge them. I cupped my hands and slurped water into my mouth, swishing until I couldn't stand the soapy flavor any longer, then spit. I knew it would take quite a few rinses to clear my mouth out, which meant I had plenty of time to think.

About how it wouldn't have happened if I hadn't been forced to go to church. About my punishment for taking the Lord's name in vain. And about what Dad had muttered as he shoved the bar of soap past my lips: "Just a g—d— good-for-nothing kid."

8

It was sometime after the soap incident that heaven smiled down on my father and blessed him with an unexpectedly awesome weapon.

He saw a report on television about a World War II tank soon to be auctioned. The Military Inn, a fixture of the Dearborn veterans' community, needed to get the M19 off its property. The proprietor owned one of the largest private collections of weapons in the world, but the tank had to go. Dad dialed the number on the screen.

"What's the story on the tank?" he asked the manager at the television station.

"It'll be auctioned off to the highest bidder. If you're interested, you need to place your bid before the weekend."

"It might be worth six hundred bucks to me," Dad replied. He gave the manager his name and phone number and then hung up.

On Monday morning the phone rang. "Mr. Bouman, how are you going to move your tank?" Turned out Dad wasn't just the *highest* bidder, he was the *only* bidder.

Dad drove over to Dearborn to see his new acquisition. The M19 was twenty tons of steel with twin 40mm guns in an open turret. The barrels and breaches were torched so they couldn't be fired, and the engine hadn't been run in years, but that didn't bother Dad. The Navy had taught him how to repair just about anything that burned gas or diesel. He contacted a heavy moving company, then contacted Mom.

"A *tank*?" Mom thought she'd misheard. "You haven't even finished your *house* yet, and you bought a tank?"

"I got a good deal."

"The last thing this family needs is you spending money on a *tank*!"

"Money, money, money—is that all you think about?"

"It wouldn't be if you'd quit spending it like we have lots of it. And spending it on *toys*."

She couldn't do more than complain, though. Dad was the owner of a tank, and there was no going back.

Blakely Drive wasn't much wider than a single lane, and since it was unimproved gravel, it didn't have shoulders. When the moving equipment arrived, with the M19 on top, it was almost as wide as the road, so none of our neighbors could get past until the tank was delivered. Dad had the moving crew drop the tank on our property within spitting distance of the road.

Jerry and I didn't say much—we didn't have to. We just kept play-punching each other on the arm and nodding our heads and grinning. Even Sheri was excited. Having a tank was definitely at the top of the list of good surprises we'd enjoyed.

It didn't take long for the Dietz clan to come over. "I was wondering why the road was blocked," called Mr. Dietz, "and now I know. You bought a tank!"

"Yeah," Dad said, practically bursting with pride. "Thought I'd build my own army."

The Dietz boys ran up behind their father.

"Is that a real tank?"

"What are you gonna do with *that*?"

"How big's the engine?"

"Geez, those guns look like they could take out a *house*!"

Dad laughed, patting the air with his palms as if to slow the flow of questions.

"It's got two 125-horsepower Cadillacs, and they run, but I gotta do some work on 'em," Dad said, as if repairing tanks were something he did every day.

Now Mrs. Dietz had arrived as well, and she marched right up to Dad. "Bouman, what have you gone and done—are you going to get into trouble with that thing?" Then she laughed and stepped closer to the tank so she could pat it.

Jerry and Sheri and I had already climbed onto it, and the Dietz kids were right behind us.

"What are these for?" Mike Dietz wondered, opening and closing some boxes beside the guns.

"I think they hold the ammo," I answered, running my hands along the barrels.

"But why are there holes in the guns?" asked Sheri.

"Looks like the holes were cut out with welding torches, see?" I stuck my finger into one. "Maybe to make sure you can't start a shooting war?"

We all grinned, and Jerry jumped down into the gunner's seat, pretending to blast a passing car.

"Don't, Jerry!" I warned. "We might get in trouble for something like that!"

"Aw, they can't really shoot," he said, pretending to attack a nearby building.

We crawled from one end of the tank to the other, and from top to bottom, searching out every compartment and hatch and cranny. Inside the tank, where the driver sat, was easily the coolest. Mrs. Dietz agreed.

"I gotta try this, Bouman—how many housewives around here can say they've sat in a tank?"

Dad climbed up and helped Mrs. Dietz, who completely disappeared down the hatch.

The Dietz boys couldn't contain their glee.

"Mom's gone!"

"She's so short she can't even see out!"

"Watch out, Mom! Turn left!"

Her happy voice shouted back from the driver's seat, "At least I can reach the pedals! All right, Bouman, help me outta here!"

As Dad helped pull her out, he looked at Mr. Dietz. "Want to give it a try, Les?"

"Nope, I'd probably end up crushing something," he joked.

"Lemme have a turn then!" one of the boys chortled. "I'll run over Mom!"

"You just watch yourself!" she threatened with a smile, sliding back to the ground and dusting herself off. That made me think of our mom, and I looked all around, but she was nowhere to be seen.

Once the excitement faded and our neighbors got tired of staring, they headed home, and Dad got to work, disappearing inside the engine with his tools. After a few days of banging and clanking, and a few hundred curses, Dad declared the engine was ready to run for real. The three of us—Mom was still avoiding the tank—gathered in a knot to watch as Dad lowered himself into the hatch. The engine choked, sputtered, and belched thick clouds of blue smoke. The noise was incredible—like a hundred cars stacked together—and I guessed the whole neighborhood knew that my father had finally gotten his new tank working.

• • •

The tank made my father a local celebrity, and not just when neighbors came by to drive it over anything crushable. Most places he went, people knew who he was. Sometimes it was just whispers he overheard—*there goes the guy who got himself an honest-to-goodness tank*—and other times it was a free bottle of Coke or game of bowling. So it wasn't long before he got it in his head to upgrade, and he put word out that he was looking for a new engine. A man called him soon after, a man who had the 450-horsepower Ford engine from a World War II M36 tank retriever. "It's still in the crate," he told my father. He'd purchased it to install in one of the construction cranes he owned, but it had been too large to fit in the casing.

"What do ya gotta have for it?"

"Oh, how about two hundred bucks?"

"I'll give ya one fifty."

Dad borrowed a truck and lugged home the new engine, then promptly set about removing the old Cadillac engines from the tank. Of course, he hadn't bothered to check whether *his* casing was big enough to fit the Ford engine—it wasn't—but he didn't waste time moaning about it. He simply rotated the new engine and dropped it in backward, and it fit just fine. He didn't bother to dig up a manual for the new engine either, so he took his best guess at how to hook up the transmission linkage. Once he got everything installed, he took his tank out for a test run. The new Ford workhorse ran like a champ and gave Dad a hair over ten miles an hour driving forward, but in reverse it went over thirty. "Too much work to fix it now!" he declared, and that's the way his tank remained, faster backward than forward.

That summer, Dad got a call from a few towns over, asking if he would drive his tank in the annual Fourth of July parade and if he'd be willing to park it at the police station a few nights early, to set the mood for the festivities. Dad was thrilled—until two nights before the parade, when someone broke into his tank and tried, unsuccessfully, to take it for a joyride. Dad didn't like that idea one bit, but the hatch didn't have a lock. Figuring the thief might strike again, Dad carefully affixed a military smoke grenade, the kind meant to mark a landing site for helicopters, to the underside of the driver's seat, setting it to go off if a person sat down.

The police called Dad the next morning to tell him that the tank was still in the parking lot, but the driver's compartment and the hatch were bright red. Dad must have told that story a dozen times that morning alone, and when it came time for the parade, and we all drove over to watch, Dad kept his head on a swivel for anyone with a guilty look who happened to be the color of a tomato. He never discovered the would-be tankjacker, but he did discover that the attention his tank brought was like a drug.

We could see it just by looking at him when he was with his tank: the way he held his head higher, the frequency with which he puffed out his chest, how he would look off into the distance as if he possessed vision that others did not. The greater the attention Dad received, the more he ignored us. Driving his tank down a boulevard filled with cheering spectators came naturally to him.

Once at a gun show, when he went to pick up a special order, Dad told me that most people are sheep. I knew that Dad wasn't most people, though, so I guessed that made him the shepherd. Seeing Dad in his tank, I felt certain that what he said was true. Some people really were born to lead, which meant the rest were born to follow.

One of the men who liked to hang around Dad helped him paint the tank with authentic World War II camouflage, and when the project was finished, they selected a prominent place on the side, just above the treads, and added an iron cross, one of the military symbols of Nazi Germany.

It was official. In the eyes of everyone in town, as well as within a fifty-mile radius, Dad had become the Tank Man, and that meant I had become the Tank Man's son.

PART TWO
A TANK

9

It DIDN'T TAKE LONG for my new identity—the Tank Man's son—to spread past Blakely Drive. One of my classmates learned about the tank, and he stopped me outside the door to our classroom. "My dad saw your dad parking it on a hill," he said, nodding to himself, "so *that's* how I know it's true!"

The news spread like spilled milk across a cafeteria table. A knot of kids formed around me.

"Your dad really has a tank? A *real* army tank?"

"Yeah," I answered.

"And he gives you rides in it?"

"Yeah, all the time."

"No way! Do you get to shoot the gun?"

That question was answered for me by another kid. "The guns don't work, dummy!"

"But why did your dad buy an army tank anyway?"

That question was trickier. Why *had* he bought the tank? Probably for the same reasons he bought all his toys. Because he liked it, and because he could.

I shrugged. "Just to have one, I guess."

My classmates' opinion of Dad soared. To them my father was a legendary figure: a bold, fun-loving man who bought and drove an army tank for no other reason than the thrill of it. I knew a more complicated reality, but I saw no reason to change their minds.

And part of me had to admit they were right. It *was* cool, sometimes, to be my father's son. One ordinary school day, when Mom was picking up Jerry and Sheri for some reason, I rode the bus home alone. Emma, our driver, was so short that she'd asked the guys down at the maintenance yard to add wooden blocks to the clutch, brake, and gas pedals. She was shaped like an apple and had a tongue like a whip, and we kids rarely dared to test her.

As the school bus slowed down near my stop, I could hear—even over the pounding of the bus's compression braking—another roar that could only be Dad's tank. I strained my eyes to see through the trees. Sure enough, Dad was chugging down the hillside, cutting toward the bus at an angle. He had the tank pushed to its limits, and smoke belched behind him as fans of dirt churned up from the treads. Dad beat the bus to the head of our driveway by a few seconds. When the bus stopped with a jerk, Dad was waiting, revving the tank's engine and watching from the driver's hatch, his mouth a half grin. All the kids jumped from their seats and ran over to gawk, and Emma didn't say boo. Even if they'd heard of the Tank Man, few had actually seen him driving. I walked the aisle toward the front, while every kid stayed glued to the right side of the bus, staring at my dad, with him staring right back.

I climbed down the steps and hopped to the ground. Dad motioned for me to get in the other hatch. By then I'd had enough experience with the tank that clambering up the tread, across the deck, and into the gunner's hatch was second nature. Once I was inside, Dad punched it. The sight of a bus full of astounded kids, their faces plastered to the windows, was the last thing I saw as we drove up the hill toward home.

• • •

Later that same school year, there was an overnight ice storm that coated absolutely everything in crystal. Each tree looked like it was made from glass, and even the sandburs had a certain kind of beauty. As we waited for the bus at the end of our driveway, the few cars that passed by sounded different—quieter and more hesitant. I plunged my hands to the bottom of my pockets. My breath came in regular puffs of white that hung in the air before drifting away. When the bus finally arrived at my stop, it didn't actually stop. Instead, wheels locked, it *tried* to stop but slid right off the road and into the ditch, the whole thing happening in slow motion.

I knew there was no way that bus was getting out of the icy ditch. I heard Emma give it gas, and the tires spun like the dickens, but she knew as well as I did that her vehicle wasn't going anywhere anytime soon. I saw her pick up her radio handset, probably to call for help, and when she did, my brother and sister and I shrugged at each other and started back up the driveway.

The ice made it hard to get back up the hill. I had to keep my hands out of my pockets, and by the time I reached the front door, I couldn't feel the knob when I opened it. For some reason, I yelled for my father— probably because the situation involved a large vehicle. Dad threw on his jacket and went outside, and I followed him. Looking down the hill toward the road, we could see the bus still resting at an odd angle.

"Huh," Dad said.

He stepped off the porch and climbed into the tank. The engine fired right up, belching clouds of exhaust into the frigid air, and before he drove off, I scrambled up beside him. We rode down the driveway together, the tank paying about as much attention to the ice as a windshield to a fly.

Dad pulled the tank in front of the bus, hopped out, and walked to the bus door, which Emma levered open.

"Want me to pull you out?"

Emma paused before answering. Normally nothing rattled her, but maybe the prospect of hooking her bus up to a tank was simply too much. At last she shrugged and stammered an answer.

"I . . . ah . . . well—I guess so?"

"Then stay behind the wheel," ordered Dad, "and steer the bus so it comes out of the ditch gradually. I don't want to pull it out at too much of an angle, or it might tip over."

"Okay, but—" Emma still sounded worried.

"It'll be fine."

I climbed out to watch the proceedings. From the road, I could tell Emma wasn't at all convinced that adding a tank to the equation was going to help. She was wearing her believe-it-when-I-see-it expression: one eyebrow raised, lips tight. My father's tank was big, sure, but nothing close to the size of a school bus. But Emma must have figured she didn't have anything to lose. If it didn't work, she'd still be stuck in the same ditch, no worse off than before—and able to blame that crazy Tank Man if anything went south.

"Get the chain from the bin!" Dad yelled over to me, and with numb hands I pulled several dozen feet of chain out of a locker on the tank. Dad maneuvered the tank so it was on the road directly in front of the bus, pointing the same direction, then positioned the chain onto the road between the two vehicles. Working quickly, Dad attached the ends of the chain to the bus's axle hooks and lifted the middle of the chain up and over a steel clamp on the body of the tank, directly between the treads. Then he climbed back into the driver's hatch and gave Emma a thumbs-up. She just stared. From where I stood, only her gray, permed hair was visible above the wide steering wheel.

Dad gunned his engine, then put the tank in gear and shoved the drive sticks forward. The bus jerked, and Emma disappeared for a second before sitting back up and adjusting her glasses. The bus shuddered, and Emma spun the wheel to keep the bus from sliding farther into the ditch. The tank was powerful, but the bus was huge, and nothing further happened beyond the morning quiet—and the icy surface of the road—being torn to shreds by the increasing roar of the tank's treads. Dad was kicking up a miniblizzard of ice crystals and frozen gravel, his tank actually sliding a bit from side to side as it grappled with the mass of County Bus No. 32.

Then, just when I thought the whole operation would be a bust, the tank's treads dug into the gravel beneath the ice. Once they did, Dad had plenty of traction, and the bus began to move, at first by inches and then by feet. All at once it came sliding out of the ditch, its wheels still locked and skidding across the ice. Dad continued to pull forward until the bus was squarely in the middle of the road. And there it sat, looking like a school bus was supposed to look, like it had never been in the ditch.

Yes! I thought. *We did it!* Dad motioned to me to unhook the length of chain, and Emma leaned out her window.

"I was worried for a minute," she yelled, "but thanks, Mr. Bouman! Now I don't need the tow truck."

Dad nodded, then spun the tank and drove it back up the hill toward the house. Suddenly it occurred to me: I still had to go to school! Not that I would have anything particularly fun to do at home. With everything outside iced over, I would probably spend the day inside, watching television if Dad wasn't and doing nothing in my room if he was. I sighed, fogging the air in front of me with a larger-than-normal cloud.

Just then Emma popped open her window and hollered down at me. "School's closed on account of the ice. Just heard it."

With that she revved the engine and began to ease cautiously down the road. I watched the bus disappear around the bend until I was alone on the road. I looked toward the house and picked out the shape of Dad's tank crunching its way up the driveway. He'd left without me. With both vehicles gone, I could hear my breathing. I could hear the occasional crack of a branch breaking under the weight of ice. I started up the driveway, hands out, carefully picking my way up the slick slope. The easiest route was to follow the tracks of my father's tank.

• • •

Dad's buddy Dale, the ammo man, was a big fan of the tank, and he was the fastest and most accurate reloader, which made him valuable to Dad. One crisp, sunny afternoon, Dale decided to be a good boy and ignore his guns, instead taking his mother for a drive. He'd just purchased a new Toyota sedan, and there wasn't a single blemish on its pearly white surface. After the drive he came over to our place so his mother, Vera, could chat with Mom—and, of course, he knew there was a good chance he could sneak in some time on the gun range.

Jerry and I were playing outside, and I watched Dale drive past the house, parking his car in an open, sandy area away from anything else. As he and his mother walked toward the house, I heard her asking him why he had parked so far away. Dale said something about keeping it cherry, but Vera was having none of it.

"You've been warned not to park away from the house, Dale," she chided. "I mean, at the Bouman place you never know—"

"It's fine, Mom," Dale interrupted. "Just head inside. I'm going to see if we can take the tank for a spin."

Dad was way ahead of Dale. He already had the tank warmed up and was motoring across the field toward the house. "Ready to go for a ride? Hop in!" he shouted. Dale jogged down the driveway, jumped onto the tank, and lowered himself into the other hatch.

"I'm going inside, Mark," Jerry said.

"I guess I'll just stay and watch the tank," I told my brother. I knew I couldn't ride in it, but I didn't want to go inside with the ladies, either. I knew Dad had the throttle levers jammed all the way forward by the pitch of the engine. Whenever he turned, the treads tossed dirt into the air. The ground they drove across looked a lot like a war zone: every scrap of vegetation, from the tallest tree to the smallest blade of grass, had been torn down, twisted up, or otherwise mangled into oblivion. The ruts in the ground were deep enough to lie down inside.

Before long, the tank began to head straight up the hill toward the spot where Dad usually parked it, behind the house. He always positioned the tank there so it could be seen in silhouette from the road, with the tank's twin 40mm guns pointed outward to intimidate anyone driving by. It was cold enough outside that the men had probably decided to head inside and take over the couch, sending the women into the kitchen.

Dad powered up the hill and across the crown, then swung around in a smooth, tight spin. He had done it so many times that the top of the hill, as well as the back slope of it, had a sort of natural road embedded in it, free of all trees and bushes.

Which is why Dale had chosen that spot to park his brand-new, scratch-free car half an hour earlier. Dale must have realized the path Dad was taking, because I heard the growl of the engines drop suddenly, as if Dale had shouted a warning. But twenty tons of moving steel can't stop on a dime. Dale's car was a trapped lamb with a wolf bearing down on it.

I heard the impact even over the noise of the tank. When Dad killed the engine, everything was silent for a moment. The next noise was Dale's voice screaming, "No, no, no! Not my car!" as he clambered out of the hatch and jumped down onto the ground.

"Mark, what *happened*?" Jerry yelled from behind me. He'd heard the noise and sprinted out of the house.

"Dad hit Dale's car! Come on!"

Dad was still sitting at the controls, and Dale motioned frantically with his arms. "Back it up! Back it up!"

We stared in awe as Dad reversed the tank, ever so slowly, and Dale's car began to move backward with it. Part of the tank was embedded in the softer metal of the car, and for a moment it looked like they couldn't be separated. Then, with a sickening noise of metal ripping metal, the tank broke free, leaving Dale's car rocking softly on its shocks.

Dad killed the tank's engine as Dale raced to inspect the damage. The front of the tank had slammed squarely into the trunk, flattening it onto the chassis with the power of a hydraulic press. Amazingly, the rear window of the car was intact, but from there the trunk sloped steeply until it was only several inches thick at the rear bumper.

Dale threw himself onto the ground, face first, and pounded his fists into the dirt. "My car, my car!" he sobbed over and over.

"It's not too bad, actually," Jerry remarked, trying to be helpful. We'd seen Dad do some serious damage with the tank. Considering what could have happened, the small white car had gotten off easy.

Dale disagreed, and wailed all the louder. Mom, Vera, and Sheri arrived then, discovering a damaged car and a grown man who was groveling in the dirt, tears streaking his face.

"What hap—" Sheri started to ask.

"Shush," Mom interrupted, putting her finger to her lips and frowning.

For a minute the only sounds came from Dale, who was curled into a whimpering heap, and the only action was the six of us watching him. It was strange to see a grown man flopped like that, his black hair waving back and forth as he shook his head like a dog.

Finally Vera broke the silence, embarrassment fighting anger in her voice.

"Dale. Get up. Get *up*."

He reluctantly climbed to his feet and stood with his head down. His pants and hands and even his face were streaked with dirt. Then he spun and kicked the tank as hard as he could, producing a dull clang.

Then Dale just stood there, the mirror of a little kid who has just had his favorite toy taken away, from the pouting lower lip to the heaves that still shook his shoulders. Mom had made it clear that we kids weren't to speak, but she hadn't told us we had to leave, so we hung around to see what would happen.

Dad spoke up at last. "Sorry, Dale. I didn't know your car was there." Then he added, "And . . . I *have* told you not to park there. So . . ."

With that parting shot, Dad climbed back into the tank, fired it up, and backed away from Dale's car. Then he parked in his usual spot nearby, climbed out, and strolled down the hill. Dale got into his car and slammed the door.

Mom glared at us to ensure we wouldn't blurt anything in front of Vera, and then Mom, Vera, and we kids walked back toward the house.

Probably no one was more surprised than Vera when, partway to the house, Dale drove up next to us. From the rear doors forward his car still looked brand new, and the engine was humming along quietly. Without saying good-bye to Mom, Vera opened the passenger door and climbed in.

Mom, Jerry, Sheri, and I watched the car bounce down our driveway, turn onto the road, and disappear.

Dale was never able to convince the repair shop that the damage had been caused by a tank, but his insurance company eventually believed him, and that was all that mattered. His car soon looked like new again, and he didn't hold a grudge against Dad. After all, Dad still had the best private gun range in a hundred miles—plus a tank that Dale still wanted to ride in.

And Dale's car wasn't the only victim of Dad's tank. A few weeks later, a rainstorm turned the ground into a morass. The next night, plummeting temperatures turned the wet ground rock solid. In the morning, Dad climbed into his tank and fired it up, planning to take a short drive around the property. He threw the tank into reverse, not realizing that one of the treads was trapped tight by the frozen mud. One tread immediately began to roll while the other held fast, and rather than backing up in a straight line, the tank pivoted. He hadn't expected that but figured the best way to break the tank free was to keep going.

By the time he saw the hood of his pickup protruding from under one side of the tank, it was already far too late. The truck was a complete loss. As was our septic tank, which Dad accidentally ran over a week later.

10

After the incident with Dale—a guy Dad would have said was one of his best friends—Mom said something that caught my attention.

"Your father values things and uses people."

Mom was right, once I thought about it. Dad *did* value things. His guns and tank and books and knives and records meant a lot to him. And it wasn't only the valuable stuff he cared about either. He cared about everything that was his, *because* it was his. It didn't matter if it was his drugstore watch or his Sears catalog shoes: ownership meant worth.

He was forever telling us to be careful with his stuff, despite his lack of concern for anyone else's stuff. He might decide to use one of Mom's baking pans to catch oil during an engine rebuild and shrug off her anger, yet woe to the one who broke anything of his. He ruined countless things that belonged to others—Mom's towels and sheets and pots and pans, a sled that belonged to us kids—yet demanded that nothing of his be damaged.

These demands began to be enforced with violence.

"Did you break this hinge off the shed door?"

"Dad, it was an accident. I—"

Smack.

"Did you bend the antenna on my truck?"

"Dad, we were playing, and—"

Smack. He was unstoppable. One blow from his hand—nearly always openhanded and directed at our left cheeks and ears—could knock any of us down. The explosion of pain and heat and noise often caused me to drop like a sack of potatoes. Even Jerry, who was taller and stronger than me, usually crumbled. Even Mom. And the slaps and smacks were landing with greater frequency.

Not on Sheri, though. It seemed like Dad never hit her, for reasons we couldn't fathom.

So it didn't take long for the tank to lose its appeal—to become just another thing Dad did at home, like shooting his guns and learning German and always keeping ice cream in the freezer. Cool at first, then something he cared about and we had to be careful with. Luckily for us, the chances of hurting his tank were next to nil.

The ice cream was another story. Dad began keeping the freezer stocked with it, and he forced Jerry and me to fetch him bowls when he was reading on the couch.

"Go get me some ice cream," he'd growl without looking up. The trouble was that our freezer kept the ice cream rock hard, and we couldn't scoop it out without letting it thaw. The first time I was sent to get him some, he cursed me from the other room.

"What the hell is taking so long?"

Jerry had to fetch it the next night, and like me, he found the ice cream nearly impossible to scoop. Dad stood and waited for him to deliver the bowl to the couch. Once the dessert was safe in Dad's left hand, he lashed out with his right, slapping Jerry on the side of the head so hard that Jerry's glasses flew across the room and clattered off the wall.

While Jerry crawled over to recover them, Dad sat back down and calmly ate the ice cream. Jerry and I learned to use a thick kitchen knife to hack out the ice cream faster.

All of which proved Mom's point: Dad was using Jerry and me to get his ice cream, and it seemed like he cared more about his dessert than us.

●　　●　　●

It wasn't like Dad was a monster, though. There were bad moments, but there were good moments as well. For instance, the more weapons I fired, the happier Dad seemed.

Dad and I would climb the gun tower and blast away at targets on the hill, and he'd keep feeding me more ammunition or a different gun. Sometimes we'd just go out back and wander around, blasting things.

"Here, Mark. Try the Luger."

The pistol pulled my hand down as I took it. "Wow, it's heavy!"

"It's a German officer's gun. Now try hitting that old milk can."

I held the gun up and fired off a round. It felt like someone had punched my wrist and shoulder.

"It's got some kick. Now keep going at that can—I filled it with water."

I took a deep breath and tried to prepare myself for the recoil. *Boom. Boom boom boom.* I kicked up dirt behind and beside the can. Dad watched, his arms folded.

Boom. The can exploded, spraying water in all directions.

"Great, Mark! You got it!" Dad gushed, giving me a wide smile. "Now this gun is a little harder to shoot."

He handed me a pistol that was even heavier than the Luger, its shape thicker and more rectangular.

"What's *this* one?"

"A forty-five auto. Issued by the US Army as a sidearm in World War II. See this bullet?" he asked me, sliding out the clip and letting me study it.

"Bigger than the Luger bullet, right?"

"Right. This'll punch a hole in a Jap, for sure." He slapped the clip back into the pistol and handed it back to me.

"Now lean into it. This has even more kick."

Boom.

"It's really hard to hold steady, Dad!"

"Take your time. Try to hit that second can."

I tried to slow my movements and breathing. *Boom.*

"High and left, Mark."

Boom.

"Closer. Aim a bit lower."

Boom.

A cloud of water bloomed in the air, and Dad let out a whoop beside me. "Good job, Mark!" he smiled. He extended his hand. I engaged the safety, rotated the pistol in my hand, and placed the grip in my father's palm.

We were the Bouman men, brothers in arms.

•   •   •

Until we weren't. That kind of camaraderie didn't last when Dad's friends came around.

Once, Dad called me over to the base of the gun tower. He was standing in a loose circle with about six guys, and when I got close enough, I could see he was holding some kind of rifle I'd never seen before. It was almost as tall as I was, and when Dad handed it to me I nearly dropped it. I knew he expected me to fire it, so I aimed it as best I could at one of the metal targets out across the field. I could barely hold the barrel steady because of the gun's weight, so I knew my chances of an accurate shot were close to zero.

As soon as I pulled the trigger, I understood that Dad hadn't been interested in my accuracy. The gun's recoil was so powerful against my right shoulder that it shoved me backward. I lost my footing and my hold on the heavy gun at the same time. Dad stepped forward and grabbed the rifle right out of the air, allowing me to collapse on my keister. Dad and his friends roared with laughter. From the wooden floor, I could see one of them bent over, his hands on his knees, guffawing like he'd never seen anything funnier in his life. Another mimed my shot, his invisible gun punching him in the shoulder and causing him to windmill his arms like a cartoon character.

I picked myself up, wondering if I was expected to say something, but by then the men had forgotten me and moved on to the next weapon, so I climbed down the ladder slowly, favoring my sore shoulder, while the men above me continued to blast away.

Another time, when one of his buddies was over, Dad went a step further. His friend, a burly construction worker who turned his T-shirt inside out whenever the outside got dirty, picked me up by the ankles. I'd been on the floor in the living room playing chess with Jerry, and Dad had been sitting on the couch talking about some battle with his friend, when suddenly I found myself upside down, suspended, my arms waving uselessly below my head.

Bam, my head pounded the floor, then *bam bam bam*, and all the while I could hear my attacker cackling.

"Dad, save me!" I screamed between slams, but the slams continued until Dad's friend became bored and released my ankles. I collapsed in a heap on the floor. I rolled over and tried to sit up, my head swimming with pain, and when I could finally see straight, I could see my father still on the couch, talking with his friend as if nothing had happened.

• • •

Dad's friends weren't always around, of course. One afternoon he was taking the tank for a joyride around the property, and since I didn't have anything better to do, I was outside watching. He'd just crushed a tree with the tank when he throttled back and yelled down to me, "Hey! Mark! Want to drive?"

Did I ever! Jerry and I played on the tank whenever we felt like it, treating it like our own personal jungle gym. I scrambled up and dropped into the driver's seat. I knew from playing in the tank with Jerry that I could reach all the levers and pedals, but now that we were out in a field, with the engine running, there was one problem.

"I can't see!"

"Don't worry," Dad said. "I'll watch where you're going."

Dad crouched, balancing himself on the lip of the hatch, looming behind where I sat in the driver's seat. He could look forward and still keep an eye on which levers I was supposed to be operating.

"Push those two together," he ordered, leaning down and waving his hand to direct me, "and give 'er some gas."

Turning left or right was as simple as pulling one of the levers on either side of my seat. If I pulled the left stick back, the left tread stopped while the right tread continued to churn, turning the tank left, and the same principle applied to the right track. Whenever Dad shouted, "Hard left! Right! All ahead!" I followed along. The sense of power made me dizzy. Twenty tons of steel responding to my direction. I was used to being the Tank Man's son, but still I couldn't stop thinking, *I'm driving a tank!*

Before too long, though, the incredible noise and vibration over-powered me. I yanked both levers to a stop and clambered onto the seat, gulping fresh air. I turned to look behind us. In my mind I could picture the sharp ruts the tank treads must have pressed into the soft earth. Like looking back along a ship's wake, I would be able to see exactly where we'd come from, even though I couldn't see where we were going. Peering past Dad, I discovered that the ground we had just crossed looked exactly like every other scrap of ground on our land. Like a war zone. Nearly every plant had been flattened or upturned, and I couldn't tell one rut from another.

"Quit rubbernecking," Dad growled. "I thought you wanted to drive!"

I climbed back into the driver's seat, engaged the levers, and shot forward. When my father told me to turn, I turned, and when he told me to give it more gas, I did. All I could see was the dark, scuffed metal of the tank's interior, and the heated odor of machine oil forced its way into my nose.

Driving the tank turned out to be more like being driven. Even as the tank powered its way across our sand, stopping for nothing, I felt like a puppet, with Dad pulling the strings.

* * *

Dad controlled Jerry, too. Since Jerry was older and stronger, Dad had been using him as a gofer for longer—long enough that it had become habit. When Jerry and I were flipping through one of Dad's military books once, Dad stuck his head into the room.

"Jerry, come on. I need you."

I heard my brother sigh, even if Dad didn't. It was probably the hundredth time Jerry had been forced to help, alone. And probably ninety-nine of those times, Dad had yelled at Jerry during the chore and called him an imbecile.

I followed them out to the shed to see what they were working on. Dad was building some kind of metal frame, and he needed Jerry's long arms to hold it while Dad sliced through sections of metal with his acetylene torch.

"Higher, and hold it there!" Dad barked. Then he flipped down his welding hood and lit the torch. It ignited with a loud pop, illuminating the inside of the shed and casting crazy shadows on the walls. As he began cutting, molten steel dripped onto the floor, and sparks leaped in all directions.

One landed on Jerry's pant leg, just below the knee, and instead of fading out, it burned a hole right through the fabric.

"Ouch!" Jerry yelled, jumping back. There was still a spot of flame on his leg.

Dad flipped up his mask and screamed at Jerry. "What the f— are you doing? Hold the damn thing where I told you!"

"But my—"

"No buts, imbecile! Just do what I tell you, g—d— it!"

Jerry quickly swatted the small fire out and tried to regain his hold on the metal. Again the torch melted the steel, spraying sparks in all directions. Jerry kept glancing down nervously, and sure enough, another dot of fire bloomed on his pants. This time he balanced the metal in one hand and swatted out the fire with his other. The same thing happened five or six more times, and Dad's cutting never missed a beat.

Dad flipped up his mask slowly, looked at his project, and simply stated, "Okay."

"Does that mean I can go?" Jerry asked nervously.

"Just a minute," Dad answered, looking back and forth between his project and some other pieces of steel scattered around the shed. "Now hold this piece."

Much later, long after I'd given up and left the shed, Jerry and Dad emerged, damp with sweat. Jerry's hands were black from handling the steel, and his pants were spotted from crotch to ankle with holes.

"It's time for dinner," I told them.

"Good," grunted Dad.

Mom nearly dropped the plate she was holding when they walked into the kitchen.

"What happened to your pants?"

"Helping Dad."

"Go wash your hands," she said, frowning at Dad, who didn't seem to notice.

Once we were all eating, she circled back to the problem. "Why didn't you make sure Jerry didn't burn his pants while he was helping you? Now you've ruined them. He can hardly use them for *anything*."

"You can't expect to not get dirty if you're working," Dad replied calmly.

"*Dirty?* Those are holes! If he's going to help you, send him back to the house to change his clothes first! Where are we going to get the money for another pair of school pants?"

Dad didn't bother to answer. He just shrugged and kept on eating.

"Jerry," I asked him later when we were alone, "is that why you sort of disappear sometimes?"

"Yep."

I waited to see if he was going to add anything. After a minute he did. "I've helped Dad so many times. I'm tired of it. Even when it's kind of fun or interesting—it might not stay that way."

II

"WHAT ARE YOU WORKING ON, DAD?" I asked as I crouched down beside him.

Dad was stretched out under a VW Beetle. It had been wrecked and the engine had been removed long before. More recently, Dad had used a torch to remove everything forward of the windshield. It looked like a piece of a car, like it belonged in a giant plastic model kit.

"It's a project I've had in my mind for a while now. I thought I'd put that old plane engine on top of this to see how it goes."

"A *plane* engine?"

"Yep. It's on that pile right over there." He motioned with his hand. Stacks of junk stretched in all directions, so I faked it.

"Oh, right. That one." I couldn't begin to imagine what he had in mind, so I let him keep working while I wandered toward the house.

At dinner that night, Mom asked Dad what he'd been working on all day.

"You know what an airboat is, right? Well, I've been thinking about this for a long time, and I think I can use an old airplane engine to power the wrecked VW."

"That sounds like fun," Jerry said. "And it'll go fast, right?"

What sounds like fun? I wondered. I still had no idea what Dad had in mind.

"I think so," he said to Jerry. "I should have it finished before Monday, and we can take it for a spin."

Mom gave a skeptical snort and passed a dish of potatoes around for a second time. Jerry used the lull to ask something.

"Can I join the basketball team at school?"

Dad set his glass of milk down on the table with a bang. "Basketball? How are you going to get to practice or games?"

"I don't know."

"Well neither do I. You'll have to find your own ride."

Jerry sighed and moved some food around his plate.

"Why don't *you* take him?" Mom asked.

"I've got other things to do," Dad shot back. "Why don't you take him if you think it's such a good idea?"

Mom didn't back down from Dad's snarl. "*I* work full-time. I make dinner every night, do the laundry, and clean up your messes. Why don't you think of someone else for once?"

"I work hard too, you know. I just want to get some things done after working all day. Can't a man have a life?"

Mom didn't know what to say to that, so no one said anything. Dad wolfed down the rest of his dinner and went into the living room. Mom left soon after, heading for the bedroom.

We kids began to clear the table and do the dishes. "Are you gonna play basketball?" I asked Jerry.

He shrugged and kept washing. I wondered what would happen if Jerry drove to school in the contraption Dad was making out of the VW and the airplane engine.

• • •

Dad spent much of the next few days on his newest *something*, as Mom labeled his projects. He stripped the airplane engine down and rebuilt it. He removed the VW's backseats. He fabricated a steel mount for the engine and welded it to the top of the car's frame. He called a buddy to help him hoist the plane engine onto the mount, and then Dad welded it into place over the rear of the car and reattached the four-foot propeller blades, encased inside a cage he had constructed to provide at least a hint of safety. By the end of the weekend, he had built a carplane.

Just one problem remained: how to actually *drive* it. After staring at his contraption for what seemed like an hour, his hands fixed on his hips, Dad stalked off toward the junk piles. Before long he shouted for Jerry and me to come help him, and we found ourselves lugging lengths of iron pipe back toward the carplane. When Dad was satisfied with his raw materials, he pulled on his welder's mask and fired up the torch. Jerry managed to wander off—who could blame him?—while I hung around to watch. A tripod of pipes took shape, the wide end attached to the VW frame just in front of the driver's seat and the narrow end reaching out past where the bumper would have been. Dad welded one of the old airplane wheels onto a pivot where the pipes met, and after testing his creation by jumping up and down on the carplane's new front end, he put his welding gear away in the shed.

He returned with an armful of cables and wheels and bolts. He grinned at me, walked back to the VW, and then crouched down at the front end. Soon he had the front tire connected, via a system of pulleys, to the VW's steering wheel. He stood up and evaluated his creation from top to bottom, front to back, the look on his face somewhere between pride and lust.

"Well, Mark," he said, eyes still on the vehicle, "want to try it out?"

Dad had seen fit to reward my patience with the opportunity to be the first kid to ride in the carplane. I jumped into the passenger seat, sitting forward and gripping the dashboard so I could see through the windshield. Behind me, the propeller blades were only about a foot past the glass. I felt like I was perched in a cockpit, ready for takeoff.

"Let's go!" Dad shouted, and with that he turned the key in the ignition. The airplane engine roared to life instantly. With the propeller a blur directly behind me, and the powerful thrum of the engine about two feet above my head, I suddenly felt an urgent question in my gut: *How in the world does this thing actually work?*

Dad must have seen my confusion. "Watch this!" he yelled, and then he reached down and grabbed a wire near the emergency brake lever. My eyes followed his hand, and I noticed for the first time that the wire ran through the back of the car via a series of eyelets before connecting to the engine mount above us. Dad gave the wire a few tugs that coincided with him waggling his eyebrows—as if his facial expressions were causing the engine to rev. Dad gave the wire a yank, and the engine became deafening. We shot forward down the driveway, Dad flinging the steering wheel every which way as the carplane slalomed its way toward the road. I held on with both hands.

As soon as we hit the bottom of the driveway, Dad tugged the engine wire the opposite way and smashed the brake pedal, and he leaped out and ran up to crouch at the front of the vehicle where the cables connected to the pivoting wheel. Then his head was at the driver's window.

"I got the cable directions reversed," he shouted with a smirk, "so when I turned right, it went left!"

He did something that seemed to solve the problem, then flopped back into the driver's seat and pulled the wire, ratcheting up the engine power, and we turned smoothly onto the road.

Dad lined up with a few small corrections to the steering wheel, and then he reached down and pulled the wire as far as it could go. The car was loud before, but now it was earsplitting and overwhelming. We surged forward, charging faster and faster down the road. And the one thought I had, spinning past again and again like the propeller, was *I'm riding in a carplane!* It felt like I was perched on a missile. I risked a glance over my shoulder and was shocked to see that the road had completely disappeared, hidden behind a cyclone of dirt, leaves, and flying rocks. I looked at Dad. He was giddy. Joyful even, in his eyes.

It wasn't a time for words. It was all about the wind in our faces and the scream of the engine as we flew down the road side by side. Dad had introduced another *thing* to our family. I was sharing it, and it was glorious.

•   •   •

Not too many weeks later, a storm had covered everything with a few inches of fresh snow, and Jerry and Sheri and I were deep into another game of Monopoly when Dad announced, "You kids come with me." He stood up from the couch and grabbed his winter coat. When we got outside, we were puzzled to see him knotting a rope to the back of the carplane.

"This'll be fun. You're up first, Jerry." With that he handed a snow saucer to Jerry. "Now run down to the road and show us how it's done."

Still a bit hazy on what *it* was, I had no time to ask Dad because he had already climbed into the driver's seat of the VW. As he fired up the engine, I jumped into the passenger seat and slid toward Dad, but Sheri didn't follow. I looked back at her through the rear window, her body blurred through the whirling propeller, and I saw her shake her head and walk back inside. Without waiting for me to shut the door, Dad pulled the wire for the gas and raced down to Blakely Drive, where Jerry was waiting. Dad pulled onto the road and stopped, giving Jerry, who had figured *it* out before I did, a chance to sit cross-legged on the saucer and get a firm grip on the rope. When he was ready, Jerry nodded at Dad. Dad nodded at me, then gunned it.

Even on the snow, the carplane could really move. Jerry held on—but I could only tell because the rope was still taut. I could see it stretching out behind the VW for about ten feet, and then it disappeared in the blizzard of snow the propeller was kicking up. Jerry was back there somewhere, and I just hoped he was on the saucer and not being dragged by one leg.

"I can't see Jerry!" I yelled to Dad.

"So?"

"So I can't *see* him!"

Dad let the cable go slack so the engine could idle. As soon as the speed of the propeller dropped, the blizzard behind us died down—and there was Jerry, completely covered in snow and still clinging to the rope. We were towing a living snowman. Dad let the VW slow to a crawl, and Jerry climbed off. I thought he'd head for home after what he'd just been through, but instead he jogged to the driver's window, wiping the snow off his face as he came.

"Dad, Dad!" he shouted. "We just need some skis! That way I'll be above the worst of the snow and can see where I'm going!"

Dad nodded, looking pleased that his eldest son was taking after him, and he told Jerry to hop in. The three of us screamed back down the road, fishtailed into the driveway, and turned around. Jerry hopped out and raced into the shed, returning with a pair of old skis that Dad had found at a yard sale a few years before. They weren't real skis—like most of the stuff Dad found, they could have been cobbled together by Dr. Frankenstein. A pair of spring bindings were nailed to a pair of small boards, and the boards were then nailed to a pair of cheapo children's skis. The result was something that nearly anyone could wear, although calling them skis was a stretch. Jerry ran past us toward the road, and we followed.

Jerry strapped on the skis, pulling the springs up and over his boots. Then he grabbed the rope and nodded to Dad. "Ready—but start out slow this time?"

Dad gave the engine just enough gas to get the carplane going, while I turned around to watch my brother. He was hanging on like a champ, his skis tracking in straight lines through the snow. Dad looked back, too, and when he saw how well Jerry was doing, he goosed the throttle. Faster and faster we went, racing down the road, the propeller kicking up the same amount of snow as before. This time the cloud only covered Jerry up to his chest, so I could still see his straight-out arms gripping the rope, his blown-back hair, and a grin that looked like it would split his face in two.

•   •   •

Dad wanted to try out carplane skiing for himself, so he ordered one of his buddies to drive over. An hour after Jerry's run, he and I were standing on the side of the road to watch. Dad's buddy was in the driver's seat, while Dad, wearing size-12 snow boots, was having a terrible time trying to pull the frozen binding springs up and over his toes. Next came goggles, a heavy pair of work gloves, a black beanie, and a complicated way of wrapping the tow rope around his forearm that, he told us, professional bull riders used. The children's skis looked ridiculous compared to Dad's large body.

"Fire it up!" he yelled.

The backwash blew off his beanie within the first few seconds, and then he was wobbling and leaning his body this way and that, like a bowling pin deciding whether it was going to fall over. We heard the airplane engine rev up another notch, and suddenly Dad was running rather than skiing. The bindings and boards had ripped from the skis, and Dad, the rope still secure on his forearm, found himself trying to sprint while wearing wooden platforms on the bottom of his boots. He was a living cartoon.

Like most cartoons, his attempt ended in a tangle of body parts. Jerry and I raced down the road toward him. By the time we got to the carplane, Dad was already back on his feet, laughing with his buddy about his exploit. Then Dad's buddy slipped over into the passenger seat, Dad got behind the wheel, and without a glance at us they roared back to the house, leaving us standing on the snowy road.

"Why'd they ditch us? And what should we do with them?"

I looked at Jerry but didn't answer his questions.

"With the *skis*," Jerry clarified, nodding downward. They were right next to each other in the snow, pointing away from the house. Both had jagged nail holes ripped in their decks.

"Well," I finally responded, "we'll keep them, I guess."

We each took one ski under an arm and trudged back home. When we got to the shed, we tossed the skis in a corner and shut the door. The VW was parked nearby, empty. Dad and his buddy were back in the house—I could see Dad's snow boots on the porch, the bindings and small boards still attached.

Jerry went inside, but I stayed out in the cold for a while longer. His guns, his tank, his carplane: all Dad's stuff, and us just along for the ride. Or not, as the case might be. I shivered. Beside me I could hear the *tick-tick-tick* of the airplane engine as it shed its heat into the frozen air.

12

OUR DRIVEWAY HAD always been a disaster, ever since the time one of its ruts tried to swallow our car whole on the night of the tornado. Whenever it rained, the driveway became a maze of rough patches and deepening ruts. Over the years, beginning when the shovel handles stood taller than our heads, Dad had tasked Jerry and me with making sure the driveway was drivable.

We never made much progress. Jerry and I could spend an entire day shoveling sand back into the ruts—something we did too many days to count—but as soon as the next rain arrived, all our work would be washed away. It was no easy job for Mom to avoid the ruts when she drove us somewhere. Veering back and forth across the driveway, Mom would attempt to steer around the worst of them, but some looked deep enough to swallow Sheri. They snaked back and forth across the path of the car, and if a tire slipped into one of them, we all knew we'd be walking the rest of the way to the house.

"Rats!" Mom snapped one of the times it happened, banging her hand on the steering wheel. We all climbed out and met Mom at the trunk. She handed each of us a bag of groceries, and we began the long walk up to the house.

"The car's stuck partway down the driveway," Mom announced in Dad's general direction as we trooped through the door. I looked back at the car, still trapped in the rut, tipped forward like it was bowing toward the house.

"What!" Dad's voice, coming from the living room, sounded like Mom had just informed him that she planned on punching him in the face.

Mom sighed. While she stacked cans of green beans on the counter, she repeated herself, first in a near shout, then more quietly when Dad marched into the kitchen.

"Again? I must've told you a thousand times not to drive it into a rut after a g—d— storm!"

Mom banged one of the cans down on the counter, then crossed her arms and faced off against Dad. "I wouldn't have driven into a rut if *you'd* fixed the driveway like *you've* promised a *thousand* times!" Mom fired back. "The last storm was more than a week ago! If you took as much time to fix the driveway as you do fixing your . . ."

Halfway through Mom's rant, Dad stopped looking at her. It was as if Mom had suddenly ceased to exist. Mom's words trailed off as Dad turned and rambled away.

"Like talking to a wall," Mom mumbled. "Worse." Then she walked into her bedroom.

Jerry reached into the grocery bag and finished unloading the food onto the counter, and Sheri and I helped him. While I worked, I thought about how Mom had gotten lucky. Their fights used to end one of two ways: shouting or silence. Dad had chosen silence this time. But there was another ending Dad had begun to choose more and more often with Mom. I'd noticed black eyes, bruises.

The time I'd noticed a cut lip, I responded the same way she did when Dad hit me.

"Mom, are you okay?"

"I'm fine, Mark, why?" Then she answered her own question, touching the tip of her tongue to her lip and running off to the bathroom.

When she came out, her lip looked fine, and she touched my shoulder and said, "Mark, your dad has been tired a lot lately. We should all do what he asks and try to make things easier for him."

That hadn't sounded quite true—*we* were all tired, but that didn't mean we needed to attack one another. But what could I say? Mom had told me she was fine. And I was fine after Dad hit me, too. What else could we be?

On the subject of the driveway, though, Mom had made a good point. Dad probably *could* fix the driveway if he wanted to—this was the guy who drove around in a tank, after all—but instead he kept yelling at Jerry and me to fill in the ruts with sand and more sand.

"As long as it's our job, Dad can blame us, I guess," I suggested.

Jerry looked at me and nodded. Sometimes Dad even tried to blame Sheri, which was a stretch, even by Dad's standards.

•   •   •

Dad wasn't much interested in anyone else's ideas. If we started a sentence with, "I thought . . . ," Dad would instantly cut us off.

"That's your problem right there: you *thought*! Don't think, just do."

We learned not to voice our opinions. Dad's opinions and ideas were the only ones that mattered. And one day he had an idea about how to fix the driveway. The perfect solution—meaning both free and involving the tank—came to Dad in a fit of inspiration: car battery cases. He drove over to a business in Grand Rapids that recycled old car batteries. They would collect the discarded batteries from all the dealers and repair shops in the area, then slice the tops from the batteries and remove the lead inside, which they would sell to a scrap-metal business. Once the lead was extracted, the battery company used a massive front loader to push the empty cases into piles as tall as two-story homes.

Dad convinced the owner that the best way to make space for more battery cases on his lot was to give all the old cases away—to Dad.

Dad must have made a good point, because one Wednesday a beat-up diesel dump truck rumbled and rocked up our driveway and unloaded thousands of chunks of old battery cases. One load. Another load. Soon we had half a dozen dump trucks' worth of plastic cases piled in mounds up and down the driveway. Dad's grin grew wider with each load. When the last driver gave Dad a quick nod and a salute before leaving, Dad climbed into his tank and fired it up.

Three hours later, the driveway problem was solved.

His tank spread and pulverized the case pieces—each about the size of a tortilla chip—in the process filling every rut in the driveway and creating a permeable, nonabsorbent surface that would instantly drain even the worst downpour. It also made the driveway look like it had been constructed by a child out of black Lego bricks, and it filled all the sand around it with hazardous chemicals. But Dad always said that progress comes at a price.

The next time it rained, the surface of the driveway held firm. Never again did we slog up a rutted driveway carrying armloads of groceries. We had our own, one-of-a-kind Bouman gravel that resisted rutting and drained water like a sieve. We also had what I suspect was the only toxic driveway anywhere in the nation. And whenever Mom complained about Dad not fixing something, he had a ready answer.

"Back off—I fixed the damn driveway, didn't I?"

13

One moment Dad, like a magician of the mechanical, could build a snowspeeder with his own two hands, yet the next moment he could slap us for any reason, or no reason, and then go back to whatever he'd been doing as if nothing had happened.

The uncertainty of what he would do wore us down. We kids didn't feel like we could ever really relax. We always had to keep our guard up—not that we had any guard that could block Dad.

"You're just grass, and I'm the lawn mower," he liked to say, and that was a promise he made sure to keep.

We all had our own ways of coping. I stayed outside as many hours of the day as I could. Jerry spent more time at the tiny, lopsided table in our room, doing and redoing his homework. Sheri would sass Dad, something Jerry and I would never dare. Once, when Dad was shouting at us during dinner, Sheri smacked her hand on the table and screamed, "I wish I lived at Monica Mitchell's house and not here!"

We froze. Dad would have beaten Jerry or me straight to the floor for even a fraction of that disrespect. But Dad just looked down at his plate, suddenly interested in his congealing mac and cheese. Mom looked back and forth between the two of them, on the edge of saying something, but then she closed her mouth and left the table. Once she was gone, Dad glanced up at Sheri. She didn't look back. And that was the end of another fine Bouman supper.

That night in our bedroom, Jerry said something for the first time.

"I hate it, Mark. How Dad treats you and Mom."

I pictured Jerry's smile, which was now missing a front tooth, courtesy of a slap from Dad the week before. I didn't wonder whether I'd be next.

"I know," I said at last. "I wish I could run away. Anything is better than this. Right?"

"I'm just hoping to get away from here as soon as I can," Jerry said. "Anything is better than this."

I sighed. Jerry sighed. We went right on sitting in our beds, doing nothing and saying nothing. I don't know what he was thinking, but I was resigning myself to the idea that things might never change.

• • •

I was lying in bed, and over the sound of Jerry's breathing I could hear wind whistling through the gap around the windowpane. Sometimes on cold nights I doodled with my fingernail on the frost that formed inside the window. Neither my brother's breathing nor the wind was loud enough to drown out Dad's shouting at Mom in the kitchen.

"Is that too much for you? To actually do something *right* around here?"

"Something? I do everything right, just like you do everything wrong!"

"The hell? You don't know how lucky you are to have a man like me!"

"Cursed, you mean! You don't work, don't save, don't help—you don't do anything!"

"If I really did nothing, you'd know it. You and your f—ing whining. I work my g—d— hands off, and this is what I get?"

"And *this* is what *I* get?"

Mom must have banged a pan on the stove to emphasize her point. What time was it? They could go on like this for hours. Mom and Dad had been out on a date, which was fine by me, until they came home arguing. I pulled my blanket up around my chin and ears, hoping not to hear the rest of their argument. Part of me was glad that Dad wasn't focused on *me*—but a bigger part of me was sad that Mom was feeling what I was more and more often, a feeling equal parts fear, anger, and helplessness.

The shouting went on and on—so far it was only shouting—back and forth from kitchen to bedroom to kitchen to living room. It grew louder then softer, like the wind, like Jerry's snores. I stopped listening. I listened to my breathing instead, and to the noise my blanket made when I slid it back and forth across my face. I wondered if I had dreamed the shouting and the slamming and the curses. Sleep whispered that everything would be better in the morning, and I believed it.

Suddenly my bedroom door flew open and slammed against the wall. "Mark, get out of bed!"

An instant later I was standing, adrenaline pumping through my bare chest. The hall light shone directly in my eyes, and I squinted at the silhouette of my father. He was holding something. "Didn't I tell you to dump the garbage before you went to bed?" he shouted.

"Yes! But it wasn't all the way full. So I—"

"Not full? Not *full*?" He crossed the room. "What do you call *this*?"

In time with the shouted final word, he raised the garbage can above my head and thrust it roughly past my shoulder. Then he turned it upside down and shook it. Everything inside slid out, some spattering my ear, neck, and shoulder, and the rest slopping across my bed.

Then he was screaming. "Clean this mess up! You want to live like a pig? Then I'll *treat* you like a pig! I should take a *belt* to you!" He threw the pail on the ground, and I watched it tumble, turn, and finally come to a rest. I glanced up, and Dad was already gone.

I grabbed the pail and set it upright on the floor beside my bed. As quickly as I could, I scooped the contents back into it. The chicken bones were easy, as long as I grabbed each one inside a fist. The mashed potatoes and gravy were trickier, so I linked my fingers and plowed the potatoes across my blanket and into the pail. The gravy was like Jell-O, so I formed my hands into small ladles, returning it to the pail as best I could. Apple cores, banana peels, burned curves of clotted oatmeal, potato peels—all of it I scooped and plucked and scraped from my pillow and blanket and sheet back into the garbage pail. Some of the food fell to the floor, and once my bed was clear, I knelt beside it and picked up the rest.

Jerry risked a quick glance from his bed, then he rolled over with a sigh and faced the wall. We were getting to the point where trying to help each other could cause more trouble for everyone.

I stripped my bed and ran to the laundry room, stuffing everything in and starting a load as quickly as I could. Then I ran back to my room, pulled on pants, grabbed the garbage, and jogged into the kitchen, since my boots and coat were by the door. Outside there was a ton of snow and no light. Holding the pail in both hands, I high-stepped toward the trash valley, and when I got near it—who could tell in the dark?—I did my best imitation of a bucket brigade and chucked the contents. Then it was back through the snow to the house, where I could see a finger of light from the kitchen door pointing across the snow.

And then I saw another light, past the house. It resolved into two: the headlights of Dad's truck slipping and sliding down the driveway. Where in the world was he going in the middle of the night?

I learned the answer back in the kitchen. It *wasn't* the middle of the night—it was five thirty, and Dad was on his way to work. Exhausted by fighting with Mom the night before, he must have fallen asleep, only remembering to deal with me after he'd woken up. If he'd waited thirty minutes, Mom would have woken me to get ready for school, and I could have simply taken the trash out then.

Dad had seen a better way to teach me a lesson, though, and he was nothing if not a dedicated teacher.

I peeled off my boots and put the garbage pail back in the kitchen, then went to the laundry room. By the time I finished putting my bedding in the dryer, Jerry and Sheri were both awake and in the kitchen, Jerry fixing oatmeal and Sheri watching him, her legs swinging beneath her chair. I wasn't hungry, and I passed through without a word. Back in my bedroom, I sat on the edge of my mattress, clamping my knees together with my hands and trying to get warm. Trying not to think about anything—to pretend it was a normal morning, whatever that meant. I could hear Jerry and Sheri brushing their teeth in the bathroom. I saw Mom walk past my doorway, a silhouette in the hallway, her hands up at her mouth, and it looked like she was crying. I could hear the wind through the gap around the window frame. I could hear me telling myself to stop thinking.

At last I grew warm, and it was time to catch the bus. Since I was already wearing my pants and jacket, I stepped into my boots and walked out into the snow for the second time that morning.

At school, I stumbled off the bus, tugged open the heavy front door, trudged down the wet hallway to my classroom, and walked to the coatroom in the back. I unzipped my jacket, and it was when I began to pull it over my shoulders that it hit me: I wasn't wearing anything under it. Before I could zip my jacket back up, another boy saw me.

"Hey, everyone, Mark Bouman came to school with no shirt on!"

Panicked, I tried to make up a reason, but all that came out was stammering nonsense. Other kids began to gather, whispering and pointing and laughing. I imagined—I hoped I was imagining—a glob of gravy dripping between my bare shoulder blades and sliding down my spine.

My teacher arrived to investigate. It took her a long moment to figure out what had happened, and an even longer moment to decide whether she could believe her own senses. I wanted to crawl under a desk and stay there forever. Mercifully, my teacher walked out of the coatroom and appeared seconds later holding a T-shirt she had retrieved from the lost-and-found bin. It was nicer than anything I owned.

"Why don't you go change in the boys' room, Mark. Take as much time as you need."

Laughter chased me out of the classroom and down the hall, and the smell of bleach welcomed me in the restroom. Every step I took echoed off the endless grid of small, square tiles that covered the floor and the walls. Standing in front of the mirror, I took off my jacket and let it fall to the floor, and a dirty, half-naked boy stared back at me. What would happen if I stayed in the restroom all day? It wouldn't matter. I was starting to understand that Dad's power could reach me anywhere.

14

"WHO. BROKE. THIS."

The menace in Dad's voice would have made any of his favorite Gestapo officers proud. The house was so small and Dad's voice was so large that pretending not to hear him was never an option. Nor were our preferences: whatever we had been doing at the time, Dad's commands took absolute priority. We left the living room and lined up in the kitchen, ready to project just the right attitude toward Dad. We had to be instantly obedient—that was nonnegotiable—but obedience wasn't the only thing he required. We had to appear beaten but not completely broken, because that would only invite more punishment. We needed to be silent most of the time so that he could deliver a speech if he wanted to, but we also needed to provide the right answer at the right time. Not necessarily the *true* answer, but the answer he wanted to hear.

Dad was holding a ceramic coffee cup in one hand and its broken handle in the other. He took a deep breath and let it out slowly, as if he couldn't believe his children were forcing him to live through such a personally painful experience. "Which one of you kids broke this?"

All three of us spoke at the same time. "Not me!"

"One of you broke it." Dad knew that beyond doubt. Mom wasn't part of the conversation. When she broke something, she'd find or buy a replacement—or sometimes start a fight with Dad about how she had no money to buy new things. And since Dad wasn't into punishing himself, it was down to the three of us kids. Dad surveyed us, and he took his sweet time doing it. Then he settled on me as his first target.

"Was it you, Mark?" He took a step toward me, and inside that small kitchen it felt like he was ten feet taller than me, his wide shoulders and angry face blocking out the domed ceiling light and the dead bugs that polka-dotted its inside.

"No," I tried to say, but it mostly came out as a shake of my head and a squeak.

It was true, though. I hadn't broken that cup. I'd broken plenty of things around the house, not all of which Dad had discovered, but we weren't talking about those other things. I couldn't stop staring at the cup and broken handle. Without the handle, Dad's hand swallowed the cup. The handle reminded me of a giant's fingernail clipping. Dad clipped his fingernails all over the house and left crescent moons lying wherever they fell. Behind Dad, both on the counter and in the open cupboard, I could see half a dozen identical and intact cups. Why was Dad making such a big deal about this one cup?

Dad was still talking. I needed to focus in case there was an answer expected of me, or in case I needed to grovel or cry.

". . . why I'm so tired of spending good money on things, just to have you kids go and break them all!" He was shouting now. I could see directly into his mouth. I could smell the sourness of each word. "When are you kids going to learn!"

He shook his head from side to side like a bear I'd seen on *Mutual of*

Omaha's Wild Kingdom. This was never a question from Dad, but always a declaration. He knew we *wouldn't* learn, despite his best efforts.

Jerry dared to speak. I don't believe he thought Dad would listen, but I also believe Jerry needed to speak all the same. Jerry was an honest brother, and if he knew that something was true, he wanted others to know as well. "We didn't break it."

Dad's scream nearly snapped Jerry's head back. "Like *hell* you didn't break it!"

Then came an instant calm. It sent a shiver down my back because Dad seemed so pleased all of a sudden, despite not having his question answered, despite having good-for-nothing kids who broke everything he spent good money on.

"*Somebody* broke it," Dad nearly smiled, "because it didn't break *itself.*"

That seemed true. I'd never heard of a cup breaking itself. But the three of us kept staring at Dad, our faces as blank as possible. What could we say? The cup didn't break itself, and we'd already insisted that we didn't break it. We were stuck. Mom would comfort us after the punishment, but she couldn't stop it from happening. Nothing could. Dad settled his hands on his hips and stared at us. Jerry swallowed. From the corner of my eye I could see his hands twitching at his sides. Sheri hugged herself and almost imperceptibly shook her head from side to side. Dad frowned at Sheri, looking like he might step toward her, but then he seemed to change his mind and his right hand drifted toward his belly. "Do I need to get out my belt?"

I knew that getting slapped in the face or punched in the ear was like the explosion of fireworks: an instant of bright agony, followed by moments of shining pain, and then a dark numbness. The belt was different—a slower buildup, a steadier pace, and impossible to forget. I nearly wet myself.

"That's it, then," Dad said calmly, and in a fluid motion he loosened the buckle with his right hand and drew the belt out through each loop with his left, *snick snick snick*, until it dangled from his hand like a slowly spinning snake. "I'm going to punish *all* of you kids until someone confesses. Follow me."

There was nothing more to be said. Now Dad's belt would do the talking. Tallest to smallest, we shuffled behind him. I walked as slowly as possible, desperate to postpone my punishment without adding to it. My heart was beating in my temples and the back of my throat. My hands looked like they were having a seizure. Not knowing exactly what was coming made the approaching cliff seem even higher.

"I did it." Jerry froze us in the hall. "I broke it when I put another cup on top of it," Jerry continued. He was staring at the floor, his voice barely above a whisper.

Dad paused in the middle of a step. Then he gave a faint shrug and kept walking. Jerry followed, and they disappeared into the bedroom.

Sheri and I remained behind, trapped in the hallway. We hadn't been ordered into the bedroom with Jerry, but we hadn't been dismissed, either, so we stood and waited. A storm had been building in Dad, and a moment later the clouds burst and he rained down suffering upon his son.

Jerry screamed. And screamed and screamed and screamed.

Here and there, like a flash of lightning, came a word or two from Jerry, pleading for mercy, but each word was lost beneath the ongoing downpour of Dad's belt. Then quick as it started, the storm ceased. Dad walked out of the bedroom, panting as he rethreaded his belt. His forehead was wet, and there were dark circles beneath the armpits of his white T-shirt. Sheri and I froze. Dad had been satisfied. He walked past us to the door and disappeared outside.

Sheri, her eyes glued to the ground, walked back to her room and softly closed the door. I went to see Jerry. He was choking back most of his screams so they came out as agonized whimpers, his body fetal and his pants still around his ankles. One arm was curled around his knees, and with the other hand he was trying to scrape the snot and tears from his face.

I knelt on the floor beside him. "What happened, Jerry? You really broke that cup?"

His answer arrived in shuddered breaths.

"No. Just didn't. Want Dad. To whip. You or Sheri."

15

WE BECAME PAINFULLY familiar with the phrase "You kids go outside and play."

When Mom said that, she meant we should go far enough away that we wouldn't hear her and Dad fighting. The sounds of their combat were simple—curse words, slammed doors, hands striking skin—but it seemed impossible to escape them. Eleven acres wasn't nearly enough. I'd seen their fights from start to finish inside the house, and thereafter I could imagine the fights, even if I went outside.

Jerry and Sheri and I had been trying to play a board game, but then one of Mom and Dad's arguments spun out of control.

"Those guns of yours are just a hole we're pouring money into!"

"I'm going to *make* money with 'em!"

"That'll be the day. You just keep buying junk. Everything we own is junk!"

"I've just about had enough from you!"

"What are you going to do, hit me?"

That was when Dad grabbed Mom by the hair and began to pull her toward the bedroom. Mom flailed wildly, screaming and trying to plant her feet, but she couldn't go limp because of the hold Dad had on her hair.

"Shut *up*!" he screamed, and he began to slap her face with his free hand. He was relentless. Like a fisherman, he reeled her in, closer and closer to the bedroom, and her fighting only made him fight harder.

And then the bedroom door slammed and locked.

"Dad's going to kill Mom!" said Sheri.

Jerry and I were speechless. Maybe he was. This was as bad as anything we'd seen. Dad certainly had the brute power to kill someone. We stared at the bedroom door, listening to the muffled shouts and the periodic crack of Dad's hand against Mom's skin. Sheri burst into tears.

After several minutes, it grew quiet. "Let's go," Jerry whispered. "We don't want to be here when Dad comes out."

We crept back to the living room only moments before Dad stormed out of the bedroom, grabbed his jacket, and headed out the door. His truck roared to life outside, then the noise faded as he raced down the driveway and up the road.

"Where's Dad going?" I asked.

"Is Mom okay?" Sheri asked.

"Just wait," Jerry said.

When Mom came out of the bedroom a few minutes later, the raised welts on the side of her face were clearly visible, even from across the room.

"Mom," Jerry asked, "are you okay?"

She looked at him but didn't answer. The skin around one of her eyes was purpling. Dad didn't come home that night, but the next day he was back, acting like nothing had happened.

In a way he was right, though. What had happened was becoming more and more common. Being attacked was a part of our lives, like the water that turned everything yellow or the sandburs that covered our shoes and clothing. It wasn't something we liked, but it was something we had to live with.

•   •   •

Mom did her best to protect us. After we'd been told to go outside, we knew exactly what it meant when Mom came running out of the house, one side of her face red, yelling at us to get in the car as fast as we could. It meant we kids were going to Grandma and Grandpa Russell's house until things settled at home. Mom never stayed with us at her parents' house. She'd drop us off and then drive away, leaving us to guess that things couldn't settle back at home without her, and they couldn't settle with us there.

Once, after yet another fight, Mom was already behind the wheel, motor running, and we were piled into the backseat, when suddenly Dad appeared outside the car and yanked open the driver's door.

Mom screamed. She tried to cling to the steering wheel, but Dad silently wrapped his large hand around her upper arm and began to pull. He was relentless. I watched her knuckles go white, her fingers slip one by one from the wheel, and then she was gone. Dad dragged her back up the driveway and into the house.

Jerry and Sheri and I stayed in the car, shoulder to shoulder in the backseat, crying and waiting for Mom to come back. In the car there were rules to obey, like stay in your seat, don't ask how long it will take, and never open the doors. Finally Mom came back to the car and opened the back door without looking at us. Her hair was tangled and her shirt was messed up and untucked from her slacks.

"Come back into the house, kids."

"We aren't going to Grandma and Grandpa's?"

"Not this time."

Mom dragged herself up the driveway to the house, and we followed. We'd see Grandma and Grandpa Russell again soon enough.

•   •   •

One visit at Grandpa and Grandma Russell's was the same as any of the dozens we spent there. None of us said a word during the half-hour drive. Mom cried most of the way, keeping both hands on the wheel while her shoulders shook in fits and starts. When we pulled up to their house, it was already dark.

"You kids wait here," she monotoned.

Minutes later, Mom emerged from the house and motioned us inside, holding open the screen door. Without a word we trooped through the dim kitchen and up the stairs to a bedroom with walls that slanted and windows that poked outward and formed little benches. There were three single beds, a lamp, and a box filled with old wooden toys that we'd lost interest in years before. Mom turned and went back down the dark stairs, leaving us alone. We knew Grandma and Grandpa Russell wouldn't come upstairs, and we knew there was nothing we could say to each other that would help. We'd just wait it out until Mom came back for us.

"G'night," Jerry said.

"Night, Jer," Sheri and I answered. Then we burrowed into our beds and waited for sleep.

In the morning, I stopped to use the bathroom on my way to the kitchen. I looked at the counter and saw the water glass where Grandma and Grandpa kept their teeth at night. It was empty, but many times I'd seen the two sets of teeth in the middle of the night, floating and foaming in the glow of the night-light. Grandma's were easy to tell because one of her teeth had a wire that stuck out of it, which anyone could see when Grandma pronounced words with lots of *e*'s in them. Beside the glass was the plastic razor that Grandma and Grandpa shared, since they both had to shave—Grandpa his whole face and Grandma just her chin.

Jerry and Sheri were already at the pink dining table, starting in on their bowls of oatmeal, and morning sunlight was slicing through the windows over the sink and shining off the metal band around the table and its metal legs. Oatmeal was one of the seven things Grandma and Grandpa Russell shopped for—along with milk, butter, eggs, bread, sliced Velveeta, and loaves of bologna—and everything else came from their garden or from bartering.

Grandma pointed me toward the oatmeal on the stove with her cigarette hand. "Get a bowl, Mark—I was just telling a story."

She was perched in her usual seat, back to the wall. Grandma could tell the same story fifty times and it never got old—just familiar and comfortable, like a favorite episode of *Gilligan's Island*. The pink kitchen table was her stage. Her stories usually started with her giggling to herself, silently wrinkling her bulbous nose, her wire-rim glasses moving in sync, and then she'd let the rest of us in on what was so funny. An ashtray lived on her side of the table, within easy reach when she pivoted her left elbow, and while her left hand always balanced a Virginia Slim, her right hand always cradled a mug of coffee. She kept a yellow sponge under her coffee elbow so that it wouldn't become sore from resting on the table for too long.

"So I remember the time during the war when I worked on Liberty ships."

"What's a Liberty ship?" Jerry asked. He knew his lines as well as Grandma knew hers.

Before answering, she leaned back with her cup of coffee and took a slow sip.

"They were called Liberty ships because they helped the war effort. Everyone had to help. I was a welder."

"A welder?" we all echoed.

"Yep, way down deep in the bottom of the ship."

"Was it hard?" Sheri asked.

"It *was* hard." Another sip of coffee, then a pull on the cigarette. "Cramped, and I had to bend over all day. Plus, I had to breathe in all those *fumes*." Her nose turned upward with the memory.

"And I had this supervisor once who came by and told me to 'get back to work' when I was sticking my head up for some fresh air." Her supervisor voice was low and bossy. "He didn't know anything about how difficult it was in that cramped, fumy space . . . so I *showed* him."

"How?" we asked together.

"I told him to take a look at my work. He crawled into that small space to take a look-see, and I stood right up against the opening so he couldn't get out! Well, he started to push and cough, trying to get out of there quick as he could, and the smoke was getting thick."

We stared at her, waiting for the punch line.

"And when I finally moved out of the way, he came out of there so fast, he just about fell over!"

We burst into satisfied laughter, and Grandma giggled as she finished her tale. "I told him now he knew why I needed air—and after that, he never bothered me again!"

After breakfast, Grandma told Jerry and me to go find Grandpa, while Sheri had to stay inside with her. The womenfolk were going to organize what Grandma called the "savin' bins," where she kept nearly everything: old bread bags, rubber bands, hairpins, pennies, buttons, and all manner of bits and pieces that could be useful but, as far as I knew, had never left the bins. Grandma even saved the old curls and scraps of soap bars in a large glass jar.

Grandpa was outside in the garden doing man's work. At least half his work consisted of sitting in a fraying lawn chair, listening to gospel music on his radio, and smoking an endless supply of plastic-tipped cigars that came in a box with an old-fashioned American guy wearing a curly white wig. Grandpa's skin was dark red and wrinkled from all the time he spent in the sun, and he pulled his hair straight back across his skull in thin white lines. He had been a carpenter until he got hurt on the job and shattered his hip, and now he and Grandma lived on Social Security and his homegrown vegetables.

"Mornin', boys. Been waitin'. Got some weedin' for us today."

Grandpa was typically a man of few words but many chores. Jerry and I sighed but dutifully wandered into the garden to look for weeds. The garden covered more than an acre, and Grandpa could be counted on to find endless chores in it for Jerry and me. It was strange, working so hard in a place where Dad never showed his face, but Grandpa had a set of lungs on him, too, and I got my share of tongue-lashings. Grandpa had turned the color of one of his prized beets the time Jerry accidentally shredded a row of flowers with the riding lawn mower. As long as we did our chores correctly, though, things were dull. And dull was a nice change sometimes.

I was weeding alone in one of the back rows when I found one of Grandpa's cigar tips. I picked it up and put it in my mouth. I mimed taking a pull, mimed Grandpa's contented face, mimed blowing a thin line of smoke into the humid air and letting the rest trickle out my nostrils. Grown-ups could do whatever they wanted. They could leave a place. They could never come back if they didn't want to. They could decide something and that thing would happen.

But Grandpa's cigar tip smelled awful, and I tasted dirt and sawdust, so I spit it back onto the ground.

The next morning when I woke up, the amount of light in the room told me I'd missed TV church. Grandpa got up early Sunday mornings, dressed in his only suit, and sat in his recliner to watch Reverend Falwell preach on a tiny television set. He expected us to sit on the green couch and watch too, although it was hard to get excited by a show that was just a guy talking—and people sitting in rows watching the guy talking—along with a bunch of people in robes singing. Still, Grandpa was very clear that the three of us kids were to watch if we were there on a Sunday.

Much better were the shows we'd watched the night before with Grandma while Grandpa stayed outside with his lawn chair and his Tiparillos. Grandma loved the *Lawrence Welk Show*, and I loved *Cannon*, a show about a fat cop with a snub-nosed .38 who, even though he could barely run, still managed to catch the bad guys every time.

After quickly getting dressed, I crept down the stairs, wondering how much TV church I'd missed and how angry Grandpa would be.

Grandpa's red face was even redder than usual, and he looked away from me quickly when I reached the bottom of the stairs. I sat down beside Jerry and Sheri, who were both watching—and who must have decided it was every kid for themselves, since they hadn't woken me. Reverend Falwell's choir was singing the closing song, and I was already contemplating how I could make peace with Grandpa, when his voice from the armchair surprised me.

"Mark, I forgive ya."

I turned around, and he nodded at me once before turning his attention back to the television for the close of the service.

We heard Mom's car in the front drive a few minutes after Grandpa clicked off the television—we weren't allowed to watch other programs on the Lord's Day. Grandma heard it too, and she went to the front door and held open the screen. We didn't have anything to gather, since we'd worn the same clothes all weekend, so we filed through the door, down the steps, and into the waiting car. Things at home must have returned to normal once again.

16

IN FACT, THINGS WERE *so* normal that Mom and Dad made it all the way through a conversation at the dinner table one night without some kind of conflict.

"This pot roast is looking smaller than last week's, which was smaller than the one before that." Dad announced this at the dinner table while he was chewing one piece of beef and cutting the next, and he did so without even a hint of anger or accusation. It sounded like he was commenting on the weather.

"The prices keep going up," Mom ventured, "so we just can't get as big a piece as we used to."

Dad chewed some more, thinking. "We should raise a beef cow."

"That might save some real money," Mom agreed.

"All right then."

"I like cows," added Sheri. Dad nodded at her, Mom smiled at her, and that appeared to be that.

I snuck a look at Jerry. He widened his eyes the tiniest bit, one of our brotherly expressions of surprise that we could almost always hide from Mom and Dad. Who were these strange adults sitting at our dinner table, discussing the price of meat so calmly? Was this what other family dinners were like all across the great state of Michigan? It was almost impossible to imagine, but I spent the rest of our peacefully quiet dinner trying: mothers and fathers chatting about raising cows and other such topics, children listening in and offering their opinions whenever they liked, and everyone basking in a sense of harmony.

•   •   •

Ike became part of our family the next week, and he caused us headaches from the moment Dad prodded him out of the truck.

The first hitch was that absolutely none of our eleven acres was fenced. Ike could wander wherever he wished, and it became immediately obvious that he wished to wander almost everywhere, causing Dad to add a new sentence to the list of chores he growled at us.

"Go get Ike."

That usually meant Mom had returned from town and it was time to feed our cow. In order for raising a cow to actually save us money, Mom had started scavenging food from the Dumpsters behind the grocery store, which yielded things like rotten vegetables, moldy fruit, and an occasional intact watermelon. Mom would pack the whole sloppy mess into boxes and bags as best she could and then dump it all behind the house. Then Jerry and I had to find Ike and convince him to walk back toward the house, where the pile of decomposing food was waiting. He was enthusiastic about the watermelons, but once they were gone, he would look at us and moo pitifully before poking his nose into the rest of the garbage. Sheri, despite her dinnertime declaration of affection for cows, didn't help much with Ike. The day Dad brought Ike home, Sheri told him that she wanted a horse instead of a cow, after which he stared at her for a moment and then walked off, muttering.

Mom's Dumpster diving lasted about three weeks.

"People are starting to call me names around town," she announced at dinner.

"Well don't look at me," said Dad. "I'm not diving into any Dumpsters."

Then he proposed an idea that seemed simply brilliant.

"Look, everyone knows that cows are wild animals, right?"

We all nodded.

"So that means Ike is perfectly capable of taking care of himself," he finished with a grin, "in the wilds of Michigan."

Ike became a nomadic terror. Growing scrawnier by the day and craving calories, he took to covert warfare. Jerry and I were the ones who had to take out the trash from the kitchen and toss it into the garbage dump in the valley behind the house. Pre-Ike, this was a boring but thankfully brainless task. There was virtually no way we could screw it up and incur Dad's wrath, not counting the time Dad chose to dump the garbage on my bed.

Ike changed all that. He learned to lurk behind some short, scrubby trees and wait for one of us to approach the dump. If we weren't careful, Ike would charge forward and ram his head into our backs, knocking us down and scattering the garbage we carried all over the ground. Then, as we climbed back to our feet and tried to clean ourselves off, Ike would lower his head and begin eating the freshly spilled garbage. Why he didn't simply wait for us to toss the garbage into the pile was a mystery to me, though Jerry's theory was that Dad had uncovered the wild animal in Ike.

"One of you boys needs to take out the trash," Mom said one night.

"I'll get it," Jerry volunteered, "if Mark is the lookout."

I peered out the window while my brother slung the black plastic bag over his shoulder.

"Okay, he's on the far side of the yard. Try walking real slow so he won't notice you. I did that a few days ago and he never looked my way."

"I don't know . . . he *always* seems to notice me when I head to the garbage pile." Jerry stood at the door, shifting his feet.

"He's still on the far side," I updated.

Jerry made a decision. "I'm going to try to outrun him. I think I can get there and back without him horning me in the back. Hold the door open so I can get a running start."

I did, and Jerry bolted out at full sprint. Ike noticed him immediately and headed toward Jerry at a trot.

"Jerry, he *sees* you!"

Jerry had made it fairly close to the garbage pile, so he flung the bag and spun around on a dime, sprinting back to the house at full tilt.

"Run, run!" I yelled. "He's coming closer!"

Jerry tried to find another gear, but Ike caught him anyway. At full run, Ike lowered his head and slammed Jerry square in the back, lifting him into the air for a moment—and then, just shy of the door, Jerry ate dirt.

"Mom! Mom! Ike got Jerry!"

She ran past me, but Jerry was already on his feet, wailing and limping toward the house. Tears streamed down his cheeks. Mom returned, grabbed a broom, and stalked back out the door.

"That damn cow! I don't know why your father can't make a fence, or at least tie it up!" Ike was still nearby, and Mom sprinted toward him, broom held high.

"She's gonna brain him," I told Jerry.

"Good," he managed to sniff.

Ike saw the threat, however, and bolted, kicking his heels high into the air as he ran off. Mom came back to Jerry's side and lifted his shirt.

"Let me see," she soothed. "You'll be all right—just a bruise, but no blood. Go wash your face."

Such attacks were simply too much for us. Even on his diet of garbage, Ike was pushing four hundred pounds, so getting hit by him in the back didn't feel much different from getting run over by a car. Mom demanded that Dad do something about *his* cow, which it had officially become the minute it started ramming her boys.

"Fine," he said, then walked outside.

Jerry and I raced after him, morbidly curious.

"You don't think Dad will . . ." I left the question unfinished, picturing a solution that involved the tank.

"Nah," Jerry said, sounding mostly convinced.

Dad's actual solution was perfectly simple and totally ineffective. He stalked through the yard, with us trailing at a distance, until he found Ike. Then Dad picked up the closest rock.

"Hey! Ike!"

Ike stared at Dad, who let fly with the rock. Ike, being in excellent running condition, dodged easily.

Dad picked up a second rock. Ike stared.

"F— you!" Dad yelled, tossing the second rock. Ike dodged again.

Dad returned to the house, grabbed the broom, and came back. Marching straight up to Ike, who unwisely stood his ground this time, Dad raised the broom above his head—"I said, 'F— *you!*'"—and brought it down with enough force to snap the handle in two across the cow's back. Ike jumped, spun around, and raced off through the trees.

"Don't know why I have to solve all your mother's problems," Dad griped, and then he walked back to the house.

Soon after that—probably sensing that the grass was literally greener on the other side of the Boumans' nonexistent fence—Ike made a trip over to the Dietzes'. Despite the trouble Ike caused us, Dad had been bragging about how smart he was to be raising his own cow, so the Dietzes had got themselves a cow too. Theirs was still a calf that they kept tied up near the house. When Ike discovered the calf, he rammed it at full speed and killed it. Not finished with his mischief, Ike entered a staring contest with the mermaid who sat at the center of the Dietzes' cement water fountain. She must have blinked first, because Ike rammed her as well, and the fountain was reduced to rubble.

Dad had to pay the Dietzes back for the dead calf—though not, for some reason, for the mermaid—at which point even he couldn't pretend that Ike was saving us any money. Still, Ike soldiered on, eating oak bark and ramming us and leaving mounds of poop in the sand.

Until one Sunday morning when a strange knock woke us up early.

"Who's at the door?" Mom said, still in bed.

"Just a minute, I'll see," Dad said, pulling his pants on. He opened the door to find two police officers, guns drawn.

"Freeze! Police! Hands in the air! Now!" One lowered his gun and pulled Dad out of the house, while two more officers pushed inside.

"Who else is here, Mr. Bouman?" came the shouted question.

"My family," Dad answered.

"What's *happening*!" yelled Mom, peeking her head out the bedroom door.

"Who *else* is here?" the officer demanded.

"Our children!"

"Well, keep them out of the way!"

Meanwhile, another officer had cuffed Dad. "Mr. Bouman, did you sell a machine gun to Robert Kovalcek?"

The question caught Dad off guard.

He grimaced. For years Dad had kept a fully operational machine gun around, and he'd take it out periodically and fire it for his buddies. It was awesome—and incredibly illegal. Recently he'd sold it, but before doing so he'd replaced the barrel with one that was plugged so it couldn't be fired. Apparently Robert had re-replaced the barrel, bragged around town about his automatic weapon, and then ratted out Dad. The sheriff had come to check out the status of Dad's permits, but permits and Dad weren't the best of friends. That was probably why the sheriff decided he needed to pay a visit to the so-called "Tank Man" with six heavily armed deputies in tow.

"I want to talk to my lawyer," Dad growled. *What lawyer?* I thought.

"Hey, there are tons of police cars outside!" Jerry whispered to me. "How much trouble is Dad in?"

Dad was escorted to the closest car. "He's headed to jail, I guess," I speculated to Jerry.

That was when Ike burst out from behind the house and blindsided one of the officers at full speed. The man's hat flew off and he hit the dirt, face first.

"Ike just rammed a cop!" Jerry shouted, partly terrified but mostly giddy.

Ike spun around and kicked his heels in the air, then raced off.

"What the hell was *that*?" shouted the officer, getting shakily to his feet and jogging for the safety of his squad car.

"A damn cow!" shouted another officer, scuttling for safety behind his car.

Meanwhile, two more officers were searching the house from top to bottom, looking for any other illegal weapons, and Dad was finally being loaded into the back of one of the squad cars.

Less than ten minutes after it had all begun, we stood outside with Mom. Dad and the officers were gone, Ike was gone, and things seemed eerily quiet.

"Well, I suppose we should go eat breakfast," Mom said.

All of which explains why Dad's one-day stay in jail coincided with Ike disappearing, only to return to us several days later in the form of a month's worth of T-bones, rib eyes, and ground beef.

Family dinners didn't always feel good, but finally eating Ike sure did.

/

17

One day, while Dad and I were cleaning the shed, I saw him crouch in front of a small, wooden box with rope handles. It was partly hidden beneath some other junk and covered by a thick layer of dust. Dad brushed his fingers across the side of the box, revealing some words I couldn't make sense of. Dad stared at them for a moment and then stood up and faced me.

"Mark, come help me pull this box out and set it on the work table."

After grabbing the rope handles and swinging the box up, we hovered over it like doctors beside an operating table. Dad used a small knife to pry off the cover. The inside of the box was about two feet long, one foot wide, and six inches deep, and it was filled with what looked like brown candles that someone had dripped dark, sticky honey across.

Dad froze. That was never a good sign. "Mark, grab your handle again. Let's get this thing outside. And *slowly*."

Dad walked backward, I shuffled forward, and soon we had the box resting in the sand a short distance away from the shed. I had no idea what I was looking at, and no more information seemed to be forthcoming. "So . . . what *is* this, anyway?"

"Dynamite," Dad replied. "It's left over from a job I had blowing stumps to clear a new runway. I guess this box found its way home with me when I quit." Then his voice became more serious. "I need to do something with this, though. I've had it way too long."

"Why, what's wrong—are you talking about all that honey?"

"That ain't honey. Dynamite's just sawdust mixed with nitroglycerin and wrapped in paper, and when the dynamite sits too long, the nitroglycerin bleeds through the paper. Very sticky," he said, letting the tip of one finger graze the dynamite, "and *very* unstable. Even a sudden change in temperature can set this stuff off. We've got to get rid of this before something bad happens."

Dad stood up and put his hands on his hips, slowly scanning our property. That was how he did his best thinking. Sometimes he'd stay that way for a dozen minutes or more, elbows out, eyes staring into the distance. And when he finally worked out a solution, nothing would stop him—he was like a bulldog with a bone. This time the answer came to him after only a minute or two, but that was plenty long to be standing next to a boxful of bombs, as far as I was concerned.

Dad dropped his arms from his hips and strode down the hill. "Go get your brother," he called over his shoulder, "and grab some shovels."

I raced off to find Jerry. "Dad found a box of dynamite, and we're gonna help him with it!"

"Help him do *what*?"

"I don't know—he just said to grab shovels!"

"So it sounds like we're gonna help him *dig*."

Shovels in hand, we caught up with Dad at a huge tree stump. He was looking at it with a smug expression. The stump was waist high and three feet across, and it probably weighed a thousand pounds. It was all that was left of a mighty oak that had been destroyed by the tornado.

He kicked it with his black leather shoe. The stump sounded thick and solid. It didn't move an inch.

"Okay, boys," he announced. "That dynamite we found is gonna make my life a lot easier. I need you boys to dig a hole—and make sure it goes all the way under the stump. It's gotta be deep enough so the dynamite will lift it."

"Got it," we both said, then set to work digging with a will. We threw shovelful after shovelful of dirt into the air.

Jerry held up his hand for me to stop after a few minutes. "Mark, don't throw the dirt too close—some of it's falling back into the hole, and we'll have to dig it twice."

"How deep do we have to dig?" I asked.

"Not sure, but Dad said make it deep enough to get underneath the stump."

I sighed. "Yeah, but this stump is huge. It'll take us forever."

"Just keep digging." Helping Dad with dynamite was looking worse by the minute. Still, I wasn't keen to have the dynamite blow up on its own above the ground, so I dug with a bit more enthusiasm than normal. Dad watched as our shovels cut through a foot of sand, then another foot. We had to dig a foot or two sideways for every foot we dug down, owing to all the sand that kept sliding down the slope and refilling the hole. From time to time Dad returned, each time carrying something he'd need for the project: blasting cap, a roll of fuse, matches, and last of all, the box of dynamite, which he dragged along the sand at a snail's pace.

With every trip, he looked at our hole and said the same thing. "Nope, not yet."

At last—long past the time my arms had begun to feel like spaghetti—Jerry and I stood at the bottom of a six-foot-deep hole that was at least ten feet across—and arching and twisting all around us and above us was the stump and its network of roots. Taproots as thick as my thigh snaked off in all directions, and the body of the stump itself was massive.

"That should be deep enough," hollered Dad, and we scrambled out of the pit, panting, and knelt at the edge of the hole to watch Dad. He lifted out the sticks of dynamite, one at a time, and set them in a pile directly below the stump. It reminded me of a tiny log cabin.

"That'll do," he pronounced, looking at the pile of explosives. But then he looked back at the box, which still had half a dozen more. He gave a small shrug. "You know what? Let's just use it all on the stump—it'll be all right."

Jerry and I were ecstatic. We grinned at each other like maniacs. All the digging had been worth it. Dad was going to blow up the entire box at once! Dad attached the blasting cap and fuse, climbed out, and ran the fuse to a safe distance.

"You boys go hide under the tank," Dad told us. "You'll be safe there." He readied a match to strike as we sprinted off, calling a final warning: "And do *not* come out early!"

We sprinted to the tank and slid underneath its near edge, then commando-crawled backward until it covered us. Past experience had taught us that safety was never at the top of Dad's priority list, so if he told us to put twenty tons of steel above our heads, something big was about to happen.

"And make sure you plug your ears!" Dad yelled.

I grinned at Jerry and shoved a finger in each ear. Dad touched the match to the fuse, and then he sprinted away from the stump as fast as he could.

The trail of smoke from the burning fuse took forever to crawl across the sand to the stump. Ears firmly plugged, I could hear only the sound of my heavy breathing and the beat of my heart. At last the smoke trail reached the edge of the pit and disappeared into the hole. Any minute now . . .

The entire world hiccuped. The ground punched me in the stomach just as the loudest sound I'd ever heard hammered my body. Everything became a violent blur of brown that resolved, an instant later, into a towering column, like Old Faithful made of smoke and sand. Fear and wonder flooded my body. I watched the smoke column drifting slowly from right to left, growing taller and more transparent.

I turned toward Jerry. He looked like he'd just been run over by a school bus, but he was grinning at me.

We scrambled out from beneath the tank. "Did you plug your ears?" Jerry yelled at me.

"Yeah, why? Did you pl—?" I began.

"I didn't!" Jerry yelled proudly.

We saw Dad jogging toward the pit, so we did too, and before we got halfway there, it started to rain wood. Pieces of all sizes were falling around us, the larger chunks hitting the sand with audible thumps while the smaller bits and splinters cartwheeled and drifted down. Dad threw his arms over his head but stayed where he was, and we did the same. As the cloud of sand and dust slowly dissipated, the rain of wood continued for five seconds, ten seconds. Jerry and I stood in awe. It was the most incredible thing either of us had ever witnessed.

When the wood shower finally dried up, we sprinted to where the stump used to be. In its place was a crater filled with pure sand, about twice the size of our bedroom. It was as if the stump had never existed.

"Guess maybe we didn't need *all* that dynamite," Dad said happily.

The three of us were like clones, each grinning at the hole in the ground with our hands on our hips. Mom, with Sheri following, came tearing out of the house. One hand held a sponge, and an apron was tied around her blouse. "What in the world just happened? I heard a *boom*, the roof went *bang*, and then the power went out!" She stopped in front of the hole, panting and waiting for my father to answer.

Dad didn't say anything. He was still staring at the hole. But Jerry, who'd turned his attention to the surrounding landscape, blurted out much too loudly, "Hey—what's that sticking out of the roof of the house?"

It was part of the stump, of course. The dynamite had launched a huge hunk who knew *how* high into the air, and it had arced across the fifty yards to the house before punching right through the roof and the ceiling. We discovered, when we all trooped back into the house together, that a small section was still embedded in the roof, but the remainder of the chunk had plowed straight on through, coming to rest on the floor just in front of the couch. It was surrounded by a scattering of insulation, ceiling tiles, and splinters of wood. When I looked up, I could see the sky through a hole the size of a five-gallon bucket.

"Well I'll be . . ." reflected Dad.

"And what about the *power*," chided Mom.

"Mark," said Dad, "go check the breakers and see if any are tripped."

I reported back to Dad that all the breakers looked good, which perplexed him—why *was* the power out? He stood for a long while in the living room, looking at the stump. We stood in the living room, too, looking at Dad look at the stump. Suddenly Dad ran outside.

"Wow, the stump just *barely* missed the couch," Jerry yelled.

"Amazing," I added.

Sheri stood mute at Mom's side, unable to take in what had just happened. Mom alternated between staring at the hole in her ceiling and asking, "Are you two all right? Sure?"

"We're fine," I reassured her. "We were safe under the tank."

"One of these days your father is going to kill someone," Mom said, disgusted.

I kept staring at the hunk of stump, comparing it in my mind to the original. "I wonder what happened to the rest of the stump—this piece isn't even that big."

"It *had* to have been blown up," Jerry said, his volume returning closer to normal. "I saw, like, a million pieces flying through the air."

He turned to Mom and Sheri. "They were landing *all* around us."

"Yeah!" I added. "And a couple big pieces landed right next to us!"

Mom frowned. "I thought you said you were—"

Dad burst into the house. "Found it!" he said triumphantly. "Knew I'd figure it out! Come on!"

We followed him outside, then down the hill about a hundred yards.

Another chunk of the stump had flown along a different trajectory, crashing not into the roof of the house but directly into the transformer atop the power pole at one edge of our property. The transformer wasn't built to withstand the impact of a dynamite-propelled stump, and it had been knocked right off the power pole. It was lying on the ground, its insulators shattered and a huge stump-shaped dent marking the side of its casing.

"Well, don't expect me to pay thousands of dollars to fix something that wasn't my fault!" Dad proclaimed, looking at the ruined transformer.

"Not your fault?" clarified Mom.

"It was an *accident*," Dad answered, "and therefore not my fault. Jerry, clear out the chips and splinters near this power pole. I'm gonna drag this big hunk clear with the tank."

Mom threw up her hands. "Come on, Sheri, we're going back inside, and *hopefully* no more *trees* will land on us!"

It wasn't fifteen minutes later that Dad was speaking with someone from the utility company.

"Yeah, I need to report a problem," he began, and there was no way, once he started his story, that the guy on the other end of the line was going to come out ahead. Dad was a great storyteller, and he never thought twice about embellishing the facts—or inventing some out of whole cloth.

By the time Dad hung up the phone a few minutes later, the power company was convinced that a freak lightning storm had knocked our transformer to the ground. Or, if they weren't quite convinced, there was nothing they could do to prove otherwise—especially when the guy complaining was the Tank Man.

"They said they'd come right out and take care of it," reported Dad.

When the lineman arrived, he didn't make even a single comment about the blue skies we'd had for days on end or about the lack of burn marks on the transformer. He did remark that in all his years of repair work, he'd never seen lightning damage a transformer in quite that way. But if he didn't believe Dad's story about lightning, so what? It's not like he would have believed the real story either.

18

THAT SUMMER, Grandma Jean said I was old enough to go to Grace Bible Camp for a week and that she'd pay. She told me there would be archery, a lake to swim in, a camp store, and hundreds of kids my age. Most of that sounded okay, except for the part about the other kids. If the camp kids were anything like church kids or school kids, I'd stick out like a sore thumb.

The week before I left for camp, Mom came into my room holding a pair of blue jeans. "These are for you to take to camp, Mark. I wanted you to have new ones to wear."

I didn't know what to say, so I didn't say anything.

Mom walked over to my dresser and opened the bottom drawer, setting the new pants inside. I'd been worrying about what camp would be like, and I'd planned on spending most of my time swimming. Mom turned to leave, but she stopped in the doorway. It looked like she was about to say something else, but she just tried to smile at me, looked at the floor, and then left.

I couldn't resist trying out the jeans early. I didn't want to get them dirty outside, so whenever I was in my room I'd pull them on. After I'd looked at a book for a while, or just relaxed on my bed, I'd take them back off, fold them neatly, and return them to the drawer. After a few days of this, I noticed that the jeans, which had never been washed, had turned my best pair of underwear a light shade of blue. That wasn't terrible news, in a way, since the hard water from our well had already stained my other underwear dark yellow.

When the time came to leave for camp, it took me about five minutes to pack. My towel, which was barely long enough to wrap around my butt and legs after a shower, didn't take up much space. Mom got all our towels as free promotional gifts for buying a certain amount of laundry soap—each box had a code on it, and Mom dutifully saved each one inside an old manila envelope, earning us three or four free towels per year. Of course, three or four free towels were equivalent to one proper, store-bought towel, and our free towels were all the color of urine. I decided that at camp, when I opened my suitcase, I'd say something like, "Aw geez, looks like my old lady packed me a yellow hand towel."

The zipper on my sleeping bag didn't work, so I used a length of old rope to keep it rolled. I tossed a few other things into my suitcase, pulled on my new jeans, and headed for the door. Halfway there, the suitcase popped open and everything fell out. Dad watched it happen.

"Here you go," he said, taking off his belt and handing it to me.

I winced as I knelt in front of my suitcase, feeling the leather belt run through my fingers. Eventually I decided to use it—I had to use it—but I considered forgetting the belt at camp on purpose.

Mom drove me, the humid summer air pouring in through four open windows and blowing our hair. The trees grew thicker, houses fewer and farther between, and then we turned onto a dirt road and drove beneath a wooden arch that announced we'd arrived. We parked beside a long, low building made from logs.

"You'll have a good time at camp," she said across the front seat, "and I'm sorry I don't have much money to give you."

She reached into her purse and pulled out a one-dollar bill. My face must have betrayed my thoughts.

"I'm so sorry, Mark, but I just don't have any more."

I knew I shouldn't, knew it was rude, but I couldn't help staring at the neatly folded bill.

"I don't have anything else," she said. "I'm sorry."

My heart dropped into my bur-covered shoes. I leaned back so I could jam the money into the pocket of my new jeans. I didn't want to get out of the car. I wanted to drive straight back home, or better yet, to drive somewhere no one knew me. It was bad enough having stained underwear and a swim towel that was really a dish towel. Now I'd be the only kid at camp with no money.

"You'll have a good time, honey?" her reassurance came as a question.

"Okay, I will," I replied, not believing my own words. I climbed out, grabbed my broken suitcase, and stood on the gravel, looking through the open window at Mom.

"Bye, Mark."

"Bye."

She pulled away, and my eyes followed her car. I was suddenly aware of a large spot of rust near the bumper.

I watched until the car disappeared, then reached into my pocket, pulling out the one-dollar bill. I didn't blame Mom, but it took me a long time to refold it and shove it back into my jeans. I kept thinking about all the things I couldn't buy with it.

•   •   •

The first night, sometime around midnight, I crept out of my bunk and snuck across the room. Then I slipped the wallet from the pair of pants draped over the end of my cabinmate's bed. I grabbed the wad of bills—six dollars—returned the wallet to the pants, returned the pants to the bed, and snuck back to my bunk. I shoved the stolen cash into my own jeans, then climbed into my bunk to sleep.

In the morning, I woke to the sound of sobbing and a counselor trying—and failing—to get a word in edgewise. My victim—I didn't even know his name, but the day before I'd sized him up as a rich kid—was a wreck. His eyes were puffy and red, and he kept shaking his wallet in the air as if he were trying to fling water off it.

"My money was *here* last night—I *know* it! Someone *stole* it, I'm telling you!"

"Sorry to do this to you, boys," sighed our counselor, "but I need you to turn your pockets out for me. We'll get to the bottom of this."

All around the cabin, boys climbed out of their bunks and began complying with the counselor's orders. I put my suitcase up on my bed and opened it, and then I took my jeans off the end of the bed where they were hanging and laid them out flat. When the counselor asked to see what was in my pockets, I reached into the left one and pulled it inside out. Empty. Then I reached into the right one, and my fist came back out with a roll of bills. I looked at the counselor and he raised one eyebrow. I unfolded the bills and laid them down.

One, two, three, four, five, six, *seven*.

"Wait, is that my six dollars? Did he steal my money?" The crying boy peered past the counselor, bouncing up and down on his feet and beginning to shout again. "Why is that *seven* dollars? Are my six dollars in that pile of money?"

The counselor calculated my net worth in a single glance. "Well," he asked, "are they?"

I shook my head. The counselor sighed again, then moved down the line to the next bed. I turned around and pulled my new jeans on. Then I repacked everything and slid the seven dollars back into my pocket. By the time I had everything squared away, the rest of the cabin had been searched. Lots of dollar bills had been discovered, of course. The crying boy was no longer crying. Instead he was sitting on his bed, mumbling to himself and looking through his wallet. He kept closing it and reopening it, as if on the fourth or tenth try his missing money would appear, the happy punch line to a magic trick he hadn't wanted to volunteer for. I yanked my shoes on and left.

It was too early for anyone to be swimming, so no one else was at the lake. The surface was a mirror of the pale sky, except for where bits of mist still floated above the water. I walked to the end of the dock and sat. The sun rose all the way, and I counted the bits of mist as they burned toward zero. When the surface of the water was clear, I stood up and walked back to my cabin. Everyone was gone, and I took the six dollars and stuffed it into the back pocket of the other boy's jeans.

That night the boy discovered his money. It was quite the camp mystery: the case of the disappearing and reappearing cash.

I wanted to disappear too—and sometimes I actually managed it. For five minutes at the archery range, or an hour of swimming in the lake, or a few hours at a time in my bunk—there were times when my mind went blank, and I didn't think about anything.

But always the picture of who I really was returned to me, made clear by the other campers. They were kids who had friends, and real towels, and regular parents. Looking at everyone else, I realized I was different— different in a bad way. They were all normal, but I was the Tank Man's son, and at the end of camp my Mom would drive me back to the eleven acres I couldn't seem to escape. At camp I wanted to crawl under a rock and disappear. At home I knew I never could.

During one activity time, I found myself sitting next to one of the camp counselors.

"What are you working on?" she asked.

"A candle," I managed. "We're supposed to make candles."

"Oh, candles! Lovely!"

Her voice was so full of genuine interest that I looked up at her. She was smiling.

"I'm trying to decide what color to make mine," I ventured.

"Well, I'll make a yellow one," she said brightly. "I've always loved candles! I really wanted to make one of my own, but I've never done it before."

"I know how to make them," I said. "My mom made them with us when we were younger."

"You do? Would you show me?"

"Of course!" Now I was smiling. I helped her gather everything she needed to make her candle, and we chatted the whole time. When we finished, she thanked me over and over again.

"I love it. It's beautiful. I just *love* it, Mark. I can't tell you how much I have enjoyed doing this with you."

She put her hand on my shoulder, and I found myself wanting her to stay beside me for the rest of camp. But that was silly—I didn't need a counselor following me around like I was a baby. The craft session ended, and I moved on to the next activity.

Helping her turned out to be the only truly enjoyable thing I did at camp, and I never saw her again after that hour we spent making candles together.

•   •   •

Mom tried to make up for it when I got back home. She scrounged up the cash for me to play Little League baseball. Practices were after school, so I could hitch a ride with one of the other kids, but for games I had to bum a ride from Coach—Mom was always busy, either working in town or working at home, and I knew better than to ask Dad.

We made it all the way to the championship game, losing 4–7 against some rich kids from the next county over.

When we got to Coach's truck after the game, he told me to hang on before climbing in the back, and then he leaned into the cab and dug something out of the glove box. "You earned this, son," he said, handing me a small ribbon with a medal attached.

It was a cold ride home that night. Dad hadn't come to a single game all season, even though I'd told him when we made the play-offs. In the bed of the pickup, small leaves swirled in the corners and my hair whipped across my eyes. I pictured displaying my medal on top of my dresser, or maybe I would pin it to one of my bedposts so I could see it when I was falling asleep. It probably wouldn't be allowed in the living room—it was already cluttered with Dad's LP cabinet, speakers, records, books, and guns—but my medal wouldn't take up much space. Maybe there was a chance.

It was an even colder walk home. Coach dropped me off a mile up Blakely Drive, and I carried my glove and bat over my shoulder like a hobo walking the tracks. Up our long driveway at last, I opened the door, and Dad was reading on the couch. He didn't look up. Bat and glove in one hand, medal in the other, I closed the door behind me with my foot and stood for a minute, waiting.

When I realized that nothing was going to happen and that no words were going to be said, I walked to my room. I dropped my equipment on the floor and climbed into bed with my uniform on, still holding my medal.

19

"Mark! Stand here, boy."

Dad speaks my name like it is poison—like he can't wait to spit it out of his mouth.

He hurls my name at me like a curse, and after my name come questions I can't answer. I understand there is no right answer, even as I long to know the answer that would halt the single motion with which he removes his belt and lets it hang loose from one hand. It is a strip of pure evil, and I hate it. I am a slave in my father's world, controlled by the bitter sound of my own name.

I know the beating that is coming. I have joined Jerry in the brotherhood of the belt, old enough now to feel the full weight of Dad's anger. Only my sister is still innocent. The terror that rears at the sound of his words feels like a living thing, like a spider I can feel crawling across my body. *Not the belt again. Anything but the belt.* The spiders are multiplying. Their legs make my skin shiver. My neck. My forehead. The backs of my thighs where the belt likes to bite.

No, please no—I'm going to soil myself. I'm supposed to be standing at attention in front of my father, but instead I'm leaning forward, bending my knees, shoving my hands sideways against my butt cheeks as hard as I can. Praying through clenched teeth that it will stay inside me. I look up and Dad is watching me, and he nods toward the bathroom. Unbearably grateful, I shuffle quickly down the hall. I'm not even seated all the way when a wave of it pours into the toilet. Then another and another. Then nothing's left, and the only thing left to do is stand up. I don't bother to pull up my pants.

When I finally force my fingers to pull the door handle, Dad is there, waiting. Ripples fall along the belt dangling from his left hand. His right hand floats at his side. "Didn't I tell you to clean this place up after school today?"

"I . . . I thought that—"

"Who said you could *think*, Mark? That's your problem right there. You thought. I don't want you to think. You're not allowed to think. Just do what I tell you. And that's all."

His hand explodes toward my face, and I hear the slap before I feel it. I'm already on the floor when the pain shrieks into my skull.

"Get up!" He's screaming now. "Not very smart, are you, kid? Get up!"

I can hear the deadly silence that follows, even over the ringing in my ear. "Bend over. Put your hands on that chair." Dad is breathing behind me, and I know the belt is alive. The plywood floor creaks, and I know he's digging in. A loud intake, held, and then I hear the sound of my screaming, and it doesn't stop. Dad is screaming too—that I need to shut up or he'll really give me something to cry about—but I can't stop. It doesn't matter that he picks and chooses his targets, alternating between my butt and thighs and back. I bite my lip and squeeze my eyes and tense every muscle and still the screams escape.

After one minute or one hour comes a new sound that is impossible to ignore. It is the scream of a creature who knows it is dying but who wants to live, primal and desperate. The sound fascinates me because it's coming from my own throat. It's roaring from some deep place inside that I never knew existed. Carried by that howl of anguish, I turn and face my father. I raise one arm like a shield, my other arm covering my bare butt.

"I promise!" I scream. "I promise!" I don't know what I'm promising, but I promise it anyway.

"You promise? What good is that, coming from you? You *disgust* me." Dad is breathing hard, his words coming in short bursts. "Put your hands back down. Bend over."

I can't. For the first time in my life I'm completely unable to do what my father wants. I can't put down my arm. Holding it up is the one thing that is keeping me from disintegrating. I know it will cost me. I want to live, but I'm going to die at age eleven, facing my father with my arm still raised.

Dad's belt finds my face. Then my wrist. Then stomach, ear, flank, and ear again. And the sound is one long scream.

Mom's voice comes from a great distance. "Stop it! Stop it! You're killing him!"

I open my eyes and see her wrestling with Dad, one of her hands around Dad's left wrist and the other clinging to the belt. Dad looks at me over Mom's shoulder.

"Someone needs to teach this kid a lesson! He never learns! He's *nothing*!"

"Enough!" Mom screams, then pleads, "Enough enough enough enough!"

She's still white-knuckling the belt. Dad turns away from us both and drops the end of the belt he's holding. And then he's gone.

"Wash your face and then go to your room, Mark." Mom's voice is a bare whisper.

I want to pull up my pants but the effort seems impossible. I shuffle down the hall and return to the bathroom. It still smells like my bowel movement. In the sink mirror I see my face and the shape of punishment painted in red on my skin. I pool cold water in my hands and splash it upward. I don't dry because the towel will be too rough.

In my room, I collapse into my pillow, sobbing. Every part of me is burning. I will never learn what my father is teaching.

PART THREE

A SHIP

20

THE FACT THAT Dad could lash out at us, at any moment for any reason, didn't stop life from happening. We still plodded through school. We still did chores and played board games and ate dinner. We even started roller-skating as a family down at the Bloomfield Hills roller rink. We'd spend Sunday afternoons grooving to the hits beneath the spinning disco ball. Dad would always take the spotlight, shirt flapping out of his khakis, skating backward and forward with equal ease, looping and twirling through the crowd, lost in a world of one. We were still a family, and sometimes we seemed happy.

With summer fast approaching and his three kids out of school for more than three solid months, Dad decided he needed to be even happier, so he pulled the trigger on his lifelong dream of boat ownership.

It started with a small, close-knit group of scuba divers who dove on shipwrecks in Lake Michigan, and between Dad's mouth, his gun range, and the fact that he owned his own equipment and didn't need to be babied, he had become part of their inner circle, diving on wrecks whenever the weather was good. Since it was free, Mom didn't care when he left, and neither did we.

One of the divers told Dad the story of a state-owned patrol boat that had sunk at its dock and was just sitting there, waiting for someone to raise it.

Years before, the story went, a certain Captain Allers had suffered a tragic accident on the boat. While on the job inspecting fishing nets, the ship's propeller had become tangled in a line. The captain's son dived into the water with a knife to cut the line, and while he was in the water, the propeller slipped back into gear, decapitating the boy. Captain Allers, who witnessed the whole grisly accident, dived into the water and immediately suffered a heart attack and drowned. No one wanted anything to do with the boat after that, until a man bought it, moored it in a small harbor, took out a large maritime insurance policy, and then sank the boat and collected his windfall. At least that was the story Dad was told, and it sounded plausible enough that the next time he and his buddies motored down the Grand River, which fed into Lake Michigan, Dad suggested a detour.

The derelict, called *Patrol One*, was right where it was supposed to be, its pilothouse sticking out of the water like a tombstone. Dad claimed it weighed in at nearly one hundred tons and was at least seventy-five feet long. As he finned along its hull in the dark water, he could imagine himself inside the boat. Not as a diver, though—as a pilot. A captain. He needed the *Patrol One* to be his.

Two weeks later, Dad scraped together $3,500 and purchased the submerged wreck. His friends wondered why he'd spent so much money on a ship that was mostly underwater and half buried in mud, but that was because most people thought differently than Dad did. Including Mom.

"I can't *believe* you bought that stupid boat!" It was dinnertime, and Mom had moved past anger into complete disbelief. "We don't have enough money to fix up the *house*, and you bought a boat? What's *wrong* with you? You've never even painted the house, and it has a bright orange *door*!"

Dad gave it back as good as he was getting it. "Don't change the subject. I can *use* my boat to make *money*!"

"Oh please! That was your story with the guns, and you went to jail!"

"For one day! And this boat'll be a cash cow! I can run dive trips, fish, use it to—"

"It's sitting on the bottom—you don't even know if it will float!"

"It'll float, believe me. All I've gotta do is . . ."

But Mom had already been broken. She fled the kitchen, sobbing, and we heard her bedroom door slam. Dad shrugged and refocused his attention on his plate, tucking into his potatoes au gratin with gusto.

• • •

Dad reported his plans for raising the ship. He scrounged up some large sheets of canvas, donned his scuba gear, and with some well-executed underwater hammering, nailed the canvas sheets around the hull, a bit like one of the pigs in a blanket he loved to wolf down at breakfast smorgasbords. He figured he could then pump water out of the boat faster than the water could flow back in through the canvas. He figured right, and in less than twenty-four hours he had the ship floating again.

Talking to a couple of locals who came out to watch the operation, Dad filled in some missing details. The *Patrol One* had been built all the way back in 1901, and besides being used to inspect fishing nets on the Great Lakes, it had been used to transport moose to Isle Royale in Lake Superior. It was powered—or would have been powered if it hadn't been a rotting, sludge-filled hulk—by a four-cylinder Kahlenberg diesel that weighed in at eighteen tons.

"Heavy as three bull elephants," he told us, "and a propeller about as tall as Mark!"

Everything about the ship was oversize, which was a scale Dad loved to work in. Next came some critical hull repairs that let him pull off the canvas sheets and shut down his extra pumps: new lumber over the holes, waterproof paint, tar and caulking, and bilge pump repair. After that Dad tackled the engine, and despite needing to take apart, clean, and reassemble the entire thing, he got that beast running within a couple of weeks.

With the *Patrol One* floating—low in the water, but floating nevertheless—and the engine running, Dad was officially the captain of his own ship. It was nearly summertime. Mom was working full-time in a factory and trying to keep her household from falling apart or being swallowed by sand. Jerry was spending more and more time in our room, studying for his end-of-the-year exams, while Sheri was trying to spend as much time at her friends' houses as she could. I was imagining a summer in which I left home every morning, striking out for the deserted woods.

As usual, our plans didn't matter, because once the boat dried out, we would be saying good-bye to our house on Blakely Drive for the summer and moving on board the *Patrol One*.

"Here, Mark, take this suitcase to the car. We're going to stay on the boat for a while," Mom said when the time came.

"How long are we going to be gone?"

Mom sighed. "Not sure. Come back and get this one when you're done—and don't drop it. It'll—"

"It'll spill if I don't hold it closed. I know."

I stuffed the first suitcase in the trunk of the car. Dad had already claimed most of the space with boxes filled with greasy tools and other items from the shed. Once the last bit of luggage was loaded, the three of us kids crammed into the backseat, squeezed between bags of food Mom had packed. She was waiting in the passenger seat, fanning herself. It was near a hundred degrees in the car. I could feel Sheri's sweaty leg against mine, but there wasn't enough space to move.

Dad eventually wandered over with another box. "Here, put this on your lap, Jerry," Dad said, thrusting the dirty cardboard through the rear window. I looked over and saw a random mess of bolts, nuts, and pipe fittings, stuff that had been lying around the shed for years. Dad backed the Ford past the tank and then stopped, giving the house a quick scan before dropping the car into drive and pulling away.

"Hope it's still here when we get back," Dad said. With that he punched the gas and we sped down the hill. I heard the occasional pop from a car battery chip slapping the underside of the car, and then we pulled out onto the road.

21

WHAT I DIDN'T REALIZE was that moving on board meant, well, a boat-load of backbreaking work. Dad had known, but he didn't want to spoil the surprise.

The *Patrol* was a two-level ship with twelve rooms, including five bedrooms that Dad insisted on calling staterooms. At the bow, on the top floor, was a large open room called the fish house, which the Department of Natural Resources had used to check that commercial nets were regulation size. Moving back along the top floor, we'd reach the pilothouse, the kitchen—Dad made us call it the galley—and the dining room, which had a large table bolted to the floor, and at the back of the dining room was a narrow, nearly vertical stairway with metal pipes for handrails. Belowdecks came the parts room, the engine room, the five staterooms, and finally the claustrophobic chain locker at the tail. Beneath all of that ran the bilge, extending the length of the ship.

And *all* of that space needed to be fixed.

The ship had been underwater for years, so every room was a maritime disaster area: thick, sticky mud caked the ceiling, dried on the walls, and covered the floor; the wood was so waterlogged you could press your thumb into it; and dead fish in various states of decomposition were wedged into countless nooks and crannies. And added to all that was the feeling that you were inhaling tiny, damp bits of the ship whenever you took a breath. Dad left a portable heater running inside the ship day and night.

Mom had taken one look at the ship and shaken her head. "I'm not living on that thing. No one can live on that thing. It's disgusting."

"It'll be fine," crowed Dad.

"No, it won't."

"The ship'll be fine."

"No, it *won't*. Look at it!"

Dad looked, and it looked fine to him. "I need the kids every day to help me fix it up. It'll be great. You'll see."

Mom didn't wait around to see and declared that she would be living at home and doing *actual* work. And thus began our summer vacation. At first Jerry, Sheri, and I made day trips with Dad to the *Patrol*. We spent weeks using individual buckets to carry everything small to the rail of the ship—scraped mud, garbage, fish carcasses—and tossing it overboard. Dad told us to make sure we didn't let people see what we were doing, though the polluted Grand River wasn't a sparkling gem to begin with. Little by little, the ship became less like the water it had been stewing in and more like a place people *might* actually be able to live.

When the ship started to dry out, however, that presented its own set of problems—problems which Dad chose to view as opportunities to put us to work. Without the mud and sludge coating every surface and with the heater running, the wood finally began to dry in the warm summer air. As the wood hardened, however, things shifted. Doors shrank out of alignment with their jambs. Closed windows couldn't be opened, and open windows couldn't be closed, and everywhere we looked there was paint peeling and bubbling off, sometimes in tiny patches and some-times in great wide swaths.

One afternoon Dad took a deep breath and declared, "Smell that dry air? Time to move in."

My stateroom had a single bunk, a single porthole, and a tiny lightbulb hanging from the ceiling with a small pull chain attached to it. Jerry and Sheri got the same setup, while Mom and Dad got the largest stateroom.

The next day we helped Dad carry what seemed like hundreds of gal-lons of white paint up the gangway and onto the aft deck. After lunch, Dad found us in the galley.

"Bought you something," he stated, tossing a paper bag our way.

Jerry reached inside and pulled out three new paint scrapers. Without a word he handed one to me and one to Sheri. Dad pulled his own well-used paint scraper out of his back pocket and walked to the nearest sec-tion of rough, bubbling wood. "Like this," he said, and scraped a patch of paint down to the bare wood. Paint flecks floated down like snow.

Then Dad walked off to another part of the ship, leaving us in no doubt about what was supposed to happen next.

"I can only reach halfway up the walls," complained Sheri. "This is the worst summer ever."

"Just scrape the low stuff," Jerry said, "and I'll get the parts you miss. Mark'll help too, right, Mark?"

"Right," I grudgingly agreed.

"Look, if we finish fixing the boat, we can play. Like at home. Dad will eventually run out of chores for us."

And so scraping decades of paint from a foul-smelling ship became our life for the following weeks. Sometimes the wood was so rotten that it scraped right off with the paint. Every morning Dad would tell us which part of the ship to work on, and we'd trudge in and begin scrap-ing. The walls all had multiple layers of paint, some so thick that I could see down through the years like I was a geologist looking at a canyon. White, gray, red, gray, dark gray, black, green, more gray.

"Who would paint a door so many times?" I asked Jerry. "And why would they switch colors each time?"

He answered with a question of his own. "And what was so gosh-darn great about gray?"

We scraped until our arms ached. We breathed in time with the back-and-forth motion, and paint flakes slowly covered us from head to toe. We inhaled some of the smallest flecks and tried to blink others out of our eyes. Our shoes were constantly transformed with new colors, and a fine grime of paint chips gummed up the knots and twists of our shoelaces just as thoroughly as the sandburs back home.

Occasionally Dad poked his head into the room to check on us, and that was our signal to sweep everything into a bucket and throw it overboard. The current in the Grand River was minimal where Dad was docked, but the sluggish water was so dirty that our paint chips hardly seemed to make a difference. No matter how much paint we dumped overboard, there was always more scraping to do—until one day we finished. We had scraped every surface that could be scraped, from the crow's nest down to the bilge.

The next morning Dad brought us something new: a paper bag with three paintbrushes in it.

"Doors, doorjambs, ceilings, window frames, chairs, stairs, railings, chain lockers, hatches, porthole frames, decking," Dad listed. "If it isn't brass or glass, paint it!"

At first we tried to paint the right way, but we quickly discovered that slopping on paint as thick and fast as possible was the best technique. When the paint was thick enough, it filled in the cracks and gaps in the old wood, and we only had to apply a single coat. Sheri painted low while Jerry and I painted high. All Dad's paint was oil based, so by the end of each day we stank of thinner—which we used to wash the brushes—and gasoline, which we rubbed on our skin to remove the paint.

Hour after hour, day after day—until one day Dad declared the painting finished.

Once the *Patrol* had been bathed in white and Dad was starting to think about taking it out onto the Lake, I was given my first taste of bilge duty. Sheri was exempted because Dad declared it a "man's job," and Jerry was exempted because he was terrified of the dark, confined space, forcing me to do it alone. After putting on my swimsuit, I climbed down to the lower deck, lifted the access hatch, and lowered myself through, splashing into a dark and claustrophobic canyon. Dad lowered a five-gallon bucket after me on a rope, inside of which were two Folgers coffee cans.

"Get whatever might foul the pump," he instructed.

In the light of a single bulb, I sloshed around in search of something solid to fill my cans. I discovered gummy sludge that was stuck to the hull, along with fish, oversize snails, and frogs, all of which were in various states of decomposition and mummification. Whenever I filled the five-gallon bucket with my Folgers cans, I called up to Dad, and he disappeared for as long as it took him to dump it over the deck rail. I waited for him in the bilge, hearing the slow slap of water on the sides of the ship, listening for Dad's returning footsteps. Several bucketfuls of gunk satisfied Dad that the pump would run again, and I was granted permission to climb back out.

"Now, into the river!"

Covered head to toe in filth and slime, I leaped over the rail and into the water. Some of the stuff I'd just scraped out of the bilge was floating there, waiting for me, but Dad tossed me a bar of Ivory soap before striding away.

•   •   •

The repairs were mostly finished, but they were a means to an end. Dad didn't want to anchor in a harbor somewhere and set up a lounge chair on deck. He had arranged to dock the ship near the coal quays on the Grand River—actually a small peninsula. Great piles of coal surrounded the city's main power plant, but not much else besides a few marshes, a scattering of small ponds and meandering waterways, and the water discharge channel from the plant. But it was a short sail down the river to Lake Michigan, and Dad wanted everyone to marvel at the *Patrol*, which meant taking it out on the open water.

"You ready to go out to sea?" Dad asked Mom when she came to see the progress.

"I suppose. Once or twice, anyway."

"You'll change your tune," Dad said, but Mom frowned in reply. I suspect the only thing worse than being cooped up with Dad at home was being cooped up with him on the boat.

Out on the water, Dad was king, and he played his role to the hilt. Squinting from beneath the brim of his captain's hat, which he donned whenever he took the helm, he would man the ship's wheel like he was a born mariner. Compass, throttle lever, gauges for fuel and oil pressure, running lights, air horn, UHF radio console—he loved everything about running that mighty machine. The *Patrol* gave him the chance to be 100 percent in charge. While he was driving the tank or shooting guns, life might suddenly inconvenience him. Mom might yell at him about money or a neighbor might come over to complain about something or he might have to go to his job. On the water, though, Dad was truly the captain of his own ship.

When it came time to sail, Dad would start up the Kahlenberg, and the noise and heat it generated were almost unbelievable. Each of the four pistons was as tall as Dad and thicker than my body. The engine shook the entire ship, and we could feel the vibrations through our shoes until it seemed even our teeth were in motion. Then we'd pull in the gangway, release the mooring lines, and off we'd go, plowing down the river toward the Lake.

When we were under way, Dad would often ignore us. Once, when I got tired of watching Dad steer, I went looking for Jerry. I checked the main cabin first and found Sheri. She was playing with her dolls and had them scattered, along with their various accessories, across the carpet Dad had hastily laid down to cover the floor.

"Where's Jer?"

"I don't know," she answered, not looking up. "I haven't seen him in a while."

I searched the rest of the ship before I thought of one place I hadn't checked: up. Standing on deck and craning my neck, I could see him far above in the crow's nest. It was the tallest point on the ship, but a quick hand-over-hand climb took me the thirty feet to the top.

"Move over a bit," I said, squeezing onto the small platform next to him. It was really only made for one person, but we figured out how to place our feet so we could both fit.

"Seen anything?" I asked.

"No, it's pretty quiet." He had Dad's binoculars with him. A large strap around his neck kept him from dropping them onto the deck below—the crow's nest could sway more than ten feet from side to side.

"No ore carriers?" At many hundreds of feet in length, they were the largest ships on the Great Lakes, and Dad's boat looked like a toy next to one of them. The land was a distant glimmer on the horizon, but when I took a turn with the binoculars, the high bluffs that lined Lake Michigan were clearly visible.

"I'm going down, move over," Jerry said, and he scampered down the ladder. I stayed for a time, enjoying the view. Everything was blue to the horizon, save for the white propeller wash trailing behind the ship.

Being at sea started out as an adventure—the lure of wide-open water and endless possibilities. The *Patrol* was a world away from the sandy hills at home, and the water never infested our socks and shoelaces with sandburs. Most of our chores at sea involved operating the boat, and that tended to be more pleasant than what Dad came up with at the house. The galley usually had a supply of Wonder Bread, jars of peanut butter, and a sack of apples, which was plenty to get by on.

It wasn't paradise, though, and the ship quickly got small after a few days at sea. We played card games and board games, but we were still antsy kids. The great part about living on eleven acres was that at least you always had eleven acres. There was really only one way to exercise when we weren't docked, and that was to play hide-and-seek. The ship was filled with hidden places, and Dad had given us so many chores that we knew them all. Some of them were so small that our little bodies would barely fit.

Jerry instigated. "Hey, let's play hide-and-seek."

"Okay," I agreed. "Sheri, me and Jerry will hide, and you find us."

She covered her face and began to count, while Jerry and I ran back to the galley and down the stairs.

We wedged into a dark, narrow crack, silently congratulating ourselves. Soon we heard the sounds of Sheri's search, and it was all we could do not to laugh or call out to her.

The minutes stretched. We couldn't hear Sheri anymore. And I didn't know about Jerry, but I was starting to lose feeling in my legs.

"Come on," I said, "let's give up."

We wandered upstairs, only to discover Sheri back in the main cabin, playing with her dolls.

"Hey, why'd you give up?" I reprimanded her.

"I couldn't find you, and it's *dark* down there. I got bored."

I got ready to retort, but then I heard Mom's voice in my head. *You boys need to play with your sister. You have each other, but she has no one.*

Living on the ship was getting worse and worse.

Dad had expectations for us too. I loved to stand at the rear rail when we were under way, watching the propeller churn the water into foam. The *Patrol*'s wake would unwind itself behind us like a forever snake, and I could stare at it for hours. Dad, however, had a radar for boys who were doing nothing—and the ship was too large for him to operate entirely on his own. Dad taught us to navigate so we could share the workload.

"Take the helm, boys," he'd say, and Jerry and I would jog off toward the wheelhouse.

I felt a sense of pride: Dad was putting me in charge of steering the entire ship. He'd told me that the Kahlenberg cranked out more than 250 horsepower, and I imagined I could feel every bit of that power vibrating up through the throttle lever and the brass wheel. He never let us steer the ship into port, of course. He wanted to be seen at the wheel. But in open water, he was content to trade our lack of expertise for his comfort. Dad might be gone for a minute or an hour, but either way, steering the ship would be up to one of us kids. We had a hard time giving navigation the attention it needed, and more than once we got up close and personal with navigation buoys and fishing nets, but that sort of marginal navigation seemed to be good enough for Dad.

In fact, once we'd taken a few turns at the wheel without causing a serious accident, Dad realized that we were an untapped source of nighttime labor. Why should he, or his diving buddies who tagged along for the ride, steer the ship when there were perfectly capable children on board? Dad began giving us overnight shifts, allowing us to use the bunk in the pilothouse.

"Share the shift with your brother if you need to," he told me one night, "but just don't leave this heading." He tapped the wide face of the compass for emphasis. "South by southwest at one-nine-five, got it? Do *not* leave that course. I'll relieve you at oh-seven-hundred."

That was a long nine hours. The dim light on the chart table reflected from the inside of the darkened pilothouse windows, making it impossible to see anything beyond the ship. The time passed like this: look at the compass and make sure it was pointed at 195; adjust the wheel if needed; grab the brass handle that controls engine speed, then release it since I wasn't allowed to change speed anyway; look at the compass again. When it was my shift, I longed to sleep but didn't dare. Although I grew more and more groggy and I allowed the ship to wander off course several times, I never actually fell asleep, and by the time the sun crept up over the edge of the Lake, I made sure we were smack-dab on course.

Jerry and I learned later that our overnight course corrections had cost the trip more than an hour of sailing time, but that was how things tended to go on the *Patrol*. You had to be ready for the unexpected—and you had to make it seem like the unexpected wasn't your fault.

22

THE SHIP WAS A PERFECT platform for Dad's scuba diving. The Lake was littered with wrecks—everything from modern fishing boats that had gone down in storms to massive, three-masted vessels that had been resting beneath the cold water for more than 150 years. Since Dad had a huge boat and an unlimited amount of free time, he had no trouble getting in touch with the right people who knew things or who knew a guy who knew things. Dad's posse knew things even the Coast Guard was in the dark about.

Finding the wrecks was like following a spoken treasure map. Once Dad heard that if he lined up with a particular pair of smokestacks at the power plant, then eased along until a certain tall tree on the shoreline was exactly opposite the starboard beam, and finally turned perpendicular to shore and motored out to a depth of exactly eighty feet, he'd find a wreck. Sure enough, the depth finder pinged a moment after we first hit the target depth, showing that the bottom jumped up where the bulk of the sunken ship rested. We'd hit it dead on—and that kind of thing happened all the time. There was *Walter L. Frost*, a lumber hauler that had gone down in a storm, and *Westmoreland*, nicknamed the "Treasure Ship" for the old coins scattered around its hull. *Montauk, Flying Cloud, Rising Sun, Three Brothers, Francisco Morazan*—we heard all the names over and over, like they were the names of distant relatives we were going to visit that summer.

Sheri and Mom didn't want anything to do with Dad's diving, but Jerry and I would come out on deck to watch him don his gear. He wriggled his way into his black wet suit first; then came twin tanks—the color of a canary—hooked to a single-stage breathing regulator, face mask, waterproof flashlight, dive watch, and a nine-inch survival knife strapped to the underside of his left forearm. Once he was ready, he'd walk to the rear of the *Patrol* to a gate, through which he would leap into the water feetfirst while pressing his mask to his face. We'd watch his bubble trail until we got bored and then wander around the ship until we heard him clamber back on board.

One day when Jerry was off somewhere by himself, Dad asked me if I wanted to learn to dive, and I jumped at the chance.

"First thing you need to learn is buddy breathing," he said, "in case you run out of air and need to come up with the help of another diver."

Diving was starting to sound less fun already, but I couldn't turn back.

"This is the J-valve," Dad continued, "and you just pull this lever if you ever run out of air."

The thought of running out of air terrified me. The tanks were so heavy it seemed unlikely I would have any control or be able to maneuver my hand behind me to reach the valve. If something went wrong, I would just die. And it would be a horrible death.

"You've got plenty of air," Dad explained, "but just in case something goes wrong, remember this, and never go below sixty feet. You'll get the bends if you do, and your blood will boil when you come up. You do *not* want the bends."

I agreed! Now I didn't want to die underwater if something went wrong, and I didn't want to come back up if something went wrong. Diving was sounding worse and worse. I would have no way to know how deep I was anyway. Dad carried a depth gauge on his wrist, but I knew he'd never let me use it.

"And remember to clear your mask like this," he motioned, "and always follow your smallest bubbles to the surface."

That sounded impossible. Smallest bubbles? And didn't every bubble race up as fast as it could? That's what I planned on doing. I decided I'd rather die of the blood-bubble thing than the blacking-out-and-drowning thing.

"Let the air out of your lungs slowly as you surface, and don't hold your breath or your lungs will burst."

For Pete's sake, I thought. *Now I've got to worry about my* lungs *bursting?*

"Remember, kid," Dad intoned, and he rapped his knuckles on my forehead. "Now let's get to buddy breathing."

Dad tossed the air tank over the side and allowed it to sink. He nodded at me. "Dive down to the tank," Dad instructed, then added, "Don't worry. I'll meet you there."

Dad jumped into the water and disappeared. I knew the water was close to twenty feet deep, so it would take all my effort to reach the tanks before running out of air. Dad was wearing flippers and a lead weight belt, so he could shoot to the bottom in seconds. I took the biggest breath I could, held my mask to my face, then jumped.

The cold water shocked my whole body awake. Down, down I went, my ears aching and my lungs feeling fit to burst. I could see Dad, waiting in the murk, holding on to the air tank with one hand and waving me over with the other. Desperate for air now, I reached for the regulator that was in his mouth. Dad took the regulator out and pushed it toward my face. I snatched it with both hands, crammed it into my mouth, and pulled in air with huge gulps. The feeling of fresh oxygen flowing into my lungs made me hang on to the regulator with a white-knuckle grip. Great clouds of air bubbles exploded from the back of the tank as I exhaled the air almost as quickly as I took it in. All too quickly, though, Dad reached across and took the regulator back, but he only took one gulp of air before handing the mouthpiece back to me. And so it went, back and forth, Dad giving me an extra breath or two, and when I'd calmed down, we slowly finned back toward the surface, buddy breathing all the way, until at last my head broke the surface.

"Okay," Dad grunted as he climbed onto the boat, "now you know in case you need it. Buddy breathing has saved more men than you could count in a month."

From then on I was qualified to dive, and I always dived alone. Only Dad had a wet suit, whereas I had to trunk it. When the mood hit, I'd ask Dad to lower the heavy tank into the water on a rope. I'd tug on a set of flippers and a mask, then jump into the Lake, surfacing beside the tank and treading water while I slipped off the rope knot and worked my way into the tank's stiff harness. Then I'd clear my mask, clamp the regulator between my teeth, and give Dad a thumbs-up.

Then down I finned, alone, into a blue-green world of liquid light.

The first few moments were always controlled panic: the icy water, the bizarre feeling of being able to breathe underwater, the sense that I was somewhere I didn't belong. And there, directly above me, drawing nine feet of water, hung the bulk of the *Patrol*, a shimmering shadow when seen from below, its massive propeller hanging motionless, slowly adding layers of blood-red rust. Soon, though, and inevitably, the quiet of diving took over. Time seemed to slow, and in the long seconds I could hear myself pulling in air, the bubbles leaving the regulator with a soft rush, like scattering birds. I could feel the water slipping around my body as I finned downward, and then I would see that day's wrecked ship below me. No matter the size of the wreck, I always felt small by comparison. Water swirled around the ship, shifting silt on the bottom, the current pulsing and pushing. I never dared approach too closely for fear of snagging my tank and becoming trapped, but each time I wondered what it would be like to enter the hull, to swim through nearly black staterooms filled with floating things best left to the imagination.

The dive had to end less than forty minutes after it began. I knew it was time to head back when the air took on the taste of metal—we never dived deep enough to require decompression stops, like Dad sometimes did, so as long as I could see the silhouette of the *Patrol*, I could make it back. Dad would help me manage the heavy tank, and if one of his friends happened to be on deck, he'd brag about what I knew how to do underwater.

"This kid has done more already than most men do their entire lives," he'd say, and he didn't need, in his words, "some government pencil pusher telling me what I can and can't do." He wasn't just the captain of his own ship—he was master and commander.

And he needed everyone to know it. Each time we pulled into a new harbor, Dad at the helm in his captain's hat, it wouldn't take long for him to befriend a curious onlooker at the dock. He was a natural storyteller, and he was an expert at projecting a kind of manly intrigue. Within minutes he would be inviting whoever it was to come aboard for a tour of the engine room. The allure started with the ship itself—what kind of man piloted a one-hundred-ton boat around the Great Lakes just for fun? That was an unasked question to which Dad's whole person was constantly shouting an answer.

Once we docked at Manistee to get in the lee of some bad weather that was heading our way. Mom and Sheri stayed on the boat while Dad told Jerry and me to follow him so we could carry some groceries back from the store.

As we stepped onto the dock, the other boats looked tiny. Dad was taking his sweet time connecting our boat to the shore power, so Jerry and I amused ourselves by picking out what we'd like to try.

"How about that one?"

"The long sailboat? Nah, too much work to rig everything up. How about that one?"

"It's nice. But *that* one's even nicer."

In fact, it was the nicest boat within sight. Significantly smaller than ours, of course, it still had every amenity. It was in cherry shape, and the man who stepped off it looked like he spent all his free time polishing and cleaning his beauty. Clearly retired, he wore a bright yellow jacket and matching hat.

Dad was just finishing with the electrical hookup when the man wandered over. "Never seen a ship like *this* before," he commented.

"Like a tour?" Dad asked immediately.

"Sure," he said, surprised to be invited on so quickly. "I'd love one."

Jerry and I groaned. We knew the "tour" would last at least thirty minutes, after which we'd still be forced to follow Dad to the grocery store. But he wasn't about to miss a chance to show off.

"Come on board," Dad said graciously, reaching out his hand to help the man up. "Let's start at the pilothouse."

As they left, Jerry told me he was going to wait in the galley, but I decided to tag along on the tour, just in case the visitor said or did something interesting. I caught up to them just as Dad was giving him the vital statistics.

"The four-cylinder Kahlenberg diesel weighs in at eighteen tons. *Patrol One*'s eighty feet long and weighs in at one hundred tons." He paused for effect. "And she draws nine and a half feet of water and has a five-foot prop."

The man couldn't respond with anything more articulate than an astonished "Wow." That was how most people reacted.

Dad continued the tour throughout the ship, ending as he always did in the engine room. The sheer size of the engine towering over us shocked most people. Dad reeled in his tour guests like fish on hooks. By the time Dad was done, the stranger looked as impressed as if he'd just been given a tour of a nuclear-powered aircraft carrier.

"Thank you for the tour. Thank you so much! It's *mighty* impressive!" As the man in yellow left the engine room with Dad, I noticed a large black oil smear on the back of his jacket. Dad saw it too but didn't say a thing. It wasn't the first time it had happened, and both of us knew it wouldn't be the last.

"Come on, Mark," Dad said once the man was gone. "Where's your brother? What are you two lollygagging for, anyway? We've got food to get!"

23

It was expensive to run the *Patrol*. Dad ran out of cash long before he grew tired of piloting his boat from harbor to harbor, so even though we took quite a few trips early on, soon we simply lived on the ship. We docked near the coal quay in the Grand River, generally carrying on as we would have at home, apart from the surrounding hills being replaced by polluted water. We still ate boring meals, played Monopoly, argued, listened to the radio, and wandered around, trying to do nothing much but just enough to keep Dad from giving us chores.

Then, as the summer trudged on, my stars suddenly aligned. Both Mom and Dad had found nine-to-five jobs in Grand Rapids, and so weekday mornings, before seven, they'd walk down the gangway and along the shore to our Ford Custom for the long drive into town, leaving us kids alone on the ship.

It was the happiest time of my life.

Every morning I'd wake up before my brother and sister. First thing,

I'd cram my head through the single porthole, which was barely wide enough, and survey the river. Nearly always it was covered by a morning mist that beckoned me to discover what it was hiding.

The ship was quiet and peaceful, and no one ever told me to do anything, which was a state of affairs that blew my mind. After stretching and looking out the window, I'd pad down the hall from my stateroom to use the *Patrol*'s single bathroom—Dad taught us to call it "the head"—which was really more like a closet. There was a shower stall, which only worked when the ship's engine was running, and a portable toilet that squirted dark blue chemicals when it flushed. Originally the shower had been designed to have a water heater hooked up to it, but Dad never replaced the broken one after raising the ship. He had a better idea. Since the ship was designed to pump the surrounding lake water through pipes in the engine room, thus cooling the engine, Dad replumbed one of the pipes so that some of the water, after flowing through the scorching engine, came into the shower instead of returning directly to the river. It was a good plan because it created hot water for free—assuming the engine was running—and cooled off the diesel at the same time. It wasn't a great plan, however, because the hot water it created was just this side of boiling. It was impossible to stand directly under the spray without being scalded. That meant there was only one way to use the shower: if I stood with my back against the wall, as far from the spray as possible, I could splash bits of water out of the spray with only mild pain in my hand, and by the time the drips reached the tender skin of my stomach or face, the heat was bearable.

Which led me to ask: Why bother to shower? By the end of most days, I'd spent hours and hours in the same river water, only outside the shower stall it was a good seventy degrees cooler. So each night, when it was time for bed, I'd simply pull off my wet clothes—shoes, socks, shorts, T-shirt—and throw them on the floor. The next morning, I'd shake the bits of green algae out of my damp socks and put the whole outfit back on.

Once Mom said to me, "You know, Mark, when Dad's friend Gary comes to stay on the boat, he washes his face, brushes his teeth, and combs his hair every morning before he goes anywhere. You should do the same."

What a clean freak! I thought. Good for Gary, but he was the first person I'd ever heard of who did such things. Dad certainly didn't. He constantly reeked of body odor, and it could become overpowering if we needed to spend much time in close proximity. He was sour and almost acidic—the smell made me want to take a deep breath of fresh air, which wasn't a helpful reflex if I was trapped beside him holding a wrench while he was tightening a bolt in the engine room. Dad treated his body almost as an afterthought. His teeth, which I rarely saw him brush, were yellow and usually caked with the remains of his last meal. He kept an electric razor in his car, and when we were driving, he'd grab it out of the glove box and flick it on, letting the dark trimmings drift onto his lap or even blow around the car if the windows were down. If we got somewhere before he was finished, he'd simply toss the razor back in the glove box and finish the job later. The razor couldn't handle his plentiful nose or ear hair, so he would reach up with his index finger and thumb and rip out a few, and then flick them away—in the car or on the kitchen floor or at a store, wherever he happened to be. I didn't necessarily want to turn out like that, but Gary seemed to be taking things too far in the other direction.

With complete freedom to do anything I wanted, I usually chose to fish with Jerry and then explore along the shoreline by myself. We rarely played with Sheri. She didn't care for fishing or exploring and always chose to stay on the boat by herself. We played Monopoly together sometimes, especially at night, but even then Jerry and I preferred to play chess against each other. Sheri hated chess. Without Mom nagging us to include our sister, Sheri spent hours and hours by herself. During those slow summer days, I suppose she played with her dolls or just waited around for time to pass—but whatever she did, she did it without us.

Despite our choosing to fish, Dad never bought us any fishing tackle. "What a waste of my good money!" he'd fume. "No matter what I buy you kids, you lose it!"

Catching anything became a challenge, but we figured out how to scavenge most things and beg what we couldn't, from hooks and lures to line and weights. There were usually a few poles around the ship, left by one of Dad's buddies for when they came to visit. The peninsula was a popular spot for local fishermen, and it didn't take us long to learn which underwater logs and edge-of-the-shore bushes snagged the most gear. Other fishermen seemed to have an unlimited supply of tackle, and the minute a nice hook-and-lure combo got hung up, they'd cut it loose and tie in a new one. Jerry and I would watch, and the minute they closed up shop and headed back to their cars, we'd swoop in, drag a sunken branch to the surface, and harvest its hidden treasures.

As we wandered from one fishing spot to the next, we interacted with quite a cast of characters. Rich and poor, black and white, young and old. The rich guys showed up on the weekends and left the best gear, but the black families—Dad called them coons, whatever that meant—were the nicest.

"Let's head out fishing," I'd suggest to Jerry, and nearly always I was answered by the same lament.

"We don't have any worms."

We had plenty of lures, but they were tricky to use. Earlier in the summer, when it was cooler and damper, we could find worms under every rock. But with the August heat, the worms had all gone deep underground, and we'd be lucky to find a single one.

"I know we don't, but I'm going fishing anyway. Maybe we can find some along the way."

We grabbed our gear, and after a short walk we arrived at our favorite fishing spot, near the base of a bridge.

"I'm going to check the rocks near the shore," I said, and Jerry, who had already split up to look elsewhere, called back, "Okay, let me know what you find."

After a few minutes of unsuccessful searching, I realized we'd have to fish without worms. Making my way back toward Jerry, I nearly tripped over a man who was sitting near the shore. He was wearing a dirty coat, and his pole was propped up on a forked stick so that he didn't need to hold it.

"What are you doing?" he asked. His voice sounded thick, like he was talking with a peppermint candy in his mouth.

"Looking for worms," I answered.

"There ain't no worms around here—too hot!"

As he spoke to me, I noticed he was missing one of his front teeth. A ragged beard covered much of his face, and the skin I could see was sunburned and crisscrossed with wrinkles. "You need to *buy* yourself some worms is what you need to do," he continued. I noticed the neck of a bottle protruding from a brown paper bag beside him. "Don't you know anything?"

I moved past him as quickly as I could, and as I did, I heard friendly voices up ahead. I came around a bend to find a black family fishing together, all sitting in lawn chairs and holding poles.

"Junior," the mother was saying, "help your sister with her pole." The pole the mom held was made from bamboo and was so long that she could reach the water without casting or leaving her chair. A small red-and-white float bobbed up and down at the end of her line.

I flipped some rocks, still hoping to find a worm before rejoining my brother.

"Honey," called the woman, "are you looking for worms?"

I glanced up, and the whole family was looking back at me.

"Yes," I admitted, hoping I wasn't taking their spot.

"You come right over here and get some from me," she said immediately. She reached in her pail and pulled out a handful of worms. "Here—is that enough? Why don't you take some more?"

"Okay, ah, well . . . thanks!" I managed. I set my pole down and held out my cupped hands, and she dropped the mass of squirming worms right into them.

"Do you have something to put them in?"

I shook my head.

"Junior, bring that cup over here." She motioned. The young boy carried over a small white Styrofoam cup. I transferred the worms, picked up my pole, and smiled at the woman.

"Thanks. Thanks a lot!"

"No problem, and you have a good day."

I found Jerry under the bridge. "I got a *bunch* of worms!"

"How? I looked everywhere."

"A black lady gave me a whole pile. She was really nice."

"Wow, lucky!"

We fished all day with those worms and still had some left over. We were able to hook a decent number of bluegill and catfish, and when we caught catfish big enough, we'd bring them back to the boat. Jerry and I would gut, fillet, and wash them, and then Mom would fry them up when she got back from work.

On our way back, we passed a man who was yelling at his son. They had fishing gear spread out all across the riverbank.

"Mark, we've got our worm container—maybe he'd help us fill it back up."

I agreed to check. I approached the man, waiting for a chance to ask.

"No, I'm *not* going to help you," he was shouting. "*You* made the mess, so you can *fix* the mess. Cut the line if you have to, but I've told you a thousand times to keep the line tight when casting!"

His boy tugged at a snarled line, then mumbled something I couldn't hear. I used the pause for my request.

"Mister, do you have any extra worms?" I held out the Styrofoam cup helpfully.

"Worms?" he snarled. "Can't you get your own worms? Oh, fine, here." He reached into a cottage cheese container and pulled out several.

"Just take these," he said in a resigned voice. "They're all I can spare."

"Thank you," I said politely. I nodded at Jerry. Now we had enough to fish with for another whole day. As I went to rejoin my brother, the argument resumed behind us.

"I still can't get it," the boy said.

"I *told* you. Cut. The. *Line*. How many times do I need to . . ."

I knew just how the kid felt, but what could you do? I was already thinking about keeping the worms in the fridge the next day and going exploring instead. I could only fish so much, but patrolling the river on my own was something I never seemed to tire of.

I would tell Jerry, then strike out on my own, spending the whole afternoon—or even the whole day—in perfect silence along the shore. For the first time in my life, *I* was the master. I was in control. I would pretend to be an explorer tasked with pushing deeper and deeper into an unknown wilderness. I would carry with me a long stick, a pocketknife, a lighter, and perhaps an apple or two, rarely bothering to return to the ship for lunch. The muddy bank was lined with empty whiskey bottles and cracked Styrofoam worm containers, and the trees had old fishing lines draped from them like spiderwebs. When I was out of sight of every other boat and fisherman, I would drop to my belly several yards from the bank and then commando-crawl, proceeding more and more slowly, until I reached the water's edge. Lying on my stomach, chin resting on my hands, I would watch, unobserved, as giant carp rose to the surface and sucked nutrients from the fingerlike roots that reached into the water. Muskrats would pass within arm's reach, leaving behind *V*s in the water before suddenly dipping out of sight.

I entered the water, too, taking my shoes off and wading into the algae-skimmed shallows. Moving ever so slowly, I caught snakes, painted turtles, crayfish, leopard frogs, and anything else that swam, slithered, or crawled. Before long I knew every curve and cove of the river like it was a map I'd invented myself: all the best places to hide, to fish, and to sit for a while and look at the passing water. I'd roast the crayfish over a small fire and crack them open with my pocketknife, savoring the sweet burn. Sometimes a guy just needed to think about nothing except what was right in front of him.

My favorite animal, by far, was the painted turtle. I spent countless hours in chest-high water, sometimes wading and sometimes standing still, watching for the telltale ripple of a turtle making its way from log to log. The bright green algae would build up on my chest in thin layers as I sloshed forward, and behind me the dark surface of the water would be visible for long minutes until the algae closed back over it. The turtles weren't much bigger than a silver dollar, and when they swam, only their tiny, dark heads were visible. There was something magical about those creatures, able to glide through the water and then, whenever they wanted, they could just disappear.

Mesmerized, I often let the turtles swim right past me, watching while they pulled themselves out of the water and into the sunlight, where the red and yellow stripes across their heads would shine brightly.

Sometimes, when I managed to catch one, I would hold it up close to my face and study it. They tended to pull their heads back into their shells, and I'd speak to them.

"It's okay, little guy. You're okay. You don't have to be afraid. Look, I'll find you some food. You're safe."

I could usually find a dead or dying bug floating nearby on the surface of the water, and I'd place it in the palm of one hand and wait for the turtle to poke its head out. When it did, I'd say good-bye and release it back into the water, setting my palm level with the surface and letting the creature climb off and stroke away. Each painted turtle was pure and wild and innocent.

Most times I explored, I chose to stay out until after Dad and Mom returned from work. Dad would blow the ship's horn—a mighty blast of air that echoed across the marshes—to let me know it was time to come back. After chow, Dad would usually wander off toward the engine room while Mom would wash dishes in the galley.

Every so often Dad would warn Jerry and me, "Stay close; I might need you." That meant we needed to be within shouting distance of the dock in case he called. Otherwise I was free to roam the shoreline until it was too dark to see, and then I would slip back onto the ship, slide into bed, and wait for the sun to rise on my next day of freedom.

•   •   •

I didn't *always* stay in at night. Once, after a long day of exploring, I lay awake on my bed, listening to the heat and the hush of the river. Restless, I stood to look out the porthole and saw across the water the sparkling lights of a carnival. I stuffed my feet into my socks and wet shoes and tugged on my damp T-shirt. Mom and Dad were in their room. The boat was dark, but I knew my way around by feel. I found the door to the deck and stepped out into the relative brightness of the night. There was the inky water, the black shoreline, and the lights across the river, which drew me like a moth to a flame.

I walked almost a mile upriver to the nearest bridge, following the outlined strip of stars above my head since the path was pitch black, and then traveled another mile downstream on the other side. I stood at the entrance an hour later, and the full panoply of the carnival exploded before me: countless game booths, illuminated food stands, the Tilt-A-Whirl, hawkers and barkers and wandering clowns, and spinning over everything, the Ferris wheel, winking like a neon eyeball. I'd been to a carnival back home during daylight hours, but at night it was a different animal.

The smell of caramel corn and hot dogs and cotton candy thickened the air, and grizzled carnies shouted at one and all. Frantic music blasted from each ride and booth, combining and echoing, overloading my senses. I rooted for this man to prove his strength with a mallet and for that woman to make three shots in a row with a basketball. My eyes and head followed the roller coaster, round and up and down, leaving me dizzy and gasping. And everywhere, people and always more people.

Couples that looked like Grandma and Grandpa Russell, holding hands and strolling. Teenage boys punching each other in the shoulders and then checking that their hair was still slicked back and solid. Between two tents a boy and a girl, kissing, both of his hands locked around her waist. It was a carnival devoid of children, save me, and I felt myself to be a man.

I wandered for hours before I turned back toward the darkness and walked home. When I climbed the ramp back onto the boat, I could see a dim light glowing behind the windows of the main cabin, and when I opened the door, a yellow rectangle fell across my body.

Mom was waiting in the main cabin. She was sitting in a chair, an open book face down on the table to her left, and her hands were folded in her lap.

"Where were you, Mark?"

I was surprised by her question. Mom rarely knew where I was.

"I was across the river at the carnival." I motioned back through the open door with my whole body. "Why?"

"You need to be more careful from now on." She fixed me with her look of serious concern. "I heard about a man who dresses up as a clown and kidnaps boys, Mark. He kills them. It's not safe for you to be out alone like that."

I stared. Her words hardly made sense.

"Mark, promise me you'll stay on the boat at night. With us, where you'll be safe."

I promised. Then I walked to my stateroom knowing that we'd only be on the boat a few more weeks. Then it would be time to go back home, where life would return to normal. School, chores, and eleven acres. And Dad. I sailed off to sleep, the music of the carnival sailing back toward me across the black water.

PART FOUR
A FRIEND

24

Dad had worked for Otto Freicky's marine salvage company, running equipment on the barge and diving. Otto, who practically lived on his barge, was a seaman from the old school, and Dad always spoke respectfully of him. Otto seemed like he was a foot shorter than Dad, and his skin looked like it was made out of old leather. As our summer wrapped up, Otto bragged to Dad about his luck: he'd purchased a red Chevy Corvette for only five hundred bucks. There was one small catch, he admitted—his new muscle car was underwater—but it would be a cinch to pull up with his heavy crane. When Dad pressed him for details, Otto said that the previous winter, two teenagers had stolen the car, raced it around town until it was nearly out of gas, and then, for some reason, driven it out on the ice, at which point they abandoned it. The next day, before the car could be recovered, the ice started to crack and shift, and a small group of locals watched the Corvette tip into the water and sink. The insurance company had already compensated the car's owner, but Otto knew a guy at the insurance company, which is how he was able to buy the title.

Finding the car was easy—just a matter of reading the insurance file and then looking for something red beneath the water—and so was hoisting it. Dad was the one who dived onto it and hooked the crane's cable to the car's chassis. Otto was grinning until his car broke the surface and began to drain, revealing not the bold curves of his Corvette but the blocky lines of a Ford Falcon.

"What the—I thought he told me it was a *Corvette*, and that's *not* a Corvette! I guess I shoulda looked at that title closer."

As his crew stood on the barge and watched muddy water continue to pour from the car, Otto kicked a deck cleat and asked heaven and anyone else who was listening, "What in the world am I gonna do with this thing?"

Dad had an answer. "What do ya gotta have for it?"

He bought the Falcon off Otto at a 70 percent discount, then had it towed to the parking lot near the *Patrol*. Once it dried out, we saw that the Falcon had a two-tone paint job, but not the good kind. The mud had eaten the paint from the half of the car that had been buried, so the front was a different color from the back. It only took Dad until the end of the day to get the Falcon running again, and despite the discovery that there were more than a few dead fish trapped in the heating system, Dad had come out ahead. Otto's brag-worthy story had been reduced to a chapter in Dad's.

Raising the Falcon was our last adventure of the summer. After months of boating, scuba diving, and learning for myself the ins and outs of every bay and backwater within a half-day's walk of the *Patrol*, it was time to head back to Belmont. The school year was barreling toward us, along with colder weather, and even Dad was ready to hang up the captain's hat and winterize the ship. For me, moving out meant nothing more than walking down the gangway, carrying a few clothes crammed into a grocery bag in one hand and some board games tucked under my other arm.

I was carrying a secret in my pocket, though—I was taking home a turtle.

On our last day at the river, I'd felt a pit open in my stomach when I thought about waking up at home without the prospect of seeing one of my little friends, and it hadn't taken much thought to figure out a solution. One last trip up the riverbank, one last wade into chest-deep water, one last patient wait, and I walked back to the ship carrying a hard-shelled emblem of the peace and solitude I'd discovered that summer.

I drove back with Dad in the Falcon. When we hit the highway and Dad got the car up to speed, it began to weave back and forth across the lane.

"Otto must've warped the chassis when he yanked her out of the mud," Dad growled. He battled the swerving for a mile or two, then swore and slowed down. The swerving wasn't noticeable as long as Dad kept the car below forty. Other cars raced past us, some honking, but Dad chugged on, headed home at *his* speed.

"It's not just the coons—it's the unions and spics, too," Dad said as we drove through the city. "Taking all our g—d— jobs. Gotta be a change in this country, and it's gotta be soon."

I hadn't heard my name, and nothing he'd said had been a question, so I went on staring out the window. Dad said stuff like that all time, and it rarely required more of a response than a noncommittal grunt. I reached down with my right hand, slowly, and patted my pocket to make sure my turtle was still there. I could picture it, legs and head retracted into its shell, waiting for my signal that it was safe to come out again.

Soon we were crunching down our gravel road, then crunching up our driveway made from car battery cases, and then I was looking at our house. Something was different, and it took me a minute to realize I was seeing new colors. When I'd left for the ship, the house had been cinder-block white with only the sunny-orange front door providing variety. Now one entire side of the house was orange as well. I walked around to get a better view and discovered a sprinkler hooked to the end of a garden hose and rotating back and forth, back and forth—*chick chick chick chick chukkachukkachukkachukka*. It was watering a shrub as well as the side of the house, and both the plant and the wall had been stained the unmistakable rusty orange of our hard water, as if the sprinkler were really a spray-paint nozzle.

I could tell Dad was standing behind me, so I froze. "Someone left the damn water running while we were away," he said, and then I heard him walk off.

I knew it hadn't been me—I'd been at the ship! Dad must have known he was the only one who had returned to the house recently, so nothing more was said about it. A minute later the sprinkler shut off, and I saw Dad go into the house.

I stayed outside, surveying. Water continued to drip from the shrub and run down the side of the house. I noticed that even the sand had been tinted orange. I pictured what would happen if we put the sprinkler in the middle of the roof and let it run for a few days, and the thought made me smile. I looked down at my shoes, and the laces already had several sandburs tangled in them.

"Well, turtle," I said, patting my pocket again, "here we are."

•   •   •

Every boy imagines worlds in which he is the hero. The previous years at my elementary school, when my teacher pulled down the world map over the blackboard, I became an Antarctic explorer making the final push toward the South Pole. I daydreamed during gym class, a sniper poised to bring down the commander of the enemy convoy. I doodled baseballs and bats in the margins of my history quizzes, the record-setting slugger who was never at a loss for friends.

One glance at my new junior high school shattered those brittle hopes. My old school, which had been out in the countryside, had a playground surrounded by acres and acres of grass and was guarded by large, twisted trees. I could smell hay and cows when I played football and baseball at recess, which was my favorite time of every day—the only time when I didn't need to pay attention to the teacher or to Dad. When I was playing sports, I felt free and easy, and the other kids liked me and picked me for their teams. My new school hulked at the center of a recently built subdivision, and everything was brand-new, from the saplings to the sidewalks to the students. As I stumbled off the bus on the first day of school, I realized that everything had changed, except for me. New kids, new classes, new teachers, new expectations, and countless new ways to mess up . . . and at the center of it all was the same old Mark Bouman.

The hallway was a fast-moving river filled with what seemed like five hundred unfamiliar fish, and I was just a small fry trying not to bump into anyone my size or get eaten by anyone bigger. I made it through the day by keeping my head down and speaking only when spoken to, and instead of drawing baseballs, I outlined the humped shapes of turtles.

When the final bell rang, I trudged to the parking lot. There were buses lined up as far as I could see, and I froze, overwhelmed by the number of choices. All around me the other kids chatted and laughed as they found their rides home. Then one of the buses started its engine, and another followed, and soon they were all idling while I was the only kid left standing on the curb. I jogged up and down the sidewalk, searching for my ride, but every bus looked identical. One by one they dropped into gear and pulled out of the parking lot, driving off in all directions like bees from a hive.

I was alone. The smell of diesel hung over the empty lot as I hitched my backpack a bit tighter to my shoulders and tugged up my hand-me-down jeans. I didn't know my bus, but I knew which streets would take me home, and I guessed it was an hour's walk, so I needed to get started.

•   •   •

As soon as I got home and figured out that Dad wasn't home yet, I raced to my room to find my turtle. Jerry was already back, sitting at the tiny folding table he called his desk, his textbook open beneath the tiny lamp, biting his pencil as he stared at a notebook. The turtle was where I'd left him that morning, half submerged in the shallow water at the bottom of a cast-iron pot on the dresser. It was time to make him a home—he didn't deserve to be trapped in my house all the time—and on my walk I'd thought of just how to do it.

At some point Dad had brought home an ornamental cement fountain, and now it sat beneath a good-sized poplar tree. We'd never used it for anything, apart from the times Jerry and I hid behind it while playing army, and Dad had never shown any interest in it, so I figured it was fair game for me to use. I knew it wouldn't hold water because there was a hole in the bottom, probably where a pipe was supposed to run, so I rummaged around in Dad's shed until I found a container filled with sticky white goop that seemed like it would seal the gap. After slathering the goop in the hole, I spent the next ten minutes searching for some large rocks to place at the center of the fountain. Then I connected two garden hoses together, set the open end beneath one of the rocks, and raced to turn on the tap. While water poured into the enclosure, I grabbed the turtle from my room. Back at the fountain, I carefully set the turtle down on the rock pile in the center, stepping back to survey his new home as it filled with water.

"Okay, little turtle, this is your home now," I said.

He extended his neck toward the splashing hose, as if to get even closer to the water. My gaze traced the thin, red lines arcing above his eyes and back onto his neck, continuing up the curve of his shell. His shell was only about an inch across, though his neck seemed nearly as long as my thumb. Over the sound of the running water, I heard a sort of click. It took me a moment to find the source: a beetle had fallen out of the poplar above, landing shell down on one of the rocks. The beetle struggled for a few seconds, legs waving in the air, and then it rolled down the side of the rock and disappeared into a crack. My turtle had been watching as well, and it followed the beetle down into the damp darkness, vanishing from my view.

"Enjoy." I grinned. "I'll see you soon."

•   •   •

My turtle filled my imagination at school. I pictured what he was doing without me, and I could almost feel like I was there with him at the fountain. Algae and moss had begun to grow in the water, green stains competing with the bright orange color so familiar from our hard water. My turtle loved to leave one of his feet in the water while he sunned on a rock, and when he dived, he always spun toward the side of that trailing foot. His tiny head, no bigger than one of my fingernails, lanced across the water at the point of a wide, expanding V, sometimes disappearing completely before reappearing, seconds or even minutes later, in some other part of the pool.

When I wanted to hold my turtle and speak so it could understand me, I would find a beetle and hold it in the water, and more often than not the ripples would attract him. When he swam close enough, I'd slip my hand into the water behind him, scooping him in a motion so smooth that his legs continued to swim the air, even as his head retracted in surprise.

"It's okay, it's okay. I just want to say hello. You're safe."

I would have been content to stay inside those memories from the homeroom bell to the release bell, but school knew the trick of lifting me back into reality. It always started with the sound of my name.

"Mark, where is your homework?"

"Forgot your gym clothes again, Mark?"

"Why does Mark have to be my partner?"

My name became a synonym for something unwanted, unpleasant, and all I could think about was how to escape. I had grown up hearing the story of a hunting trip Dad and Mom had made to Montana. Dad had shot a black bear and two mule deer, and for the trip home he tied the bear to the hood and lashed one deer to each door. When they stopped for fuel and a restroom break, they were forced to climb in and out of the windows. I imagined what it would be like to escape to such a place, a wilderness filled with animals. A place of endless trees where my name was never spoken.

As the school weeks stumbled past, my daydreams began to coalesce around the very place where my parents had traveled. One day during social studies, the word *Montana* took on an individual and urgent voice, walking into my head and whispering of endless forests and vast lakes, isolated places where I could wander forever without hearing the syllable of my name pronounced. In Montana I could choose my own name, maybe, a new name that would make me a new person. And there were turtles there just waiting for someone to find them.

"Mark? Isn't he the weird one?"

"Mark always gets the worst grades."

"This seat's already taken, Mark."

Time and time again I was called back to a classroom or a locker room or a lunchroom filled with kids who were smarter and faster and cooler, while I was stuck being Mark, living on a hill of sand with a bookworm brother, a kid sister with a ton of friends, a dad who smiled before he hit me, and a mom who seemed powerless to stop him—and no amount of imagining was going to get me to Montana.

●　●　●

One day Sheri announced that she'd won a goldfish at school—which drew an apathetic grunt from me—and then she said that she had put the goldfish into my pond. "Now your turtle can have someone to play with," she gushed.

That elicited an outraged grunt, along with a half-shouted, "He doesn't want someone to play with. He has *me*."

"But *you* can't swim with him, dummy. He wants to have another creature to swim with."

I could feel the anger rising. "You're the dummy, and your fish is even dumber. I hope my turtle eats it!"

Sheri giggled. "He can't eat my fish—my fish is almost as big as your tiny little turtle!"

She ran off while I raced down to the pond, fuming. Every so often I caught a glimpse of my sister's fish, a quick flash of bright orange and a tiny ripple in the surface of the water. My turtle was sunning on the largest rock in the center.

"C'mon, boy, don't you want to go get that stupid fish?"

Either my turtle didn't hear me or it didn't care. But I did. My sister's fish was an intruder. I'd created the pond for my turtle so it could be safe and happy and do what it pleased. I didn't want it to have to compete for space or fight for survival. I wanted the pond to be a place of solitude— and now Sheri was horning in on it without even asking me. A goldfish was a little girl's pet. It made my pond feel like a toy. The turtle pond was my slice of riverside, my reminder of the peace that I'd discovered during the summer. The only times I'd been content since coming back from the river were when I spent time with my turtle. I hated school, and I hated how there was nothing to do in my room and how everything in the house seemed to be broken or breaking.

Just recently Dad had walled off part of the living room to make the master bedroom bigger, and since that blocked off the entrance to the living room, he used a power saw to cut a new doorway in the kitchen wall, directly through the middle of the cabinets and the counter. Worse, Dad discovered a bunch of pipes on the floor, across his new doorway, and decided they would be too much trouble to move. His solution was to toss a small, dirty carpet over them and tell us to "get used to it." I didn't have to think about that kind of thing when I was with my turtle. I could sort of shut down my brain and just sit without thought or worry or fear.

I tried to calm down, hoping everything would get back to normal soon. The fish was bound to die. I studied my turtle's shell, which still carried a faint shine from the last time he'd climbed from the water. After several minutes of sunning himself, he turned and slipped back into the water. He could go anywhere and do anything—which at that moment, sadly, did not appear to include attacking and killing my sister's fish. I decided to feed the turtle, and after a few minutes of searching the nearby trees, I discovered a praying mantis perched on a twig. I pulled off its wings, carried it back to the pond, and set it afloat on a leaf. My turtle slipped off the rock and disappeared beneath the water, and a moment later he reappeared beside the mantis, pulling it into the water and devouring it.

• • •

School didn't get any better with time, and home—apart from my turtle—was how it always was: moments of fun, moments of terror, and lots of sitting around waiting for time to wander past.

Jerry and Sheri seemed like they were each on a raft, and both were drifting away from me in different directions, while I was stuck on an island. I knew what life was like on that island, and I knew they might end up somewhere better than me, but I just couldn't seem to move.

Sheri had a whole pack of friends, and she was constantly at a sleepover or a fair or a restaurant with one girl or another. Jerry seemed like he was digging deeper into his books, finding a place to escape that eluded me. None of us understood what was happening at home, like what it meant when Dad would choose one of us to teach a special lesson to, or why we could never afford new clothes. What could we say to one another? What could we do for one another? It seemed the only thing that worked was to put our heads down and try to live in a world of one.

The kids at school knew who my father was, and plenty of them would have been first in line to come over and ride the tank or shoot guns, but that idea terrified me. Dad might be fine, but he might *not* be. It was safer to never invite anyone over and safer still to never speak about what happened at home.

I had plenty of time to think while riding the bus to and from school each day. I'd imagine my way inside the houses we passed, watching kids sit at clean kitchen tables, watching fathers announce their arrival home from work with hugs and questions about school, watching mothers fold fresh laundry and bake cookies. When we left the neighborhoods behind and drove through the countryside, I'd imagine I was standing on an expanse of black steel and an unseen force was pushing me toward the edge of an abyss. Closer and closer, yet I never quite fell in. And so my thoughts would turn to my turtle—the closest thing I had to a friend, though it didn't seem like much.

One afternoon, home from school, I noticed the water level was dropping in my turtle pond, so I hooked up the hoses and draped one end over the rim.

It wasn't until the next morning, when I stopped to watch my turtle on the way to the bus stop, that I discovered the hose was still running. Water was slowly pouring over the rim, and while Sheri's fish was still swimming, my turtle was nowhere to be seen. I dropped to my knees on the downhill side, where the sand was wet, hoping to discover the telltale tracks I knew so well from the hours of stalking up and down the river. Seeing nothing, I ran in circles, wider and wider, scanning the ground for any sign.

Nothing. My turtle was gone. Panting, not knowing what else to do, I turned off the hose. I could hear the bus coming, and I ran. The whole trip to school, my chin kept wanting to shake, and I wove my fingers together to keep them still. Dad was right: it really was pointless to waste good stuff on us kids, since we'd lose or break it anyway.

•   •   •

That week I replaced my missing turtle by stealing David Visser's. He had brought his pet for show-and-tell, bragging about his fancy aquarium with its fake island and its heat lamp while the whole class oohed and aahed.

"Well, wasn't that just delightful and so fascinating," chirped Mrs.

Woolerth. "If you have any more questions for David, you may ask him at recess. Class dismissed—except for you, Mark."

I sighed and sat back down while everyone else poured out the door, laughing and shouting. I hadn't completed my homework, again, and my teacher decided that keeping me inside would teach me a lesson. Left alone in the classroom, silent except for the playground noise that seeped in through the windows, I couldn't take my eyes off the turtle. And when it turned its head to look at me, I quickly walked to the front of the room, grabbed it out of the aquarium, and jogged back to my desk with the turtle in hand. I shoved it deep into my desk, pushing my cupped hand past crumpled papers and books and pencils before releasing the creature as far away from the opening as I could.

I was just in time. Mrs. Woolerth opened the door and held it wide while the rest of the class trooped back inside. David Visser hadn't been in the room more than ten seconds when he freaked out.

"My turtle is gone! My turtle is gone!" He was hopping up and down at the front of the room, his hands flapping at his side like bird wings.

Mrs. Woolerth knew exactly what had happened. "Mark Bouman, did you take David's turtle!" It wasn't really a question.

"No," I shot back, "I didn't!"

"I don't believe you. You give David his turtle back this instant!"

Why had I said I didn't take it? I was dead meat. Before I could decide what to do, Mrs. Woolerth decided for me.

"Dick, Michael, check Mark's pockets, then check his desk—I want that turtle back!"

The boys had seen enough episodes of *Adam-12* and *Dragnet* to do a pretty thorough job of frisking me, and when I came out clean, they moved to my desk. I was going to get caught for sure. It wouldn't mean any trouble at home, because Mom and Dad would never find out, but it might mean trouble for me at school. David Visser had a lot more friends than I did. As I backed away, pulling my chair with me, the teacher's two lackeys crouched down and peered inside my desk.

It was a pit. I probably had the messiest desk at school. Looking into my desk was like trying to see through pea-soup fog, so the boys began to fumble around with their hands, gingerly, as if they didn't want to get cooties from all the junk. When that didn't reveal a turtle, at Mrs. Woolerth's urging, they began to lift things out and set them on the floor. All the while David Visser sat crying at his desk, surrounded by a sympathetic knot of kids who were trying to console him by patting him on the back and whispering insults about me.

"Teacher, there ain't no turtle in here—we checked!" complained Michael, and Dick nodded his agreement.

"Everyone sit at your own desk. Now!" snapped our teacher. She looked like she wanted to strangle me.

I sat down and began to refill my desk, wondering where in the world the turtle had gone. Two rows up on my left, I could see David Visser's head was slumped on his arms, and his shoulders were heaving up and down. Mrs. Woolerth gave us the angriest, fastest history lecture in the history of the world, then told us to write an essay until the next bell rang.

Thirty minutes later I dared to reach one arm into my desk, aiming for the spot where I'd placed the stolen pet. Ever so quietly I felt around, until—at the very end of my reach—my fingers brushed the familiar edge of a shell. Soon I had the turtle in my pocket, and the minute the bell rang I walked out the door, head down, feeling the burn of Mrs. Woolerth's eyes and hearing the fresh sobs of David Visser.

Back at home that afternoon, I left the turtle in my pocket while I went inside and grabbed a piece of Wonder Bread and a cup, then returned to the pond. After I ripped off some bits of bread and sprinkled them near the edge, I took the cup in my left hand and a fist-sized rock in my right. When Sheri's goldfish came for the bread, I scooped it up in the cup and then tipped it onto the cement rim of the pond. It flopped and flapped for a second or two, and then I brought down the rock on top of it.

I was elated. My turtle, my pond, and nothing to interfere. I took my new turtle from my pocket.

"Here's your new home."

I slipped my hand into the water and opened my palm, and the turtle slid off and swam away. I watched it circle once, twice—magic in motion—and then it climbed onto one of the rocks. I stared at it for a long time.

Then I looked down at the body of the goldfish. I had been wrong to kill it. Not just wrong. *Evil.* I'd wanted to protect my turtle, to have my pond all to myself, but I'd killed something defenseless. I quickly flicked the fish's body into the water, feeling my throat tighten.

I heard the rumble of Dad chugging up the driveway, and I shivered. I had acted just like him.

25

DAD MARKED MY BODY with his belt and his hand more times than I could count. So often it began with a phrase from which there could be no escape.

"I thought I told you . . ."

He went to great lengths to force an answer from me, widening his eyes like he was waiting for my response, or asking again and again, "Well? *Well?*"

The moment I opened my mouth—*wham!*—my words were slapped away. I tried to spread my legs wide enough to withstand the coming blow, but Dad was simply too powerful. My head would bounce off the fridge, the door frame, or even Jerry or Sheri if they happened to be standing near.

Dad's words were powerful too, and they seemed to be seared on my soul with a branding iron. How long did it take for the worst bruise to fade—a week? But I could still hear every name, loud and clear, that Dad had ever called me.

Imbecile.

The village idiot.

Good-for-nothing.

Any moment of the day—on the bus, slouched at my desk in school, on my back in bed—I could picture Dad standing over me, hands on his hips, declaring the truth.

Not very smart, kid.

Often after a beating, he would say, "I brought you into this world, and I can take you out of it." That wasn't a figure of speech—Dad was stating a fact. I was completely powerless.

•   •   •

Dad even had the power to turn me against Jerry. We were brothers in suffering, and if we never said it out loud, it was because we both knew it: we were on the same team. Dad's worsening temper, along with our differing reactions to it, had made us more isolated. Still, we were the closest thing to a friend either of us had at home, and we never forgot that.

It was always different with Sheri. When she was younger, she spent more time with Mom, more time playing inside with her dolls and her Easy-Bake Oven instead of tramping through the woods—and sure, more time being pushed around by me and Jerry. As she grew older she became a social butterfly, making countless plans and dates with her friends. The biggest difference between her and us, though, was her relationship with Dad. It became obvious that Dad was hurting us boys more and Sheri almost never. He needed no excuse to slap or beat us, whereas Sheri could sometimes get Dad to back down.

If he looked like he might be warming up to spank her for leaving the laundry unfolded, she might shout back, "Well, you didn't give me enough time to do it!" Jerry and I would cringe, picturing what would happen if we even *thought* that, and meanwhile Dad might stalk off, muttering to himself, allowing Sheri to escape scot-free.

Dad understood the bond between Jerry and me, which is why he used it against us. Once, when he heard us arguing about some pointless thing in the kitchen, he hollered at us to follow him outside.

"Thought you boys wanted to be men. From now on you'll settle things like men do. Now fight!"

Jerry and I were still standing shoulder to shoulder, looking at Dad, and the understanding of what was about to happen felt like it was reaching my brain in slow motion. We took too long to move, so Dad shoved us apart and spun me so I was facing Jerry.

"Now *fight*," he repeated.

Wanting to get it over with, I threw some halfhearted punches at Jerry, and he allowed a few of them to land before hitting me back a few times. We made the sort of noises that seemed like fighting noises, wrestled around a bit, and then broke apart, wondering what would happen next.

Dad put his hands on his hips and looked at us.

"You don't think I know when you're pulling punches? When I say fight, you fight," he said, looking us up and down. "Now fight!"

What alternative did we have? If we didn't fight, Dad would just beat us senseless anyway, and chances were his beating would hurt worse. Jerry's eyes turned flat as he came at me. He wasn't Jerry anymore.

"Harder!" yelled Dad.

And the first time one of his punches lanced real pain into my chest, I changed too. We were no longer boys but animals tearing into each other with genuine violence. Dad had forced us, for one dark moment, to hate each other.

"Harder! Harder!"

The more we hit each other, the more we hated Dad and what he was doing to us. We pummeled each other's bodies until we both were crying.

As quickly as it had started, Dad yelled, "That's enough. Now remember this next time you two want to fight."

He stalked off, leaving us staring at each other, panting and continuing to cry. We hadn't hit each other in the face—nothing could make us do that—but we *had* hit each other. Hard.

Mom called us back into the house.

"What happened? You boys should know better than to fight! Now go clean up, and don't let me catch you doing that again."

• • •

On the ship Dad had briefly become a different person. Authoritarian still, but less evil. Like the movies he'd watch by himself in town, starring men like James Cagney and Humphrey Bogart, Dad played a role when he was at sea, and I wondered if he simply liked being *captain* so much that he forgot to be the father who beat his family. He assigned jobs to his crew and directed the whole show, a confident and capable man of leisure who had the means to vacation on a ship he owned and piloted.

Back home, though, Dad became himself again. One morning, after Dad had really laid into me for losing something of his, I limped down the driveway to wait for the bus. On the ride to school, the bumps were painful, but I didn't give it much thought. It wasn't the first time a beating had made the day just a little bit worse. When it was time for gym class, I stood in front of my locker and pulled my pants down to my ankles, stepping out of them so I could pull on my athletic shorts. I glanced down at my legs and panicked: they were completely covered, from thigh to shin, in purple, red, and yellow bruises. I tried to leap into my shorts, only to realize that they weren't going to hide a single mark.

Then, from behind me, came the words I dreaded. "Hey man, what happened—did your dad beat you?"

My mind raced for an excuse that made even a shred of sense. I came up with nothing. "Yes," I admitted, "he did."

My classmate's reply was a snarl. "If my old man tried to beat me, I'd kick his ass."

I didn't respond, but as I walked out to the field, I thought, *You'd be dead if you said that to* my *dad.* Maybe his dad was smaller than mine. Or less mean. Jerry was the biggest of us kids, and even he wasn't close to a match for Dad's thick arms and solid body.

Gym class was torture that day. I tried to move slowly and carefully. I tried to keep my legs hidden. And I tried not to think about how my latest pet turtle—the one I'd stolen—had also disappeared. My efforts were not successful.

26

One Saturday I decided to earn some extra money, not because I had anything I was saving up for, but because I wanted to be more like other kids. I'd heard a boy at school bragging about how much money he made mowing people's lawns, and that sounded promising—how hard could it be to mow a lawn? Dad never tired of reminding Jerry and me that we knew how to do things most grown men couldn't do—which really meant we were used to doing chores that only adults did, like wielding a shovel for five hours straight. We did own a lawn mower, which Dad had picked up for next to nothing, just in case he got the urge to mow down the sandburs, and we always had gasoline around.

Neighbors were few and far between, and after the Dietzes, I had no idea who the next closest neighbor with grass might be, but I figured there had to be someone—it wasn't like we lived at the North Pole. I walked up the road, away from town, until I found an employer about a mile away. A man was standing outside his house, looking at the road, and he had a lawn big enough to land a small airplane.

"Hey, mister!" I hollered. "Can I mow your grass?"

He looked at me, looked at his lawn, and hollered back, "I'll give you three dollars."

Three dollars was a pretty good chunk of change. I jogged the mile back to my house to grab the mower, and just as I reached the driveway, I spied Mike Dietz in a nearby field, riding his two-stroke motorcycle. I waved him over, and after I explained my good luck, he agreed to help me by towing me and our lawn mower back up the road. I grabbed the mower out of the shed, used a jerry can to fill it with gas, and then pushed it down to the road. When I met Mike, I flipped the lawn mower around so its handle was facing up the road, and then I hopped on behind him, grabbed the mower, and told him to punch it.

Punching it meant going pretty slow up the road, it turned out, but it was still faster than pushing the mower. When we arrived, the man was nowhere to be seen, but I fired up the mower anyway and got to work. Nearly finished, I reached the back corner of the man's grass, and I spied something that made me stop and stare: a kennel full of bounding, whining puppies. I dropped the mower, letting it turn off, and beelined for the kennel fence. The dogs were all the same kind—floppy ears, long legs and tails, colored with large patches of white and candy-bar brown. They crowded the fence where I was standing, forcing their wet noses and long, rough tongues through the gaps toward me.

Suddenly I knew what I was earning money for. I raced back to the mower, finished my job, and then sprinted around the property until I found the owner, and before I could think better of it, I asked if I could buy one of his dogs. He looked at me like he was measuring something.

"Yep."

"Okay—lemme ask my mom!" My answer came out as a single word, shouted as I was already sprinting back down the gravel road. One mile later I raced to my front door, threw it open, and yelled, "Mom, Mom, can I have a puppy?"

She was in the kitchen. Her look said I wasn't giving her enough information, and when I stumbled through an explanation, she said, "If you promise to take care of it. You'll have to feed it and give it water and do all the other stuff that comes along with having a puppy."

"Promise promise promise!" I called as I bounced up and down. Mom gave me a smile that had a drop or two of sadness in it, and then she turned back to the dishes she was stacking in the cupboards. I waited half a beat to make sure there were no further conditions on my dog ownership, and then I spun and raced back out the front door, on the way collecting Jerry from the living room.

"Jer, you should see him," I panted, as we jogged up the road together. "He's just. So cute. And perfect."

"Cool."

"Maybe you. Can get. One too!"

We reached the man's house, and I quickly led my brother around to the kennel. The man—I still didn't know his name—was waiting for me there, leaning against a corner of the garage and chewing on something. When I raced up, he spit on the ground and then pointed to one of the dogs.

"This one should be a good hunter." As he said this, he leaned over the top of the kennel fence and picked up one of the animals. "He goes hunting with his mama every chance he gets. He's yours, no charge."

With that pronouncement, the man placed a wriggling puppy in my waiting arms. My dog. I held him in the crook of my left arm, the fingers of my hand splayed out to cradle his front legs. With my right hand I stroked the top of his head, and it was the softest thing I'd ever touched.

That afternoon, Jerry helped me slap together a doghouse in the corner of the shed, and then I tossed some hay inside. We cut a hole through the wall and built a square chain-link enclosure outside with some fencing and pieces of lumber we found lying in a scrap pile.

"This is where you're gonna live, Zeke," I told my dog, and since that name sounded right, I kept on using it.

That first night Zeke whined and howled for what seemed like hours. I lay awake in my room, terrified that Dad would hear him. I knew from experience that making my father angry in the middle of the night was about as bad as bad ideas came. Zeke was so small that a well-placed kick would seriously injure him—or worse. But Dad seemed to be sleeping through the noise, or ignoring it, and at last I drifted off to sleep, soaking up the feeling of receiving something I hadn't even realized I'd been longing for.

•   •   •

Zeke became the fourth kid in our family, and like the rest of us kids, he felt Dad's wrath on more than one occasion. When I left for school, I'd make sure Zeke was in his kennel, and then I'd tell him to be a good dog while I was gone.

He didn't always take my advice.

One morning, with nothing better to do, Zeke began to gnaw an opening between two boards of his doghouse. At first this project went entirely unnoticed. Day by day he shaved away little bits of wood, gradually loosening the nails and random screws that held the whole thing together. It took Zeke months of focused chewing, but eventually he created a hole large enough to stick his head through.

Now when Zeke began that project, he didn't have an endgame in mind. Biting through the wood was just something to keep him busy. Fate was on his side, however, because the first time he crammed his head through that hole it had taken him months to create, he discovered something amazing: a giant rubber chew toy.

Dad owned an inflatable life raft—a yellow, six-person affair he stowed on the ship whenever we were living on it. During the winter, however, he deflated it, rolled it up like a sleeping bag, and stored it in the shed, on top of Zeke's doghouse. When Zeke poked his spotted head through the hole he had created in the roof of his doghouse, his eyes must have doubled in size. It was like doggy Christmas.

By morning the raft was in about seven thousand small pieces, strewn all across the shed as if a small bomb had gone off inside the tightly rolled boat. I discovered this when I heard Dad screaming. I raced outside in time to see him stomping back toward the house.

"What in the holy hell, Mark? Do you know what that stupid dog of yours did? Do you? I should ram my shoe so far up his ass that his teeth shatter!"

I ran toward Dad, intending to throw my body between him and Zeke. He was a good dog—so good that I guessed my life for his would be a fair trade. He probably had a brighter future than I did.

"I'm sorry, I'm sorry, I'm sorry! I'll pay for the raft, I promise! I'm sorry!"

I kept shouting my apologies again and again, straining to be heard over the top of Dad's cursing. Dad was stomping around outside the shed rather than going for one of his guns or bladed weapons, so Zeke wasn't in any immediate danger, but just in case, I stationed myself at the entrance to Zeke's doghouse.

By this time Jerry, Sheri, and Mom were all standing outside. My brother and sister wisely kept their distance—this was my fight with Dad, and Zeke was my dog. Mom, though, walked straight toward the shed. She stuck her head past me to survey the damage and then turned to face my father.

"It's your own fault!" she yelled.

We froze. Even Dad.

"You were a fool to keep that raft anywhere near Mark's dog—what did you *think* was going to happen?" She snorted derisively and walked toward the house without looking back.

Dad stood there for a few seconds while we waited for him to explode . . . and then he walked away. Jerry raised his eyebrows at me as if to say, *Close one!* Then he and Sheri went back inside to get ready for school.

The only ones left were me and Zeke. I could hear him whining, so I went and sat beside him on the dirt. He laid his head across my lap, waiting for me to knuckle the spot right between his ears. After a few minutes

I told him I needed to clean up, and he seemed to understand. While I picked up the pieces of rubber and shoved them into a bucket I found, I thought about Mom. Sometimes she could do that: stop Dad's anger in its tracks. The trouble was, it didn't work every time and not as often as we needed or wanted. At least it was something. I guessed a desert had to take rain whenever it came, not complain when it didn't.

It took me three buckets to get all the pieces. Dad's raft was busted, like so many other things around our house. Like the carplane. Dad had raced it down a dead-end road, deep into a valley, and he couldn't get it back up the hill without opening up the throttle. The engine had shaken so hard that the muffler ripped loose and slammed into the propeller, tearing off more than six inches of one of the blades. He'd limped the contraption home, parked it out back with the rest of his junk, and forgotten all about it. Why fix it when you could let it rust?

I hammered a few scraps of wood across the hole Zeke had made. It wouldn't hold him for long, but now I knew what to look for. "And I'll be looking," I promised Zeke, because who knew what would happen the next time he angered Dad. "I gotta get to school," I told him, holding his head between my hands, "so be good while I'm gone."

• • •

Mom saved Zeke's bacon another time too. One night while I was in bed, he managed to climb up and over the chain-link fence, no doubt egged on by a raccoon that had been visiting a mountain of garbage.

The next morning, while I was fixing breakfast, I heard Dad screaming at me to come outside. The minute I saw him, I knew something bad had happened. Zeke was out of his kennel and keeping his distance from Dad, and Dad looked as mad as a hornet.

"Look what your dog did!" he screamed at me. "Look at it! I'm going to kill him this time, I swear!"

I looked where Dad was pointing, but all I saw was a patch of sand just outside Zeke's kennel and an upright fuel drum—one of the fifty-five-gallon kinds that was too heavy even for Zeke to knock over. What was I missing?

"Your f—ing dog knocked open the valve on that drum last night—there's not a drop left!" He grabbed the fuel drum with both hands and rocked it back and forth. "Do you have any idea how g—d— expensive fuel is?"

My stomach dropped. I raced over and dropped to my knees. That close to the ground, I could smell the truth of Dad's accusation. The sand stank of gasoline, and the valve—which was a simple handle that flipped open and closed in a ninety-degree arc—was open all the way. Positioned just where it might be if a dog landed beside it on the ground and then ran off, whacking the handle with one of his paws.

Dad was walking toward Zeke, hands swinging loose and ready at his side. Zeke, looking from Dad to me and back to Dad again, moved slowly backward, head and front legs low to the ground. I chased after Dad, begging him not to hurt my dog.

"I'll pay for it, Dad! I promise I'll find a way to pay for it!"

Dad answered without turning. "Yeah, boy, you'll pay all right."

I knew the footsteps behind me were Mom's, since Jerry and Sheri would never risk getting involved. We all knew that a Bouman kid suffering alone was a kid best left alone. Dad wouldn't ration his wrath. He was prodigal with pain.

"Hey!" she snapped.

Dad didn't turn around, but he did stop walking. Zeke and I froze.

"That wasn't the dog's fault, and you know it! If you don't want your stuff to get wrecked, then stop putting it where the dog can reach it! Just like that lousy life raft. Go on, Mark—get Zeke back in his kennel."

Mom's logic was a lot less sound this time than when Zeke had chewed the raft. Dad had put the fuel drum *outside* the kennel to keep it safe, and while Zeke hadn't opened the valve on purpose, it was his fault. Still—any port in a storm. I rushed forward and grabbed Zeke by the collar and led him back. We passed Dad on the way. He was standing stock-still, except for his fists. They were opening and closing. He wasn't looking at anything in particular.

Mom watched us, arms folded across her chest. "Come on now," she said when I'd lugged Zeke back into his kennel and chained him up. "Get ready or you'll miss the bus."

When I walked down the driveway fifteen minutes later, Dad was still standing outside, looking for all the world like a man enjoying a quiet morning. Sometimes Mom took the fight right out of him. Thing was, sometimes she didn't. Sometimes Dad hung on to the fight and then gave it back later.

But I was glad Dad wasn't going to kill my dog—that was all I knew for that day, and it was enough.

27

SCHOOL HAD ALWAYS been a chore. Even in elementary school I'd really only enjoyed the fact that a guy could get a free lunch. Since I was always hungry, I always cleaned my tray, and I marveled when other kids would toss away half their food. Recess was fine when I was smaller, since I could hit a baseball and tackle hard. But recess wasn't part of the equation anymore. Break time was just other kids standing around in groups, chatting and laughing, and me realizing there wasn't a single group I could join.

From what Jerry told me, high school was going to be even worse. Still, while he wasn't the coolest kid in school—his high-water pants and stained T-shirts guaranteed that, not to mention his thick, black glasses—his teachers seemed to respect him and so did certain kids. And the ones who didn't—well, he never let them bother him.

Once a blimp of a guy from the baseball team confronted Jerry in the parking lot after school. The kid had two or three chins and brand-new Chuck Taylors.

"Whaddaya think, four eyes—that I'm just gonna let you walk past?"

Jerry's answer was simple. "Yes."

"Well, I ain't."

Jerry pushed his glasses farther up on his nose, and then said, "I'm going home to study. I don't want to fight." He made a move to go around, but the other boy shoved Jerry's shoulder.

"You're gonna have to, *Fairy* Bouman."

Jerry sighed and set his books down on the asphalt in a neat stack, then straightened. He was a good six inches taller than the other kid, and probably forty pounds lighter. An impromptu boxing ring formed, a row of parked cars on one side and spectators on the other three. Jerry raised his arms to his chest, loose and easy, then tucked his chin down and waited.

"Get him!" someone yelled.

The baseball kid charged, and Jerry just stood there. The other kid threw a flurry of punches, all aimed at Jerry's face, but Jerry tried to duck and dodge, all the while backing away from his attacker. It looked like the fight was going to be over soon enough, as Jerry didn't seem to be able to defend himself.

And it was, but not in the way that everyone watching expected. Jerry'd had the stuffing beaten out of him too many times to count, and he had an incredible tolerance for pain—Dad saw to that. Jerry hadn't been retreating—he'd been luring the other guy closer, like a patient fisherman. With a sudden move, Jerry stepped inside the other guy's reach and slugged him smack on the jaw. Matching the rest of his angular body, Jerry had sharp, pointy knuckles that protruded from his clenched fists, almost like a set of brass knuckles. Without slowing, Jerry spun his opponent around, doubled him over with two shots to the kidney, then grabbed him and, using all of his considerable leverage, rammed the kid headfirst into the nearest car door with a nauseating crunch.

His huge body slid down the door, collapsing in a heap and leaving a head-shaped dent in the metal. In the sudden silence, Jerry said to no one in particular, "I don't want to fight," and then he picked up his textbooks and walked away.

Kids at school just couldn't believe that a dork as skinny and quiet as Jerry could really fight, so that wasn't the only time Jerry was forced into violence. The result was always the same, though: Jerry would absolutely destroy his opponent. One thing he'd learned from Dad, whether he liked it or not, was that the quickest way to end a fight was to make sure the other guy couldn't get up off the ground.

Jerry had confidence, and he could defend himself. I had a report card full of Ds and a single purpose in life: spending time alone with my dog.

Every minute spent at school was a minute spent away from Zeke, and that wasn't good for either of us. Before the bus was even stopped at my driveway, I would stand up and begin stumbling down the aisle toward the front, and the minute the door hinged open, I was through it like a shot, bolting up the driveway. Zeke always knew I was coming, and as I ran, I could hear his barking growing closer and closer. Then Dad's shed would come into view around the side of our house, and I'd run even harder toward the frantic barking. As I rounded the front corner of the shed, Zeke's doghouse would come into view, and we'd see each other for the first time.

"Hey, boy! Hey! How ya doin'? Ready to go?"

I had learned that Zeke was a German shorthaired pointer, but unlike most of his breed, he never had his tail clipped. His long, slender tail only added to his ability to seem entirely wild, like a small brown-and-white tornado. He was totally unable to control himself when I sprang him from the shed, sometimes leaping into midair and then, with all four legs off the ground, twisting in the opposite direction and landing in a heap. Barks, yips, licks, wags, sniffs, and all the while switching between four legs, two legs, and no legs with the speed of a bullet. To me he looked like living joy.

I don't know what I looked like to Zeke. All I know is that somehow, for some reason, he loved what he saw. Of that I was certain.

I would jam my hand into the latch to open his gate, and out he'd fly, blowing past me and rounding the corner on his way to the house. We both knew exactly what came next. Zeke would wait outside the door while I'd race to my room, toss my books onto my bed, and in one fluid pivot grab my shotgun from where it always leaned against the wall. Dad had given me the shotgun—a double-barrel Ithaca hammerless—and it was so heavy and long that without my pride I could scarcely have carried it. I kept it clean and oiled, and Zeke and I never went into the woods without it. Next came a handful of shells stuffed into my coat pocket, and I'd make it back to the door where Zeke was whining with happiness.

And that's when things slowed down. Our rush to reunite and get ready was over, and now we could relax. We had escaped—Zeke from his cage, me from school and home—and now it was time to savor our freedom. Usually we walked behind the house together, away from the road. Our house, squatting at the top of one of the tallest hills around, gave me a view that stretched for miles. While Zeke sat beside my leg, letting me know with the occasional pressure of his head that he was ready to go whenever I was, I would scan the surrounding land. Sometimes sharp in the sunlight, sometimes dark in the mist, and other times painted with the colors of fall, our land—and our neighbor's land, since we never paid attention to property lines—hid what seemed like endless places for a boy and his dog to explore.

The man who gave me Zeke had been right: my dog was a born hunter. He could sniff out any critter, anywhere, and nothing pleased him more than chasing down a scent and then making sure I kept up with him. Turned out I was a born hunter too. Running with my dog was the only thing I cared about—the only thing I let myself care about. The amount of game hidden in the surrounding creeks and hollows and stumps and burrows was astounding: raccoons, rabbits, squirrels, opossums, and even foxes.

We loved those woods. What we found there couldn't be taken from us. I was free from the constant, nagging fear of humiliation that followed me around school. Free from the stabbing fear of punishment at home, from the sense that every move I made was being scrutinized by an unfair judge, who on the strength of a single careless word could call down a slap powerful enough to knock me off my feet and into the nearest wall. And Zeke was free to be himself and to be with me, which was all he ever asked.

Jerry and Sheri and I would always be connected. No one understood our life, which meant that no one would ever understand us.

Thing was, *we* didn't understand our life either. We lived in the same house, but we almost never talked about life. The things that mattered most remained unspoken between us. We never told one another that everything would be all right. We didn't hug or hold one another. We rarely touched.

But touch is a language a boy needs to speak and to hear spoken to him. Trapped in my own silent suffering, I pined for touch. That was a constant wound, an ache that had no remedy. All I could do was cope, alone, and the only way I knew how was in the company of Zeke. Because it just so happened that touch was my dog's native language.

We would explore miles and miles of woods and streams, uphill and down, always side by side. Zeke loved to swim in one of the nearby ponds, and I would sit on the bank while he frolicked in the water before running to shore, shaking himself, and racing back into the woods. He had a funny habit of sniffing out and collecting every box turtle he could find, one by one, and then dropping them in the pond. Maybe he was bringing them back for me, as presents, wanting to fill my pond with something he knew I liked. And I would always thank him with a kind word and a thump on his flank. Then Zeke would thank me for thanking him, giving my hand a lick and turning in eager half circles, then pushing his bony head into my flank. In the silent shadows beneath the trees, alone with Zeke, I was never belittled. Never criticized. Never attacked. No one talked at me about failed tests or water-stained clothes. No one reminded me of all the chores

I had done wrong. I was never made to feel like a waste of space on God's green earth.

The end of every hunting trip was a little death. Zeke and I would straggle back to the house at the latest possible hour, and I would take my sweet time settling my dog down in his kennel. The longer I stayed outside, the greater the chance that inside Dad was watching television or reading on the couch. I could go from the kennel to my bedroom if I was lucky, wolfing down some leftover food on the way. Zeke's face—bright eyed, smiling up at me, painted with mud over the top of his brown-and-white spots—might be the last face I'd see at night.

It was the first one I thought of every morning.

28

Zeke became my escape, but it was an escape that could never be complete. I still saw Dad nearly every day, of course—there wasn't another option in an 800-square-foot home. It was true that I avoided him whenever possible, but Dad had a knack for finding me, whether I wanted him to or not.

What didn't make sense was that sometimes I still *wanted* him to find me.

The Dietzes had a large barrel that they used to store their garbage. We never understood the need for a barrel, since they had plenty of land behind the house where they could dump trash, but it seemed to work for them. We would burn our trash heap, and they would burn whatever was in their barrel.

One afternoon, when I was hanging out with Zeke near the house, I smelled the smoke from the Dietzes' burn barrel and glanced up. The smoke wafting our way didn't look normal. "Hey, Jerry." I pointed. "Look!"

"Burn barrel smoke, right? So what?"

"I don't know—doesn't the smoke seem more spread out? I've never seen it like this before."

"I think you're right. Let's go check it out!"

We ran down the hill toward the tree line that separated the Dietzes' property from ours. And then we saw Mike Dietz near the burn barrel, racing around in a panic because the low grass all around him was on fire. He was trying his best to stomp out the flames, but it was impossible. For every patch he put out, three more sprang up.

"Jerry! Mark! This is growing too fast!"

"Where are your parents?" Jerry asked, starting to panic. The grass fires were edging toward the trees.

"Not home. No one's home. Help!"

We all started to chase the flames, but it was no use. The dry grass continued to ignite and sometimes reignite even after we stomped it out.

"This isn't working!" Jerry shouted. "Mark, go get Dad!"

I headed up the hill as fast as I could. I glanced back over my shoulder once, and the smoke was thickening and filling the sky. As I neared the shed, where I had last seen Dad, my stomach dropped. What if he blamed *me*? Then I flung open the door.

"Dad! Dad! There's a fire in the field from the Dietzes' burn barrel!"

Dad looked up and read my face.

"Where?"

"Near the tree line."

He dropped the tools he had been holding and followed me out the door. I was still puffing and breathing hard from running up the hill as I stood next to Dad. He looked across the burning field.

"Go get a shovel. I'll meet you down there."

I ran toward the shed to grab a shovel, noticing as I did that Dad wasn't running to the house to call the fire department like I expected. Shovel in hand, I raced back to where Mike and Jerry were fighting the flames. "I told Dad," I panted, attacking the nearest set of flames with the shovel.

"Where is he now?"

"I don't know."

"Did he call the fire department?"

"I don't *know*."

Seconds later, Dad crested the hill in the tank. We could see him motioning us out of the way from the driver's hatch, and we scattered like bowling pins. Dad jammed the tank right up to the trees, lined one of his treads up, and plowed forward. The burning grass was disintegrated beneath the weight of the tank, leaving nothing more than smoking soil in its wake. He reached the end of the line a few seconds later, and he put the tank into a tight turn and came back for one more pass.

A minute later, the fire was almost completely out, and a wide swath of charred, fuel-free ground stood like a barrier at the edge of the trees.

He halted the tank and shouted, "Finish up what I missed!"

Then he drove back up the hill and disappeared.

It was a while before any of us moved. Mike summed up the general opinion when he said, "Whoa . . . I can't believe it. That was amazing!"

We began to scan back and forth along the ground, stomping out any embers we discovered. Our little brains, which had been on overload, finally caught up with what Dad knew: with a tank, you could crush nearly anything.

•   •   •

Other people knew that Dad was willing to use his tank to do almost anything, provided the "anything" in question was something he could brag about or do while showing off.

One day Dad got a call from a farmer a few miles down the road. The farmer had sold his land to a developer, but before the sale could go through, the farmer needed to demolish the farmhouse and the barn. "I asked myself why I should pay some demo crew when the Tank Man lives nearby," the farmer told Dad.

Several days later, Mom drove us kids to the farmer's property while

Dad followed slowly in the tank. We noticed cars parked all along the man's long driveway. After we found a spot and walked up to the house, we joined the hundreds of people who had shown up to watch the demolition, as well as a crew from the local television station. It wasn't too many minutes later that Dad rumbled up the driveway to great applause.

He took his time climbing out of the hatch, and then he and the farmer walked around the house and the barn for several minutes discussing the best way to bring everything down. The brick farmhouse had a basement, so Dad couldn't simply plow through the walls or the tank would become stuck below ground level. The barn wasn't small, either—I wondered if Dad would be able to drive out of it if the barn happened to collapse on top of the tank. Eventually, Dad and the farmer shook hands, and then it was time for an interview with the television folks.

"Mr. Bouman," the reporter asked a bit breathlessly, "are you ready?"

Dad simply nodded.

"What gave you the idea to buy an army tank?"

Dad knew everyone was watching him. The bright lights of the camera lit up his face, and he seemed to grow a few inches as he stood next to his tank. "Most people stand around and just watch the world, wishing they had the courage to act," he declared to the camera. "But I'm not most people."

The reporter took a step back, extending the microphone she held a bit farther. "You seem very sure your tank will take down this house—do you have any concerns?"

"Nope." Dad jumped up on his tank with one fluid motion, gave a jaunty wave to the crowd, and brought the tank to life.

We watched as Dad made slow but steady progress with the farmhouse, nosing the first third of the tank through the brick walls and then backing out before the tank could overbalance and tip forward. Every five minutes or so he'd gesture toward the crowd, and several men would scramble over the tank, removing the hundreds of accumulated bricks with the speed of a pit crew.

The house probably took forty minutes to knock down completely, but most people stuck around because the barn was next. It was at least fifty feet high, and it had a massive main beam holding up the roof. I knew if the beam didn't go over, the barn wouldn't either—but I also knew it was in the center of the barn. Dad couldn't just poke in the edges like he was doing with the house.

At last he positioned the tank directly outside the door of the barn, and all the folks who had stayed to watch grew quiet. Dad drove through the main door and stopped the tank a few feet shy of the main beam. Then he gunned the tank forward and the beam—an incredibly heavy piece of wood, two feet square if it was an inch—simply snapped in half like a twig.

Two things then happened simultaneously: Dad rammed the drive levers into full reverse, and the barn began to collapse like it was made of wet cardboard. The roof buckled, walls leaned and snapped, and all the while Dad's tank was powering backward. Just as the central peak of the roof hit the floor and the four walls fell inward with a mighty crash, Dad exploded out the door in reverse, seemingly spit out by the massive cloud of dust and splinters.

The crowd roared with one voice.

I found myself roaring with them, clapping and jumping up and down. How could I not? The Tank Man had triumphed again.

29

ANOTHER YEAR OF school slouched past; another summer vacation arrived. We knew from past experience that Dad and Mom would be too busy working or fighting to pay much attention to us. I knew I should be spending more time with Jerry, since he'd be heading off to Michigan State soon, but in truth what I was looking forward to were uninterrupted months of tramping through the woods with Zeke, seeing as few other humans as possible.

And then Dad surprised us.

I could tell what the pile of blue plastic and white aluminum poles was, even from across the yard, and there was no *way* Dad had gotten it for us. But there it was, sitting right up the hill from the shed: an above-ground swimming pool.

"Jerry! Jerry!"

He came tearing out of the house. "What?"

I pointed. He shrugged at the blue-and-white pile, uncomprehending. I pointed again for emphasis. "Jerry—it's a *swimming pool*!"

He grinned and punched me in the shoulder.

•   •   •

Dad assembled it that same afternoon. Sheri joined us, and we hopped around and asked questions, tossing ideas back and forth about what we'd do with the pool. It stood as high as my shoulder and formed a circle almost as wide across as our living room. Once it was up, Dad looked at us. "Well, guess you'd better fill it," he said, and with that he walked away.

"What made Dad decide to find a pool for us?" I asked.

"Who cares!" Jerry answered.

We connected three different hoses together, and before long we had a steady stream of water trickling in. And then . . . we waited. And kept on waiting. It seemed to take forever for the hose to fill the pool, and we were determined to wait until the water was high enough that we could take a real swim—no cheating! We tried to do our usual things to stay busy, but more often than not we found ourselves back at the side of the pool, peering in, trying to determine how many inches the water had risen since the last time we checked. Not even hunting with Zeke could take my mind off the pool and all its possibilities.

Finally the pool was ready. While Sheri watched, Jerry and I dragged a few old boxes over to the edge so we could get in—Dad hadn't bothered to bring home a ladder or steps—and then the three of us took our first laps around our new pool. It was glorious. Sure, the water had already started turning the blue liner a shade of orange, and it was ice cold, but the pool was ours. We could hardly believe it: as if running water and a sunken bathtub weren't luxury enough!

We soon discovered two reliable pool toys: Zeke and a plastic baseball bat. The bat, which had a hole at one end, filled with water and could maintain neutral buoyancy, like a submarine, and since it was streamlined, it made a perfect torpedo. We played a game in which one of us—two, if Sheri wasn't off at one of her friends' houses or tired of playing what she disdainfully called our "boy games"—would try to swim underwater from one side of the pool to the other, while the gunner would aim the bat and then accelerate it underwater, trying to anticipate the swimmer's movement and score a hit.

"Ping, ping, ping," came Jerry's uncanny imitation of a submarine's sonar, and that called for my response. "Flood all chambers! Dive, dive, dive!"

Once, Jerry hit me with the water-filled bat *above* water, when I came up for air, and it shoved one of my front teeth back against the roof of my mouth. Dad decided the dentist would be a waste of money, and he turned out to be right: over the course of the summer, my tongue slowly pushed my tooth back into place.

Zeke, though, was an even better toy. The easiest way to get him into the pool was to stand outside on the sand, lift him up, and then heave him up and over the edge. Getting out was, for both him and us, a matter of scrambling up the side and dropping to the ground. He loved to swim, and we loved it when he was in the pool with us. He was a yipping, tail-bashing game all by himself, and though we never knew what we'd do with him (Try to ride him? Teach him underwater fetch? Play Marco Polo?), it was always fun. We got him to understand the torpedo game well enough, though he tended to bite any incoming munitions and swim away with them. It was a summer of unexpected fun at the Bouman house, and between the pool and hunting with Zeke, I had rarely been as happy.

•   •   •

Like all things on our property, however, the pool slowly decayed. The inside liner, which had been the blue of a summer morning, turned a deep rust color, and since we weren't putting any chemicals into the water and had no filtration system, bugs began to multiply. When we were underwater, wearing our diving masks, we'd come face-to-face with bugs as big as our thumbs, spiraling their lazy way through what must have seemed an ocean. We didn't stop swimming, but we did become more careful about keeping our mouths closed underwater.

The bugs weren't the biggest problem, though. The water level had started to drop faster and faster, to the point where we had to leave the hose running in the pool for most of the day. After some sleuthing, we discovered that whenever Zeke scrambled his way out of the pool, his toenails punched small holes in the liner. Mom bought us a patch kit in town, and we walked around the inside rim of the pool, covering the worst of Zeke's tracks. From then on we gave him a boost over the side when he wanted to get out, hoping not to create any more leaks, since Mom hadn't given the impression that she'd keep supplying us with patch kits.

A few weeks later, however, as the water level continued to drop, it became clear that Zeke's toenails weren't the real culprit. Jerry, donning a diving mask and spending so much time underwater that his skin wrinkled up like Grandpa Russell's, eventually discovered a leak at the bottom of the pool, right in the corner where it met the wall. While I supplied moral support in the water, Jerry took one of our last patches and swam back to the bottom, but he found himself floating up to the surface before he could apply enough force to do the job. After several failed attempts, he spotted something that looked like a blue string right near the leak. It seemed to be waving at him, and thinking he could hold on to the string and stay underwater while he finished the patch, Jerry grabbed it.

He instantly discovered that the string was part of the stitching that held one of the pool's main seams together. Jerry's tug ripped the seam open a few inches, and that was all it took. The rip became a hole, the hole grew into a tear, and three seconds later the pool was split from top to bottom. Five thousand gallons of water exploded out of that side of the pool, leaving Jerry and me gaping like landed fish inside the suddenly empty pool. One instant we were swimming, and the next we were standing in a few inches of water on a heap of wet, blue plastic, watching our lives drain away.

Because it just so happened that the leak had been perfectly aligned with the doorway to Dad's shed.

The sound of a mini tsunami caught Dad's attention. He had been just behind the shed, and he raced around the corner in time to see Jerry and me standing atop the ruined pool in our swimsuits while a wall of water pushed hundreds of pounds of sand, dirt, and small rocks directly down the hillside toward him.

Without missing a beat, he charged for the front of the shed, yelling, "Don't just stand there—close the door!"

Too late. By the time the flood hit the shed and redirected around it, the water had deposited more than a foot of sediment inside the shed. Luckily for Dad, he'd built the shed with a raised floor and separated floorboards, so all the water drained out. Unluckily for me and Jerry, though, the mud showed no inclination to follow the water. It took Jerry and me about thirty seconds to slosh our way out of the remains of the pool and scramble down the hillside to the shed, and that was how long it took Dad to grab two shovels and plunge them into the wet sand outside, blades first. There they stood, like drill sergeants, waiting to give us our marching orders. Dad didn't even bother with words.

Jerry and I shoveled damp sand for three days, and on the first day Dad tore the pool down the rest of the way. He never moved it, and the ruined pile of plastic simply stayed there to rot.

Sometimes I'd picture that day in my mind: Dad appearing from behind the shed just as the waist-deep wall of water arrived, his face expressing something I'd never seen, and only for an instant. It was shock mostly, but mixed with a bit of fear and a dash of awe. It was the look of someone who is always in control realizing, if only for the briefest moment, that control is elusive. Those three days of shoveling blistered my hands, but it wasn't an entirely unhappy memory.

• • •

Our house continued to decay as well. One of the floorboards in the living room eventually rotted all the way out. Dad yanked out the pieces of spongy wood with the claw of his hammer, but he never got around to replacing the board. That meant there was a hole in the floor about the size of a loaf of bread. We all knew where it was—just in front of where you'd stand if you were answering the phone—so it was easy to avoid—much easier than the water pipes and cooling fins we had to step over to get through the new doorway between the kitchen and the living room. Sheri found a small rug somewhere that she placed across the hole in the floor, and that became the new normal.

One day a saleswoman rapped on our door. Dad was gone, but Jerry and Sheri and I were in the house, so we all came into the living room and lurked behind Mom to see what would happen. The woman, dressed smartly in a white blouse and blue skirt, wanted to sell Mom beauty supplies, and she just knew she had something that would be perfect for Mom's complexion and hair color. Her white high-heeled shoes clicked as she walked into the house and sat down.

"Let me open this up," she cooed. "Now let's start with some foundation. We have various skin tones and shades."

Mom might have liked to buy some, but we knew she wouldn't. Not with Dad using all the spare cash for his toys. So Mom made a kind of politely noncommittal noise—"Mm?"—and kept listening.

"Next I'd like to show you blush . . ."

We three kids sat and watched her dig through her leather makeup case, fascinated by the exotic wares. Having salespeople come to the house was a rare event. One by one she placed little bottles on the table next to Mom.

"Oh, this *is* nice," Mom said approvingly, unscrewing a cap on a vial of lotion and rubbing some of it on her skin. Sheri scooted closer so she could watch up close.

While Mom tried something else and Sheri tried the lotion, the woman asked if she could use our phone. "I just need to make a quick little call to my daughter."

"Of course," agreed Mom, still looking at the samples. "It's right over there."

As the woman rose from her seat and made for the phone, we kids became aware of a potential problem: she was headed directly for Sheri's rug.

None of us said a thing, most likely because we were too shocked to speak. What happened next unfolded in slow motion.

With a grunt that became a screech, she tipped forward. Down went her front leg into the hidden hole, the rug wrapping itself around her ankle and disappearing, while her other leg splayed backward across the floor, straining her skirt's stitching to its limits.

"Oh *no*!" Mom shrieked, and leaped to her feet. "I'm *so* sorry. There's a hole there we haven't fixed, and . . ."

Jerry ran to the woman's side and tried to help Mom lift her out of the hole. After a bit of struggling, the woman slowly wobbled to her feet, still unsure of what exactly had happened to her. Her leg slipped out of the hole, but her shoe stayed folded up in the rug below, forcing Jerry to lie on his stomach and reach into the crawl space.

"I'm *so* sorry," Mom repeated. "We all know the hole is there, so we just naturally avoid it. I'm so, *so* sorry."

"Wow, I *wondered* what had happened. The floor just disappeared from under me!"

She straightened her blouse and skirt, then reached for the phone again.

We moved back to the couch. "Why didn't you *say* something?" hissed Mom.

"I tried, but . . . ," Jerry said, shrugging.

"And we all know it's there, so . . . ," Sheri added.

Mom sighed, then we all waited for the woman to finish her call. She hung up and made her way back to the couch. "So, is there anything else you'd like to see?"

Mom could see the woman wanted to escape. "No, not now. But maybe . . . ?"

"Yes, here's my card. Call me when you're ready to place an order."

She hastily gathered her samples and haphazardly placed them in the leather case.

"It was nice to meet you," she said, standing. "Thank you for your time, Mrs. . . ."

"Bouman."

"Good-bye now, Mrs. Bouman."

"I'm so sorry," Mom said, opening the front door. Mom followed her outside, apologizing the whole way. We stayed behind, staring down into the hole.

"Did you see how fast she dropped?" Jerry whispered, motioning with his hand. "Zooooom, down she went!"

We laughed until our stomachs hurt. I wished Dad had been there to see the whole thing. He would have loved it.

30

Ever since the year we had spent an entire summer on the *Patrol*, the ship had become more Dad's toy and less a family activity. He and his buddies still used it for diving, and the five of us made only occasional trips to the Grand River—a weekend here and a weekend there. While driving back to Belmont after one such trip, I spotted a turtle on the highway up ahead. It was large enough for me to see from the backseat of our Ford, even driving sixty, and Dad saw it too. Dark and disc-shaped, the mud turtle was hauling its bulk across the two-lane highway. It was a kind I usually avoided in the waters of the Grand River. While my favorite paint turtles were gentle and safe, bigger species like the muds and snappers seemed to have an unpredictable dark side.

"Hey, Mark, want me to stop so you can grab that turtle?"

It took me too long to process what Dad had said, so unexpected was his consideration. We passed turtles on the road all the time, and Dad had never even commented on one, let alone offered to stop so I could pick one up. He decided for me, slamming on the brakes and skidding the car to a stop on the shoulder in a cloud of dust and flying gravel. Recovered from my initial shock, and still in disbelief about my luck, I leaped out of the backseat and then raced along the edge of the road before swerving toward the yellow centerline. I scooped up the turtle with two hands and sprinted back to the waiting car. There was no way Dad could change his mind now.

My door was still open, and as I slid into my seat, I held the turtle in one hand and yanked the door closed with the other. Right away Dad pulled back onto the highway, having left the engine idling while I claimed my prize. Sheri was sitting beside me, and Jerry was on the other side of her, and both leaned over to inspect my find. It was a beauty. At least a foot across, its shell was a mix of flat, dark green—like an underwater plant—and lustrous brown. It opened and closed its mouth as we peered at it, giving the impression of asking what in the world had just happened to it.

Soon we were back at highway speed, and as our car hummed along, I stared at my new friend. Dad rarely allowed talking or singing or game playing in the car. Usually we all sat in silence, but if he was in a particularly bad mood, and one of us made a noise, Dad would nearly drive off the road while wildly trying to smack us from the front seat. Having a large turtle in the backseat, however, presented a whole new set of entertainment possibilities.

My first thought was to scare my sister. Holding my new pet in both hands, I eased it upward, inching it closer and closer to my sister's face. At first she didn't notice but kept on staring straight ahead, moving her lips slightly to some internal dialogue or song. When the turtle was less than a foot from her face, staring right at her and still opening and closing its mouth, Sheri reentered reality with an audible scream and a full-body spasm. Her legs leaped off the floor, her elbows dug into Jerry and me, and her head jerked back, away from the turtle.

The sound of breaking glass was unmistakable, even over the noise of driving with all the windows down. There was only one thing it could be: the antique lamp Mom had found at an estate sale on our way to the *Patrol* several days earlier. Dad had balanced it on the shelf beneath the rear window and told us not to touch it. Sheri's head had done far more than touch it: she'd knocked the lamp backward so hard that its leaded-glass shade had shattered against the rear window.

Without taking his left hand from the steering wheel, Dad spun around and slapped Sheri hard, right across her face. "I told you to be careful!" he screamed.

Gasping, she yelled back, "But Mark scared me with the turtle!"

Dad put his right hand back on the wheel. I could see the muscles in his shoulders knotting, flexing.

"Mark," he commanded, "you throw that thing out the window!"

"But Dad, it's—"

"Do it now!"

The entire car was frozen. In the front seat, Dad white-knuckled the wheel and Mom stared straight ahead. In the backseat, Jerry gaped at me, bug-eyed, while Sheri's face was a red-welted mask of confusion and pain. I was frozen too, still holding the turtle suspended, its small mouth open. The rush of hot highway wind was the only noise.

Then the turtle peed, its warm urine running down my arm and staining my shirt and pants.

Dad broke the silence. "What are you waiting for?" he screamed. "Throw that f—ing turtle out the window!"

So I did.

With one reflexive motion, I tossed the turtle to my left like water from a bucket. When it hit the slipstream it disappeared, instantly, spinning away into oblivion.

Dad pushed the car up to fifty-five. Sixty. Sixty-five. The rest of us sat in stunned silence, pinned to our seats. I pictured the pavement behind us, unwinding like the wake of a ship. I thought of the turtle in midair, windmilling his legs in slow motion, and of how it had no idea, as it spun toward the road, what was waiting for it.

31

ONE NIGHT I WAS heating some water on our gas stove. After holding the lit match to the burner, I blew it out and flicked it into the garbage pail. Dad had been sitting at the kitchen table, reading a book, but he was in my face in an instant.

"What the f— was that? Do you have any idea what you just did?"

My shocked stare was answer enough.

"You just tried to burn down the house, you imbecile!" He reached into the garbage and pulled out the spent match. Holding it between two fingers, he waved it in front of my face. "This match was hot when you threw it in there, and a hot match still burns!"

Before I could process what he told me, he flicked the first match back into the garbage and grabbed a new match. Holding it in his right hand, he lit it and then grabbed my wrist with his left hand. Then he blew out the lit match and shoved its smoldering tip into the palm of my hand.

"How does *that* feel?"

"Ow! *Ow!*" I tried to jerk away, but Dad held on tightly.

"Did that burn you?" he asked, almost amused.

"Yes, yes," I whimpered.

"Then why the f— did you drop it in the trash? So you could burn down the house? What an idiot. When are you going to be more careful? At least you learned never to do that again."

He released my wrist, and I snatched my burned hand back. The match was still resting in my palm, and I stepped to the sink and ran both my hand and the match under cold water. Dad, meanwhile, had sat down at the table. I tossed the wet match into the trash, but Dad didn't even look up.

That was the kind of lesson Dad liked to teach. Practical, he said, and something we wouldn't soon forget.

I was learning something different, though: that I could never trust my father. I took that lesson to heart and avoided him every chance I got. He was the source of our pain at home, so less Dad meant less pain. I wasn't bright when it came to math, but even I could see the end of that equation. If less Dad meant less pain, then no Dad would mean no pain.

But could I actually kill him?

I knew how to use a gun well enough, and my shotgun could certainly kill a man. That wasn't in doubt.

What I doubted was my courage. Perhaps if he was sleeping, or facing the other way. But what if he woke up, or turned around, and I had to look into his eyes as I pulled the trigger? Then there was the possibility of missing. If Dad was alive after the first shot, I knew I wouldn't get a second. He would certainly murder me.

And what if I succeeded? Say I pulled the trigger: who would I become? I'd no longer be the Tank Man's son. Instead, I'd be the kid who killed his father. The police would probably understand my plight, and perhaps even look the other way. But even with my poor record of church attendance, I was convinced that God would still hold me accountable. And if God was anything like Dad, I wouldn't get off easy.

• • •

I spent every minute I could with Zeke. Sometimes I was too tired or too depressed to hunt, and he seemed to understand. We'd walk together until we found a patch of grass or a fallen log, and then I'd sit and pull him into my arms and cry. During the loneliest years of my life, my dog was my companion and friend.

But even Zeke couldn't shield me from a growing awareness of my near-total isolation from other people and of the constant agony of living. I felt as if darkness were clinging to me, and everything I saw was shadowed. Pain seemed to take on an almost physical form.

Pain knew all my habits, all my haunts, and there was no place I could go where he wouldn't find me. I spent most days apart from Zeke, stuck at school, but Pain followed me everywhere. I had tried for years to run from him, but he always found me. Pain covered me like a blanket, there for me after the beatings when I cried myself to sleep. He was waiting for me at school each day—in the locker room, in the lunchroom, in my classrooms—reminding me that he would never leave me. Pain greeted me when I walked the halls, when no one else would even acknowledge me.

Pain shared my silent world. He was a constant presence looking over my shoulder. Whenever my spirit groaned from not being free, he reminded me that being utterly alone would be even worse. His friendship deadened my emotions. Life began to pass at half speed. Living each day was like shouldering a heavy weight, but what choice did I have? Life was leaden, but at least it was predictable. Lift, suffer, sleep. Repeat.

Pain was rough around the edges—not the sort of friend to show off—and he didn't want to share me with others. It was easier to bend to his will. To stare at the ground instead of other people's eyes. Life became a series of wanderings through desolate places, and he went with me. I hated him, yet it seemed he was the only one who refused to leave my side. He would be my constant companion. There was nothing I could do to change that fact.

I felt altogether alone—so alone that I almost welcomed Pain's company.

• • •

Another afternoon, and more hours spent exploring with Zeke—but this time something new happened.

As Zeke ran ahead of me, I'd been asking myself what would happen when I became a man. Before Dad was twenty-one, he was already married. He already had two kids. He had already been kicked out of the Navy. I wondered if I'd even make it to twenty-one.

My only goal in life was survival. I watched other kids in school gain confidence and chase dreams and learn to do things that were unavailable to me. The world was moving forward, and I was falling behind. From what I could tell, life happened fast once you grew up. And life could get bad fast, too, and then keep getting worse. *What will I be doing in ten years?* I wondered.

From out of nowhere, a sentence rose into my head, fully formed: *You'll be in Montana, in the military.*

The voice was quiet and clear, and it surprised me—mostly because I knew it wasn't my idea. I knew Montana was just a big wilderness of high mountains and old timber—how many times had I fantasized about running away there?—but why in the world would I move there as an adult? Was there even any military in Montana? And what did it mean that I was hearing voices?

Here came the questions again. That still, small voice had seemed like something helpful for a second, like a real answer, until the thought of it faded into the dusk. It was just me and Zeke, like always—and Pain, always Pain—and the future was still far enough away that I tried to put it out of mind. However scary it was to imagine life as an adult, the terror of being a kid had a way of demanding my focus.

•   •   •

The next day after school, I sprang Zeke from his kennel, grabbed my shotgun and a few shells, and headed out. I paused behind the house to load my gun, even though I was planning on just roaming that day, not hunting. I called my dog over and showed him the gun, and he instantly went on alert, ears up and tail straight back. I waggled my eyebrows at him. "Want to go hunting, boy?" I swung the gun slowly back and forth across the tree line, pretending to be looking for animals. Zeke's head followed the barrels exactly. "Look—there!" I joked with Zeke. "There goes a rabbit!" With that I swept the gun quickly to my right where the imaginary target was, touching the trigger and saying "Boom!"

Unfortunately, when I said "Boom," so did my shotgun.

I had forgotten to set the safety after loading my gun, and I'd just discharged a real shell at a pretend rabbit. Worse, my pretend rabbit had been hopping through the weeds in the direction of a mahogany motor-boat sitting on a trailer in the yard. Dad had been restoring it for weeks.

It took me longer than it should have to cross the thirty yards to the boat, partly because I was praying so hard—*Please, God, don't let me have hit the boat, don't let me have hit the boat*—and partly because I was squinting my eyes. Through my narrowed lids the boat was a dark, flickering blur, still in a state of limbo between tenderly restored and totally ruined. When I could reach out and touch the boat, I could no longer put off the inevitable, and I opened my eyes all the way. To my horror, the boat had taken a direct hit. My gun had been loaded with pellets, and in thirty yards the hundreds of them had expanded to a cloud. It didn't look like a single pellet had missed the boat.

My brain shut off. There was no way I could process the extent of my screwup. I hyperventilated, shotgun drooping from my right hand, left palm spread on the boat's chewed-up side, head tipped forward to lean against the wood.

Then a single emotion powered me back up, jump-starting my brain.

Panic. What in the world was I going to do? Maybe Dad wouldn't notice. I stepped back a few paces. It was even more obvious. The side of the boat looked like a giant had sprinkled black pepper on it. Could I run away? It was already too late—Dad would be home in less than an hour, and that wasn't enough of a head start. But maybe that was enough time to repair the damage! I safetied my gun, set it down, and whipped out my pocketknife. Choosing the thinnest blade, I inserted the tip beneath a pellet and tried to pry it out. It was wedged in tight, though, and I had to dig around it to loosen the wood's grip. Finally the pellet popped free and I pulled the knife away. Instead of a tiny hole with a speck of metal at its center, now I was looking at a larger hole with rough edges, and the lighter colored wood beneath the exterior varnish shone like a beacon.

There would be no covering up what I'd done. I was dead. Not get-in-real-bad-trouble dead, but dead dead. Dad was going to murder me.

My body began to shake. Zeke hopped around my legs, whining and throwing an occasional yelp my way. My panic folded in on itself and became a hard knot of terror that hung in my gut. Only a few weeks before, Dad had beaten me so bad that I had trouble sitting down even three days later, all because I'd left a half-eaten pot of oatmeal congealing on the stove. I had no illusions about how shooting his boat compared to that. I'd be killed in cold blood. I became physically sick to my stomach. *My life is over.*

Then a sudden wave of calm washed over me. Since I had less than an hour left to live, I might as well go out doing what I loved. Yes: I would go for a final hunt with Zeke. It was my dying wish. I picked up my gun, cleaned it off, and walked down the hill toward the trees.

Zeke was out ahead in an instant, scouting for scents. He had already put our strange detour to Dad's boat out of his mind. When Zeke told me he'd found a rabbit, I thought about where the rabbit was probably hiding—in that shallow gully that ran crossways past the top of the pond—and how I might be able to get around the other side and be ready when he made a break for safety. I thought about which way the wind was blowing, about how many shells I had in my pocket, and about what it meant that Zeke's barking was getting louder.

I lost myself in the hunt, or perhaps the thrill of the hunt swallowed me, but the events of that day were erased, like a miracle, from my mind. As Zeke and I disappeared into the wild, all thoughts of Dad's boat disappeared as well.

•   •   •

A few days later I was in the shed, looking for some twine, when Dad called me from his workbench.

"Mark, come here for a minute." His tone told me something was wrong, but I couldn't for the life of me think of what. I'd kept a clean slate so far that day—or at least I thought I had.

Dad looked at me, still holding on to the part he was cleaning. I approached him but kept myself out of his reach, all the while scouring my brain for what I might have done wrong. Then he simply asked, "What did I ever do to you that would make you so mad that you'd shoot my boat?"

The boat! The memory came crashing back like an explosion. The shotgun, my final hunt before Dad was due to murder me, and then the strange oblivion that followed. I literally hadn't thought about it since it had happened. But Dad knew. I'd managed to live a few extra days, somehow, but *now* I was going to die.

"Dad, it was an accident!" I blurted, sure I had just spoken my last words.

"Okay, son. That's all I wanted to know." Dad turned back to his bench and continued working in silence.

I stood rooted to the floor, mouth hanging open. I watched Dad's shoulders rise and fall, saw his watch glint as he reached for a tool and brought it back into the circle of his work lamp. There was a round window in the shed, made from the lens of a searchlight, and for some reason, the light streaming through made me think of a bee's eye.

In a daze I walked out the door. Outside the sun was shining like I'd never seen it shine. The sky was blue all the way to forever. I knew in my gut that I'd just come out the back side of a miracle. It was a small one, maybe, compared to what other people needed, but that day it meant life to me.

32

"THE *PATROL'S* GOTTA GO," Dad told us at supper. As if any of us cared. His announcement simply created a blanket of silence that covered the table.

He went on and on about it. Fuel costs were rising, dock space was getting more expensive, and ship maintenance was becoming a nightmare. The hull was suffering from dry rot, which meant that the bilge pump was under constant strain as new leaks sprang. When the ship was docked, the pump could keep up, but the *Patrol* could no longer sail. Even if Dad could afford to put the ship in dry dock and overhaul the hull—which he couldn't—he was probably fighting a losing battle. And if the ship sank at its mooring, the Department of Natural Resources would stick Dad with a huge fine.

That night we heard the sound of bedsheets ripping and tearing. "The DNR is gonna ride me like a cowboy!" Dad shouted in his sleep, waking all of us up. "She's sinking, she's sinking—I've gotta plug the hole with this sheet!"

By the time Mom woke him up, the bedding was in tatters and Dad was drenched with sweat. We all went back to sleep, and over the following weeks, Dad went to work on the ship, pulling everything off that was worth more than fifty cents, from the brass compass in the pilothouse down to the life jackets in the stern chain locker. Then he hired a demolition crane to knock down the superstructure and pull it off the ship, leaving the *Patrol* as nothing more than an empty, leaking hull. Dad then ordered two dozen tons of sand and spread it throughout the hull.

Then came the wait. Sinking a ship in Lake Michigan was illegal seven ways to Sunday. It wasn't that Dad *wouldn't* do something so illegal—just that he'd be plenty careful about how he did it. If he had been worried about the DNR's reaction to the *Patrol* sinking at the dock, he was terrified of them finding out he'd scuttled his ship in deep water. That was the sort of stunt that went far beyond a hefty fine and a pile of paperwork. He'd be looking at jail time.

The perfect opportunity arrived when a cold front pushed down from Canada, bringing with it thick sheets of rain and miserable cold. Visibility on the Lake was under twenty-five yards, and the water was heaving. No sane person would be out on a boat unless his livelihood depended on it.

Dad convinced one of his buddies who owned a big boat to motor to the dock in the Grand Haven harbor, and together they attached lines to the *Patrol*'s deck. There was a harbor watchman on duty that night, but a quick scouting trip convinced Dad that he would be staying inside his shack for the rest of the night, trying to keep warm and dry.

Four hours later they were five miles out into the Lake. Five hundred feet of water would be plenty to hide the *Patrol* from prying eyes. With his friend's boat idling nearby, Dad detached the lines. Then he climbed down to the first level, scooting around the piles of sand, and found the back steering gear by headlamp. The *Patrol* would sink on its own, given enough time, but time was one thing Dad couldn't afford. He needed to ensure no one could see his boat, because no one would fail to recognize it—what he needed was for it to sink like a stone. So first he opened the ship's seacocks, a series of valves that formerly connected the engine's cooling system to the water. As more water poured into the hull, Dad picked up a tool he'd stashed when he first decided to scrap the ship: a heavy, four-foot crowbar. He knew which areas of the hull were weakest from dry rot, and he intended to help things along with a few well-placed holes.

He nearly lost the crowbar on his first attempt, so decayed was the hull. The metal punched through the wood like a needle through skin, and it was all Dad could do to keep it from continuing out the hole and into the Lake. A moment later Dad struggled to keep his footing as a great geyser of water shot into the boat. Dad could see the edges of the hole widening as the force of the water tore off bits of rotten wood. He hurried to the next few sections of weak hull and punched additional holes in them, finding the steep stairway again as water swirled around his knees. Moments later he emerged on deck and hollered for his friend to pick him up.

Dad wrapped himself in a wool army blanket, and they spent the next hour watching as the *Patrol* sank lower and lower in the water. "Fifteen minutes and she'll be gone," said Dad's friend. Dad grunted and tried to stay warm.

Except that fifteen minutes later, just as the waterline reached the deck, the *Patrol* stopped sinking. No more water could flow into it since it was already resting level with the top of the Lake. The ship was staying afloat, barely, because of its wood hull and decks. It would get waterlogged eventually, and the ship would sink, but Dad needed it to sink right then, not later. His worst fear until that moment had been the DNR discovering he'd sunk the ship, but now he feared the DNR discovering he had *almost* sunk the ship, creating a partially submerged navigation hazard. He would be able to wallpaper the living room with the tickets he'd get for pulling a stunt like that, right after he got out of jail.

Fifteen minutes became an hour. The *Patrol* was still stubbornly at the surface, clinging to its last bit of buoyancy as if it were treading water. Dad couldn't wait any longer. "Screw it—let's ram her."

His buddy maneuvered the boat into position perpendicular to the keel of the *Patrol*. "Hit it," Dad said, and the moment the bow of the other boat edged up onto the hull, the *Patrol* rolled over and slipped below the surface.

They idled in the area for the next half hour, making sure the sunken ship didn't resurface. A few boards and other bits of flotsam bobbed to the surface, but nothing of any real size. Then there was nothing for it but to motor back to the Grand Haven harbor. If the harbor watch saw the boat tie off at the dock, he must have wondered why two men had been out on the Lake on such a miserable night and why one of them was wrapped in an army blanket. It might also have occurred to him to wonder where the *Patrol* was. But the harbor watch remained safely inside all night, and Dad's operation went off without a hitch.

Still, he was shaken and sad. We stayed out of his way even more than usual. He had loved being the captain of that boat—and what could replace it? Nothing. It was a once-in-a-lifetime deal.

In the following weeks, Dad heard through the grapevine that he was a prime suspect in the *Patrol*'s disappearance. "The DNR ain't the sharpest tools in the shed," Dad proclaimed. "They got nothing on me."

He was right, though. The consequences of his actions that night never caught up with him.

33

THERE WERE OTHER CONSEQUENCES he couldn't outrun, however.

One morning Mom woke up and realized she was done. Done with absolutely everything. Done living in a tiny shack that had a sunken tub. Done working overtime to pay for Dad's toys. Done driving her car over crushed battery cases. Done forcing herself to stay in another room while Dad beat her kids. And most of all, done with Dad—and she told him so.

We learned this later that afternoon. Dad shouted at us to line up in the living room. We stood side by side, a small platoon of soldiers obeying the orders of our drill sergeant.

"Your mother and I," he said, pacing in front of us, "are getting a divorce." He stopped suddenly and studied our faces, starting with Sheri and ending with me. He was hoping to get a reaction out of one of us that would embarrass Mom into changing her mind. But he'd taught us all too well to never show our emotions. If Dad knew we were happy about something, he'd take it from us. If Dad knew we were afraid of something, he'd use it against us.

And so we were stoic, save for the one emotion it was allowable to express. It began on the outside of the eye, which tightened ever so slightly. It continued in the lower lip, which pushed out and downward. It flowed through a neck too weak to support the head, which then tipped forward. And it finished in shoulders that curled like they were cringing. The emotion was defeat, and all of us spoke it fluently.

Jerry, with the gangly six-foot-four body of a man, spoke it, from his size 14 feet all the way up to his shock of black hair.

Sheri, looking more like Mom all the time, spoke it.

And I'd known how to speak it for what felt like forever.

We were defeated, so defeat was the only thing Dad found as he examined us. When Dad was studying Sheri, I stole a glance at my brother, and he looked exactly as I did. Crushed by our father.

"Well," Dad said, as if that explained everything.

He walked outside. Mom and Sheri left next, headed toward their rooms. I looked at Jerry. He was still wearing his mask. But he whispered to me, looking at the floor, the same words I had been ready to whisper to him.

"I'm glad we're finally going to get rid of Dad."

PART FIVE
AN ESCAPE

34

ON MOM'S ADVICE, the lawyer served Dad the divorce papers while he was at work.

He quit coming home and sold the tank for a song. Leaving behind piles of broken junk stacked in the shed and scattered willy-nilly across the gun range and the sand, he took his collection of guns and books and records and moved into his mother's basement, not yet twenty years after he had moved out.

That left four of us in our house—five if you counted Zeke—and a load of fearful questions. What if Mom changed her mind? What if Dad did something crazy? He was capable of anything, and we all knew it.

None of us dared to speak a single word about what might happen. It was as if the divorce were a house of cards that could tumble down at any moment.

So we went to school. We did chores. We kept our heads down. And the three of us kids, despite thoughts and hopes that must have been nearly identical, lived like silent strangers under a single roof. We were holding our breath, collectively, waiting for the surprise ending where Dad came tearing back through the front door.

•   •   •

It never happened. Four months later, Mom told us at dinner that the divorce was final.

"So will we have to see Dad anymore?" Sheri asked right away.

"It's up to you," Mom answered. "I'm getting the house and five acres, and I'll sell it for whatever I can get. Your father is getting the other six acres. We won't stay here a moment longer than we need to."

Jerry had recently left for college, and my sister and I silently adjusted to the news that Dad would never come back home. Our home wouldn't even *be* our home for much longer. It was a lot to take in. I set the few remaining dishes in the sink, careful as ever to avoid touching the steel rim. Sometime way back, Dad had spliced some wires together during a project, and an exposed connection was touching a metal water pipe. That meant a stiff shock whenever one of us stood in the wrong spot and touched the sink. It was one of those things that had always seemed normal, like a father who drove a tank, but the idea of moving made me wonder what it would be like to live somewhere else.

In the following weeks, Mom sold her share of the land and the house for $22,000, but the buyers put a condition on the sale: the valley of trash needed to be covered. They had found someone to haul away the junk, but the festering pile of waste—now approaching the size of a large pond—was going to get them in trouble with the county.

Jerry, home to help with the move, shoveled beside me at the garbage pile, scattering a thousand shovelfuls of dirt across almost two decades of moldy, half-melted Bouman trash.

"Just like old times," I said.

"Except no Ike to charge us when we're finished."

Mom bought a small home in Grand Rapids. The day the moving

truck arrived, and while the others loaded boxes and dragged out the few pieces of salvageable furniture, I slipped away with Zeke. I looked back at the house and the hills surrounding it. Everything was quiet. No roar of gunfire. No growl of a tank. Dad had left the washing machine behind, still sitting on what was once the gun range, its rusted corpse riddled with what must have been ten thousand bullet holes. A few small saplings were beginning to spring up next to the crushed trees, and some of the ruts made by the tank treads were beginning to grow weeds. The door to the shed stood open, and inside I glimpsed a scattering of sand, the only remaining testament to the tsunami that had filled it.

I was finally leaving. Leaving the house and leaving Dad. But if I'd hoped so long for that to happen, why did part of me feel sad?

Kneeling beside my dog, I knuckled his head. A new house, a new school, a life without my brother and my father. At least I was taking Zeke with me, the only deep-down good thing I'd ever known.

35

ARRIVING WITH MOM IN Grand Rapids felt like landing on another planet. Everything felt foreign from the first moment we pulled up to the tree-lined curb. Neat Cape Cod cottages stretched down the block, one after the other, and kids played catch or rode bikes while adults watered lawns and chatted in driveways. After spending my first sixteen years either moping inside a disintegrating box or wandering the acres of sand that surrounded it, the new place felt like somewhere I didn't belong. I was a counterfeit, sure I'd be discovered and sent back to where I had come from.

Mom took Sheri and me on a tour of the house, demonstrating in the kitchen how to turn the stove knob until—*click click click fwoosh*—the burner lit itself without a single match or singed fingertip. We looked at each other and grinned. My bedroom, which Jerry would share when he visited from college, had a window that could slide open, carpet on the floor, and a real desk with a real lamp—not that I'd be using it. The closet and dresser were large enough to hold all my clothes five times over, and Sheri had a similar room down the hall.

As Mom went to her room to unpack, Sheri looked at me with raised eyebrows. "Mark, there's nothing broken in this whole house!"

"I know, and it's so quiet."

"I can't wait to invite friends over here," she said. "Now I won't always have to go to their houses."

That wasn't a selling point for me, since I didn't have any friends. I went outside to check on Zeke, who didn't seem to love his new digs as much as Sheri and Mom did. His eleven acres had been reduced to a postage-stamp yard, fenced and grassed. He whined as I knelt beside him.

"Don't worry, boy, we'll get out soon. If anyone can hunt this kind of place, it's you."

I soon discovered, when Mom asked me to take out the trash for the first time, that other people paid someone to haul away their garbage, a concept that had never occurred to me.

I also discovered, when a neighbor berated Mom through the screened front door, that I could no longer pull out my gun and shoot at something, even if the something in question was a raccoon who insisted on eating our garbage.

Sheri and I both attended a new high school that was so close we could walk to it. She made more friends on the first day than I'd had in my life, and while she was constantly going to other girls' houses and having friends over to ours, I remained a loner. Because I was the new kid, and painfully shy, other students assumed I was smart and treated me accordingly. But if I had to speak with anyone—during class or at my locker between classes—the illusion would evaporate almost instantly. I quickly learned that it was best to shut my mouth and keep it closed and simply try to tough it out until graduation. What I would do after leaving high school escaped me, but I could get a job somewhere and then . . . just work, I supposed. So I'd slink from class to class, slouch in the farthest desk from the teacher, and pass the time by letting my mind wander.

It always found memories of Zeke. Of us running in the woods back in Belmont, of the sound of his barks echoing across hills I could navigate with my eyes closed. Or of us exploring the suburban wilderness of Grand Rapids. I started taking him out every afternoon, seeking pockets of nature in which I could forget about life for a time. We discovered each secret and hidden place for miles in every direction. There were brooks that ran through backyards, unnoticed, and the farthest acres of the local cemetery were overgrown and teeming with wildlife. Sometimes we simply wandered, and other times we scouted with a purpose, running hidden traplines—highly illegal in the city limits, which I knew, though I didn't care—and bagging critters that were bigger and fatter than anything I ever saw in the country. If we were ever seen, we were simply a boy and his dog out for a walk. But we were rarely seen, and I wished our expeditions could last forever.

The minute those memories faded, though—when the bell rang, or the teacher called my name for the third time, or a boy rammed my shoulder on his way to the hallway—I was dumped straight back into reality. Months drifted by, and I hadn't made a single friend.

One day, when I was home alone, I answered a knock at the door and discovered Dad standing on the porch.

"Hi, Dad?" I tried, waving him in and instantly regretting my choice.

"I'll just stand here," he said softly.

"What's up?"

"Oh, I was in the area and thought I'd stop by." He looked through the door and listened for a minute. "Where is everybody?"

"Jerry's off at college, and Sheri must be out with her friends. She always is. Mom won't be home until later. She's taking classes after work."

Dad snorted dismissively. "Trying to *better* herself? We'll see."

I said nothing.

"I thought maybe you and me could get something to eat."

"Um . . . sure. Okay. Let me get my coat." What was happening? Why was I agreeing to this? I didn't have any experience with making my own choices, and it seemed my default was still to follow my father.

Once we were in the car, he let loose. "Your mom brought all this on herself, you know. I'm fine, but I just feel bad for you kids. I can't imagine she'll be able to afford that new house for long, and then what?"

"Mom got a job with the phone company. Union wages."

Dad hit the wheel with his hand. "Damn unions. Couldn't *pay* me to join one."

His punch was perfunctory. He seemed deflated. He was talking like nothing had changed, but I knew better. I knew—somehow with absolute certainty—that he'd never lay a finger on me or Mom again. All the venom was still there, but his poison had lost its potency. Or maybe it was starting to eat away at him.

We went to dinner together, barely saying a word. He drove me back to Mom's place and dropped me off. I watched the man who had once been more of a prison guard than a father drive away. I was free of him.

Physically free, anyway. I had thought that when Dad was gone, I would be free of my past. To my shame, the opposite was true.

My past imprisoned me more completely than anything physical ever could. I carried my prison cell everywhere I walked, and when I spoke, I struggled to make myself heard through the bars.

It wasn't only school where I struggled. I entered stores with my head down and my feet shuffling, desperate not to be noticed, terrified I'd have to interact with someone. I might leave the market without buying what I'd come for, so unwilling was I to socialize with the cashier. I was unable to look a grown man in the eye.

What I assumed was that each person I passed—students, teachers, strangers—knew the same truth I'd long ago internalized and accepted: I was, and always would be, a good-for-nothing imbecile.

• • •

With everything lost, Dad tried to reinvent himself.

He started with golf. He would march down the fairway like he was on his way to buy engine parts, hacking at the ball as soon as he reached it. It was all business, all strong-arming the ball, and his uniform—his same old white, short-sleeved, collared shirt, tan shorts, white socks, and black leather shoes—wasn't the only thing that looked ridiculous. His new toupee did too.

Eventually he gave up both, got himself fired from his latest dead-end job, and tumbled into a deep depression. He had burned through the money from the sale of his six acres in no time flat. The reality of what he had done began to weigh heavily upon him, and the long periods of sitting in his mother's basement exacted a toll.

We all avoided him. The very idea of visiting him was ludicrous: descending the basement stairs to sit on a ratty couch and chat with our father. He had no land, no tanks, nowhere to shoot his guns, no boat—the things with which he had defined himself had been taken away, probably forever, and what was left was a man filled with anger, bitterness, and fear. He was shrinking.

That knowledge made it all the more jarring when we learned that Dad had started dating. Her name was Ann, and she was a friend of the Dietzes whom we had sometimes skated with at the rink.

But . . . why? I thought. Who in the world would date Dad? He was at his lowest ebb, fresh off an acrimonious divorce, and still the same selfish, violent, racist jerk he'd always been, but further darkened by depression. And *Ann*, of all people? All I remembered about her was that she was about five feet tall and talked about Jesus a lot. What could they possibly have in common?

Still, we were used to things not making sense when it came to Dad. He could do what he wanted as long as he didn't want anything to do with us.

• • •

It was only a few months later that Dad called me.

"Mark?"

"Dad?"

"I want you to be in my wedding. Ann and I are getting married."

"Married?"

"And you'll be in it. Jerry too, of course."

I said yes because it was the first word that popped into my head, and before I could second-guess myself, Dad was already telling me the date and time, which I scribbled on the back of an envelope.

"We'll have something real nice for you to put on," he said and then hung up.

• • •

They planned the ceremony for the day I was scheduled to take the SAT. I raced through the questions, filling in bubble after bubble as quickly as I could with my pencil. Then I drove my borrowed car deep into the countryside, ignoring the speed limit, trying to find the small church where Dad and Ann were waiting to say their vows. I burst through the front door, out of breath, only to simultaneously hear the wedding march and have a tuxedo and shoes thrust into my chest.

"Man, Mark, you're late," my brother hissed. "What took you so long?"

"I got here as fast as I could—they don't let you out early, you know!"

"Never mind. Just put this on!"

I ran to the dressing room, tugged on the tuxedo at flank speed, and bolted back to the sanctuary. Dad was pacing back and forth at the front, with Jerry at his side, and I hurried to join them. Seeing me, Dad leaned over and said something to the piano player. The wedding march restarted, and the ceremony commenced. Dad looked like a stranger to me in his powder-blue tuxedo, and the white bow tie perched in stark contrast to his tanned neck. But it was the same face, still certain and in command, if slightly more haggard, and the same powerful hands, sticking out of the sleeves like boxing gloves.

Ann emerged from the back, nestled against her father's arm, and the music swelled. Everyone stood as Ann walked slowly to the front, stepping away from her father and stepping up to stand by my father's side. She seemed smaller than a child compared to him, and I wondered if she knew what she was getting into.

The ceremony floated past in a haze. None of it interested me. Dad was going to do what Dad was going to do, and it wouldn't bother me. I had escaped. He would be moving into Ann's place, several miles north of Grand Rapids, and I would scarcely be part of his life. That suited me just fine. I guessed we were all trying to start over, to move on, even if we weren't sure which direction to go.

Sheri found me right after the ceremony. "You sure took your time getting here. They had to start and stop the music twice!"

Unable to tell if she was attacking me or thanking me, I simply shrugged. What did it matter? Without speaking to anyone, I walked out the back door of the church, then looped around to the front, standing at a distance. Dad had stationed himself outside the front door, and he shook guests' hands as they exited, thanking them for coming. Ann was next to him, and she smiled and nodded, also shaking hands with some of the guests and hugging others.

I saw Dad shaking hands with one of my uncles. I hadn't seen my uncle for several years, since we'd been on the ship together. Dad had organized an impromptu family reunion one weekend, partly so everyone could catch up, but mostly to show off his new boat. Relatives had driven in from hours away, and we found ourselves on the water with more than four dozen people on the *Patrol*, motoring across Lake Michigan. When the Coast Guard pulled alongside the ship, Dad pulled *me* aside and said, "Mark, quick, take all the kids you can find, and hide inside the rear chain locker. And keep it *quiet*." I rounded up the first ten kids I could find, and we shut ourselves in, keeping absolutely silent until we heard the Coast Guard boat motor away. When we emerged, Dad didn't thank me—not directly—but he did brag that his idea had saved him from a hefty fine for not having enough life jackets. That meant *I'd* saved *Dad*.

Now his ship was chock-full of holes and resting on the bottom of the Lake, silent and stoic as every other wreck.

How had things changed so much, so quickly? That life was all I'd ever known. I squinted in the too-bright sunlight. I tried to swallow, then wiped my cheek for no reason.

•   •   •

A few weeks later, my SAT scores arrived in the mail, and they were higher than I had expected. A few months after that, a letter arrived from Michigan State University. Mom was sitting at the kitchen table, and I ripped open the envelope and read aloud.

"We at Michigan State University are pleased to offer you a financial-aid scholarship for the next school year . . ."

I looked up at Mom and found her grinning. "Mark, this is your ticket. A scholarship! Isn't it wonderful? I always said you were smart. I was worried that . . . but it doesn't matter. Mark, first your brother and now you."

I wondered what I was supposed to say. I didn't trust myself to speak, but I smiled at Mom before going to my room, chucking my backpack full of books on the floor, and heading outside to grab Zeke from where he was waiting in the yard.

Now that I knew the direction my life was headed—seventy miles due east on Highway 96—the prospect excited me.

But I also dreaded it. Most kids received scholarships because they were smart. I got mine because we were flat broke. Did I belong at college? Did I even *want* to go to college? What would I do there?

As usual, the questions didn't matter because they didn't have answers. I didn't really have a choice—I received a scholarship, and I had no other plans, so of course I would go to college.

Zeke and I headed out. We would do what we always did when I wanted to avoid thinking: run our traplines. We'd disappear into whatever wilderness we could find in Grand Rapids, and we'd stay hidden as long as we possibly could. It was somewhere between our back gate and the back of the cemetery that it hit me: when I went to college, I'd have to say good-bye to Zeke.

36

On my first day of college, Mom had to work at the phone company, so Dad drove me to Michigan State.

"I'm supposed to be living in Akers Hall. That's what the paperwork says," I told Dad, looking down at the letter in my hands, then up at a bewildering complex of massive buildings. "I think it's over . . . there?"

Dad grunted. We'd already been over there, but maybe we'd missed it. It felt like every other car was driving directly to its destination, while we were stuck in a maze. At last we spotted a sign confirming that we'd found the correct dorm. Dad didn't bother trying to find a real parking spot—he simply bumped the car up the nearest curb, sandwiching it between a legally parked car and a fire hydrant.

It felt like we were at the center of a thousand-car tornado, and every door and trunk was flung open. Suitcases were piled three and four deep on the curb, waiting to be taken into the dorms. Students streamed every direction, carrying chairs and lamps and laundry baskets and record players. Everyone I saw seemed to have new shoes, new clothes, combed hair. They were relaxed and laughing. It was their first day of *college*, and every single student was glowing with anticipation.

I felt minuscule.

I climbed out as slowly as possible, trying to keep my head down. My frayed hand-me-downs and outdated shoes shouted, "Look over here!"

I glanced back at Dad. He climbed out of the driver's seat and walked around the back of the car. Greasy fingerprints streaked the doors and the trunk lid from where his hands had marked them. The other dads lounged beside their sleek new cars, grinning as their sons and daughters prepared to conquer the world. The other dads wore sunglasses and slacks and polished black shoes. The other dads were trim and fit.

My father shuffled. His shirt was partly untucked. His authority had simply leaked out of him. Dad was no longer the man I remembered when I was a boy.

"Thanks for driving me, Dad. I'll see you later."

He grabbed his wallet, fished out a ten-dollar bill, and held it out. I took it, then shook his stained and calloused hand.

With that he got back into his car, reversed off the curb, and drove away, leaving behind a small cloud of foul-smelling smoke. I waved good-bye, keeping my arm low. When he was out of sight, I grabbed my things—it would only take one load—and began to search for my room.

•   •   •

Dave had been the star running back on his high school football team, and his girlfriend, Jackie, had been a cheerleader. Tim immediately began making plans to join a fraternity and pretty much disappeared. John's two loves were heavy metal and pot, and when he and his druggie pals really got cooking, you couldn't see across the room or hear yourself think. The fourth guy, Ted, went home every weekend.

I was the fifth roommate, and my glaring lack of social skills quickly became apparent, and I sensed that everyone had already labeled me as the weirdo. Mine wasn't the endearing kind of weirdness either, the kind that could still secure me a spot in the pecking order. Plenty of guys were weird, but they had something that made them safe and easy to understand. You could be weird and also be a druggie, or a record collector, or a Ping-Pong expert, or a party crasher, but the one thing you couldn't be was plain old weird. But that was me: a kid with no interests, no money, and absolutely no ability to make friends.

Having been around engines and machines all my life, I decided to become a mechanical engineer. Within two weeks, however, I realized I was in way over my head, and by the end of the first semester I was drowning.

I couldn't keep up in class, I couldn't keep up after class, and my sense of total isolation increased. I learned it was easier to simply avoid everyone I could. Between classes, especially when it was dark, I would step off the path when I saw someone, waiting until they had walked past to continue on my way. I arrived late to class and left early, or even skipped it entirely. I was afraid to ask for help because I didn't want anyone to know I was failing. I ate alone in the cafeteria and sat alone in my room. I looked out my window at the other students, sitting on the grass talking with each other or tossing a Frisbee. Everyone else seemed so happy and so well connected while I felt completely abandoned.

When I lay awake in my bed, I thought about Zeke, wishing I could smell his dog smell, wishing I could trail a hand down and come up against his warm fur. Mom was working for the phone company during the day and dating at night, while Sheri was busy with her friends and her homework, so Zeke was stuck in a fenced backyard with nothing to do, lonely as a sailor lost at sea. The worst part was I knew he was lonely all the time and there was nothing I could do about it.

I remembered a time years earlier. We had returned from a weekend on the ship late one fall, and I raced to find Zeke, who was beside himself with happiness at my homecoming. I noticed his water bowl on the ground beside him, and when I stooped to check it, with Zeke romping around behind me and whining fit to burst, I saw that the water in the bowl was frozen solid. In his thirst he had licked a groove into the ice. How could I have done that to my friend? Now, sleepless late into the night, I would stand at the window and look out across the campus, the brick buildings winking between the tree branches. Every curved path seemed to have a group of kids hurrying along it, off to a study group or a party or a pizza joint. I could see everyone else, and no one could see me.

One Friday, the need to be understood became too powerful to resist. I stuffed some clothes in a backpack, ripped a small square of cardboard off a pizza box lid, and scrawled the letters GR on it. Then I jogged out of my dorm and across campus until I was standing, breathing hard, at the edge of the highway, thumb in the air.

Two hours later, I was sitting in the cemetery in Grand Rapids, tears wetting my cheeks and shirt, clinging to Zeke like a drowning man. I don't know how long I held him. During that visit I must also have done the sorts of things one does on a visit from college, like eat potatoes with Mom and pretend to care about Sheri's homecoming dance, but it felt like I held my dog forever, and when I blinked, I was back at college, the same old weirdo imbecile, and no one even knew I'd been gone.

•   •   •

John's ability to score good-quality weed, as well as his prized record collection, endeared him to some guys across the hall who liked to party on Friday nights. One night, when I was sitting alone in my room thinking about Zeke, their door was open, and I could hear bits and pieces of their shouted conversation over the hi-fi that was blaring Fleetwood Mac. When they flipped to the B-side, I realized one of the voices was directed at me.

"Hey! Bouman!" It was John. "You want a beer, man, or what?"

I'd never heard that sentence before in my life. I knew as well as anyone that to be included in a party, you had to be willing to pony up for the beer every so often—and the other guys on my floor knew I didn't have a cent to my name. I had arrived at college with ten dollars, spent it almost immediately, and hadn't earned a penny since. Besides, I didn't even like the taste of beer. My father never drank, and he absolutely despised anyone who did, calling them blathering idiots. Declining the rare party invitation was easy.

But why not? I was miserable, willing to try anything.

When I showed up at the door, John's stoner buddy Keith motioned me in. "Grab a cold one from the fridge, man." He nodded, once, and I knew that he knew I had no money and that he was covering me for the night. I walked to the fridge and leaned down to open it, hearing Keith holler, "The ones on the top shelf are mine."

The beer in my hand was the armor I needed to face the room and look for a safe place to sit. I knew Dave was an accounting major. His glasses and his hair were both thick and black.

"You're Bouman, right, from across the hall?"

"Yeah."

"Heard about you," he said, taking a swig. "They said you're strange and never talk to anyone."

I tried to play it cool. "Oh yeah?"

"Yeah," he answered, as if my question had been a real one. And maybe it had been. Then, "But you seem pretty normal to me."

I studied his face for signs of mockery, but he seemed genuine. He reminded me of my brother in a way—since I knew he would tell me the bad news, I could trust what sounded like good news. I chugged half my beer, hating the taste but longing to be like everyone else. Being different was death.

Before I'd had too many beers, Tim sauntered into the room. His family owned a dry cleaning business that he was always bragging about, and he fancied himself a ladies' man. He was the shortest guy in the room, and besides having a typical Napoleon complex, he was just an all-around jerk. At least to me he was, ever since we'd been introduced and I wandered off in the middle of his boring account of which fraternities he might grace with his presence. His eyes locked on mine almost instantly.

"Where'd you get that beer?"

So he'd been the one sharing the stash with Keith.

"From the fridge," I answered.

His scream drowned out the music: "That's my beer!"

I understood two things at that moment: it wasn't, in fact, his beer, and also that his sense of entitlement made me want him to suffer. Something inside me snapped. From where I sat, I screamed right back at him, "I ought to rip your f—ing head off!"

Then I was on my feet and across the room, glaring down my nose at Tim. "I am going to *kill* you!"

The voice coming out of my mouth sounded eerily familiar. Keith pushed between us, holding me back with one arm and saying to Tim, "That's my beer, man. I gave it to him."

"It better not be my beer." Tim was weaving back and forth like a snake, trying to see past Keith. I mad-dogged right back, fists at my side but ready. Then Tim was at the door, saying something and gesturing, and I was already sitting beside Dave again, somehow, feeling the blood banging out time in my ears.

As the conversation picked up around us, Dave asked, "Man, Bouman, what happened to you?"

I had no idea.

"You scared me, man. It's like you've got a volcano in your soul!"

Without a word, I stood up and went back to my room, closing the door behind me. In bed, with my pillow over my head, I couldn't drown out the sound of my thoughts. It wasn't memories of Zeke that tormented me but the fact that I knew the sound and the name of the anger inside me. I was becoming my father.

My anger at that—my anger inside that—felt bottomless, like something that would drown me the moment I dipped a toe into it. As my bed tilted and wobbled, I realized Dad had lied to me about life. What he'd told me was most important was not important at all. He taught me how to drive a tank and a ship, shoot every kind of gun, and kill a man. He taught me to obey without complaint or question. He taught me that power and the will to wield it were the only things that mattered.

Yet such things were beyond useless. They only marked me an outcast. Dad had filled my head with propaganda. He had taught me to hate and to be violent. He had set me up to fail and to keep on failing. I wasn't going to make it—not just at college but in life. As a man.

I was the fool. Everything I had been taught was a lie, but I was the one who had believed it. I wanted to forget. I wanted more beer.

●   ●   ●

"There's no easy way to say it," Mom told me on the phone. "You have to sell Zeke."

She was right. He deserved to be happy, and seeing me whenever I managed to hitchhike home didn't qualify. He needed someone less useless than me, someone who could take him hunting and call him into the kitchen when it was extra cold outside and scratch him on his back leg, just in the spot that made his front leg shake with pleasure.

Mom helped me place an ad in the local paper, and someone responded—a man with acreage who lived outside town. Zeke would love it there, back among the oaks and ponds and wide-open skies. And just like that, it was over. Zeke's new owner picked him up from Mom's, and part of me withered away.

More bad news arrived. I'd been so busy bumming beer and weed from anyone and everyone, desperately trying to bury my sorrow, that I hadn't been to class in weeks. The university notified me that my scholarship would be canceled. If I got kicked out of college, where would I go? What would I do? The spinning I felt was myself circling the drain, and the speed seemed to be picking up. I was screwed.

That's when I remembered seeing an Air Force recruiter on campus during the first week of school. *What a joke*, I'd thought. *Only a moron would sign up for something like that.* Now I wondered whether signing on to become Private Moron was still an option. The Air Force was more palatable than moving back to my mother's house at age nineteen—why did *that* sound so familiar?—or waiting in my dorm room for campus police to evict me. Before I decided anything, though, I needed a drink.

• • •

The walls of the small recruiting office were plastered with posters of jets and a promotional slogan encouraging me to *Aim High!* for *A Great Way of Life!* There was a single desk, and in front of it was a single chair. Behind the desk sat a man dressed in an immaculate uniform, and it appeared that each item on his desk—brochures, papers, pens, a framed photograph—had been arranged with a protractor and a T square. I cut right to the chase, and so did he.

"I want to join the Air Force."

"Well, what are you interested in?"

He gestured at the chair, and I sat down. "I'll do anything, go anywhere," I said. "Just get me out of here."

"We *love* your kind, son." The man's smile was wide, and he slid a paper across the desk toward me. "Look these over and decide what you'd like to do."

I looked down at the list of specializations, pretended to read, and looked up at the recruiter. Then I pointed at random, hopping my finger back and forth across the paper. "This, this . . . or this," I said, "looks good to me."

The recruiter narrowed his eyes a fraction. "Are you sure you don't want to *read* those first?"

"These are good enough," I answered.

He took the paper back and returned it to its precisely aligned pile. "We'll just need you to take some tests and make sure you qualify for the jobs you . . . selected," he said, "and when the testing is done, we'll assign you a job and a station."

While he was talking, he opened a drawer in his desk and pulled out a packet of colored papers. By the time I'd signed my name a dozen times, I was officially "entering the system," as my recruiter called it. A trip to Detroit a few weeks later, along with a raised right hand and a repeated vow, and I had officially joined the Air Force. The United States military would take care of me, which was good, because clearly I couldn't take care of myself.

37

It took our bus the longest day ever to reach Lackland Air Force Base, outside San Antonio, Texas, smack in the middle of hot-and-dry as far as the eye could see. Gear bag over my shoulder, I shuffled down the aisle with the rest of my fellow recruits, then stumbled down the steps and onto the radiating asphalt.

"Well, boys," called down the voice of the driver from behind us, "this is the end of the line." He was smiling, and he pronounced "end" like it tasted sweet.

There were footprints painted on the pavement in four long lines. We knew enough to form a line, or at least to attempt to form a line, but that was where our initiative ended. Doing absolutely nothing on the bus had worn me out, and others apparently were feeling the same way, because one by one we dropped our heavy bags to the ground. I wondered when someone would arrive to show us to our barracks and the mess hall. Over the noise of the still-idling bus, I began to hear a strange sound, *click click click*, growing louder. Around the corner of the nearest building strode a tall man, his boots and aviator sunglasses shining, his uniform pressed to perfection. *Cli-clack*. He snapped to a stop in front of us, glaring out from beneath his Smokey Bear hat.

"My name is Sergeant Christian, and I want you to turn around and face the bus."

With varying degrees of speed and military panache, we did.

"Now I want you to wave good-bye to that bus, boys, because it's your last chance out of here."

A few guys snickered, and one standing near me drawled, "Bye-bye, bus," as the diesel huffed away in a cloud of smoke. I smirked.

"Wipe that smile off your face, a—hole!"

The last syllable was our call to attention. All around I could hear my fellow recruits straightening into a semblance of order. As I stood there with the others, listening to Sergeant Christian scream what seemed an unending stream of profanities at us, it occurred to me: *This is just like home.* I could tell some of the guys were taking it hard—slumped shoulders, bug eyes—but it was all very normal for me. Maybe the ones who had joined the Air Force because it was a lifelong dream were beginning to doubt that decision. Not me. I was here because it had seemed like my least-bad choice. Sergeant Christian could bark and cuss at me all he wanted—I knew he wouldn't lay a finger on me, and I'd be getting three square meals plus a paycheck, just for keeping my mouth shut and doing whatever I was told.

" . . . we clear on that, recruit?"

"Sir-yes-*sir*!"

•   •   •

Back in the recruiting office, I must have pointed at something to do with computers, because after basic training I was shipped to Illinois for eight months of school and then to Montana to work on our nation's nuclear weapons systems. I had a regular job about a million miles away from anything dangerous, a regular paycheck, and as the months turned into years, it seemed I had a pretty good chance of surviving.

Unfortunately, I also had a regular drug habit that had followed me from college, as well as an irregular aversion to authority.

Especially to Sergeant Simpkins. "Sarge is such a jerk," I would complain to whoever would listen, making no attempt to hide my disdain. "He's out to get me, for no reason."

It was true that he was out to get me, but everyone, including myself, knew there actually were good reasons. I failed dorm room inspections regularly. My uniform was never pressed and often dirty. Whenever I had a job assigned to me, I made sure to quit as soon as I'd done the bare minimum. I drank beer and smoked weed. I was surly to my superiors. All of which meant that I'd accumulated a ridiculous number of demerits and extra work shifts, not to mention an official personnel file filled with Letters of Admonishment and Letters of Reprimand.

Still, it wasn't all my fault. My roommate knew the right people, and when he got so drunk that he couldn't crawl out of bed in the morning, Sergeant Simpkins would cover for him. I, on the other hand, had been written up for being an hour late the morning after we switched to daylight saving time.

I hated how unfair it was, and I hated that there wasn't a single thing I could do about it, but I'd developed an ongoing—and, to that point, successful—policy: ignore everything. One day, however, that option was snatched away.

"I'm gonna need you to come into the office, Airman Bouman."

I could hear the air quotes around my rank when Sergeant Simpkins spoke. I rolled my eyes and made sure he saw me. He grinned right back.

"I'm writing you up, Bouman," he gloated as he pushed the paperwork across the desk. I didn't even read it—what would be the point? I signed it, scarcely looking at the paper, and shoved it back across the desk. We'd been through the same drill before.

Usually I got up and wandered away at that point in the proceedings, but my sergeant wasn't finished.

"I don't like you, Bouman. And guess what? I don't have to like you." He let that sink in. I shrugged. "And do you know what else?" he continued. "I'm not gonna need to put up with you for much longer."

My expression must have given me away.

"I see what you're thinking, Bouman, but you've got it backwards. See, I'm not going anywhere. In fact, I'm getting promoted. Nope. It's you, Bouman—you're the one who's going somewhere. And do you know where you're going? O-U-T. As in out of the Air Force. I'm getting you kicked out, Bouman. Your very next step is an Article 15."

I knew what an Article 15 would mean: I could never be promoted, and if I quit, I could never reenlist. If he filed the paperwork, it would be a rubber-stamp case for the higher-ups. My file was thick enough to need a forklift. I was trapped, and he knew it.

He left, chuckling on his way out the office door. I stayed in my seat, seething, clenching and unclenching my jaw until it ached. He had me cornered with no way out. Unless something happened to him first.

I left to find a drink.

•   •   •

"If I can't make it in the Air Force, what'll I do? I'm gonna end up in prison or dead, you know?"

After four beers and half a joint, my words were slurred, but the wall I was talking to didn't seem to mind. It just kept listening. I had no other friends, so the wall would have to do. It wasn't hypothetical, however— I *couldn't* make it in the Air Force. I'd proved that. And the thought of my family helping me was laughable. If I was kicked out, I wouldn't make it. I'd die, sooner or later, probably in a ditch or a motel room, probably wasted.

Another few tokes and I asked the wall, "Then maybe *God* will help me?"

I laughed as soon as I said it. I knew God wasn't going to listen to an imbecile like me, especially since I happened to be higher than a mortar round.

Then a strange thing happened. I heard a different voice—not my own, and not the wall's—and it said, "Yes, he will."

I considered that. What the hell did I have to lose? I spoke two sentences that summed up the first twenty-two years of my existence.

"Help me, God. I hate my life."

And then I stumbled to my bed.

• • •

That was late on a Friday night. Monday, before Sergeant Simpkins had filed any paperwork, and before I'd hatched any real plans for revenge, Brian, one of the airmen I worked with, cornered me.

"Hey, Mark," he said, an earnest expression on his face, "I can see you're not doing so well. So . . . why don't you come to church on Wednesday? We're going to show a movie." That was one of the weirdest things I had ever heard—who would go to church for a movie? I knew Brian was a bit different from most of the other guys, but our bosses seemed to like him. I was more worried about church than about him. Church was for good people, and I was clearly not one of them.

"I'll think about it," I said, as surprised as he was by my answer.

I was even more surprised when, two days later, I actually opened the front door of the small church. The pews were half full already, and I slipped into a seat at the back just as the lights went out and the movie started. It turned out to be one of those movies about the end of the world, and when the last frame of the film passed the bulb and someone flipped the lights on, I saw Brian sitting close to the front of the church along with some other airmen. The pastor then talked about how to be sure you were saved. Being saved definitely sounded like something I needed, but there was no way I was getting out of my pew in front of the other guys from work. I left before I was forced to talk to anyone.

Nothing improved over the next few days—not with my sergeant, who was still watching me like a hawk and counting down the days until he could write me up again, and certainly not with me. I went right back to slacking at work and drinking and doing drugs the moment I went off duty.

•   •   •

The following Sunday, though, I found myself back at church, opening the front door and sliding into the same seat, farthest pew back. I don't remember anything from the service until the part when the pastor asked if anyone wanted to come forward to accept Jesus.

I was the only one who stood up. I left my seat and began to walk the center aisle toward the front. Every eye was fixed on me—weirdo Bouman, failure Bouman—but I didn't care. I was desperate. My life was like our old house back in Belmont. Everything I was trying—pretending my past hadn't happened, relying on the military to take care of me, searching for oblivion with beer and weed—wasn't any better than slapping some paint on the chipped cinder-block walls. Paint or no paint, I'd still be the same falling-apart shack underneath.

With each step down the aisle, the heaviness of everything I was carrying seemed to increase. *Why would God ever want* me? I wondered. I had failed at everything I ever tried. I had nothing to offer. *Nothing.*

Next thing I knew I was kneeling on the carpeted steps that led up to the low stage, as if the weight of my life had pushed me to my knees.

I prayed. "Help me, God. My life is a mess."

With that, my life—that broken house built on sand—was leveled in a single shuddering instant. Something changed in me. I felt cleaner than I'd ever been. Eventually I stood and walked back to my pew. As I did, a voice I'd heard years before, back when I was a boy running the woods with Zeke, spoke to me.

I'm going to start over with you, Mark. You're going to start over.

38

After that fateful Sunday, the little church became my life. If the front door was open, I was inside. Sunday morning services, Sunday evening prayer meetings, potlucks, Wednesday movie nights, Saturday yard work. I didn't talk much about it to anyone else, and I couldn't describe it well to myself, either, but I knew that something had changed for the better in my life, and I wanted more of it. As much as I could get.

I started reading the Bible, and there was one verse that seemed to keep echoing inside my mind nearly every hour I was awake. "When a man's ways are pleasing to the LORD," it read, "he makes even his enemies live at peace with him."

Despite having invited me to church, Brian was just as shocked as everyone else at work that I had become a Christian. Most of the other guys pounced on the chance to tease me, and Sergeant Simpkins egged them on. "Praise the Lord," someone would drawl when I walked past, and the group would roar with laughter.

Brian pulled me aside one day. "Mark, they're just waiting for you to fail, watching you like a hawk. You're doing the right thing—keep it up!"

I didn't hate Sergeant Simpkins anymore, but I still had a serious problem on my hands because of him. I didn't even think about him much, being so busy with my new life, but he was still riding me harder than the other airmen, and I figured it was only a matter of time before something final happened. If I messed up once more, I was finished.

The trouble for Sergeant Simpkins was that I really *had* cleaned up my act. Before, I'd been giving him an embarrassment of material he could use to get me into trouble, but now his opportunities had dried up. Without even thinking about it, I quit beer and weed. And all the time I was doing my job, keeping my head down, I was turning that verse over and over in my mind, like a river rock tumbling down a stream.

A few months later, I heard that Sergeant Simpkins was being transferred, and I didn't know what that meant until my new boss, Sergeant Barns, called me into the office to discuss my personnel file. He was smiling in a genuinely friendly way. "Mark, I sense there was some bad blood between you and your former sergeant. We don't need to go into all that. What we do need is for you to keep this file from getting any thicker—and something tells me you're already on the right track."

I looked him straight in the eye. "Yes, sir, I am."

"Well then, Mark, I'll see what I can do to keep you on Uncle Sam's side, okay?"

I left the office, then stopped midstride in the hallway. My boss had always been my enemy—but now I was at peace with my boss. Stranger still, my problem had required no violence or anger to solve. I smiled and kept walking. And Sergeant Barns made good on his word: with his help, I was able to stay in the service and even earn promotions.

•   •   •

I didn't need to look far to discover another place I could pitch in at church. The youth group was always in need of volunteers to help at meetings and to chaperone trips, and I was a natural fit. The kids seemed to like me, regardless of my character flaws—or perhaps because of them. The more I hung out with the youth, watching all the fun things they did together—pizza parties and football games and campfires—a realization punched me in the gut. I had never done any of those things.

I had done *interesting* things, sure. Crazy things even. Things other kids had envied. None of them had ridden in a carplane or scuba dived. None of them had lived on a formerly derelict ship or seen their father's tank run over a car. None of them had fired machine guns. But their simple activities were infused with a goodness and innocence that the atmosphere of my childhood had choked away.

I had been robbed of my childhood.

I'd been learning to pray, but the realization kicked my prayer into high gear—and it wasn't always pretty. My heart ached, thinking of everything I had missed and everything I had endured instead. My list of complaints to God seemed endless. The gap between what my childhood *had* been and what it *might* have been felt like a widening chasm inside my heart, and in my prayers I pleaded with God for a way to close it.

Then one day I was reading the story of Joseph in the book of Genesis, and I found that after he had been sold into slavery by his brothers, he eventually rose up to become the second most powerful man in all of Egypt. He married and had two sons, Ephraim and Manasseh. The version of the Bible I was reading told me what the two names meant, and the instant I read the meaning of Manasseh's name, I knew that God was talking to me.

"Manasseh, meaning, 'God made up to him all the evil of his youth.'"

In that moment, I felt God was making me a promise, and I clung to that promise with everything I had. When I was a boy, I had tasted only fleeting moments of joy—in the outdoors, first alone in the hills at home and on the shoreline waters of the Grand River, and later accompanied by Zeke. As if opening my eyes for the first time to my surroundings, I found that I was living in Montana's unspoiled wilderness. All around me were lakes and forests and mountains and skies that stretched forever, but I'd been too busy screwing up to notice. I'd been too busy regretting my past to remember an important part of it: *You'll be in Montana, in the military.*

Now I noticed. Life on the base was going well. I was staying on the right side of military law. Life at church was flourishing, and I wasn't just learning about my faith—I was starting to make the first true and deep human friendships of my life. I could look other men in the eye, and I talked with them about work and God and life. And so, with the foundation of a *normal* life holding me up, I began to spend every minute of free time outdoors, often with new friends from church who also loved the outdoors. But unlike my childhood, I wasn't escaping. I was celebrating.

One of the guys I'd met at church was named Jerry, and something surprised me about him: he loved the outdoors even more than I did. Between us we had enough gear to do everything we loved—hunt, trap, fish, canoe, and just disappear into the wilderness for days at a time. We decided to share a small apartment that had a basement, which we converted into what must have seemed like an entire sporting goods store. Our motto became that if it had fins, fur, or feathers, we'd go after it.

Someone asked if I wanted a dog who needed a new owner. Of *course* I did! On Sundays, Jerry and I would load my beater truck with gear before the morning church service, then race out the door to hunt the moment the service ended. Once, we pulled back into the parking lot for evening service with two dead deer in the bed of the truck, and our mud-splattered hunting clothes didn't merit even a second glance from anyone else at church.

It was precisely what I needed.

The older ladies at church started to joke that I'd never marry since I was spending all my time hunting. At least I hoped they were joking. They did have a point, though: I had no idea how to have a conversation with a woman my age.

But God hadn't finished promising.

•   •   •

I noticed Joan the first Sunday she came to church. She was a park ranger in Yellowstone during the summertime, but during the rest of the year, she worked as an audiologist in the local schools. And since my friends at church noticed me noticing her, they urged me to ask her out on a date.

"Mark, think about it: she's a ranger, and you love the outdoors!"

That logic, which I had heard variations of for week after week, was sound. What wasn't logically obvious was why someone like Joan, whose beauty was only equaled by her gracious sophistication, would be attracted to someone like me, an obsessed outdoorsman with the social skills of a rock. But I thought about Joan all the time, and I prayed that God would have mercy on me.

It took me months to gather enough courage to ask her out, and I have no idea what she saw in me that made her say yes. My truck was beat up and in constant need of repair. My apartment was so dirty that we joked you could grow mushrooms in the carpet. Jerry and I had so much wild game stuffed in the refrigerator that there was barely room for store-bought food.

"So," I ventured one Sunday morning after church, "would you go out with me? If you want?"

"Sure." She smiled. "What's the plan?"

My brain was already completely overloaded. No one had prepared me for this. I had to have a *plan* as well?

"You can drive over to me and Jerry's apartment?" I tried.

She paused like she was waiting for more. But I was fresh out of ideas.

"Okay, great, then." She was still smiling. "I'll come over tomorrow night at seven."

When Joan agreed, I felt I had won the lottery. She seemed too perfect. By the time she arrived the next night in her immaculate Honda Accord, I'd managed to clear the dirty plates and ammo boxes and hunting catalogs and trays of elk jerky off our dining room table.

"Come on in," I invited. I'd practiced that line.

"Thank you."

She didn't run back out the door screaming, which was a good sign.

"Shall I . . . ?" she asked leadingly.

"Oh! Yeah, of course. Come over to the table. Here, let me get your chair."

She sat down, and I went into the kitchen. I returned with my dinner—a Banquet frozen chicken dinner I'd microwaved, along with a container of cottage cheese.

"Are you eating?" she asked.

"Yep. I'm pretty hungry. Don't worry, there's enough for you."

"You didn't tell me we'd be having dinner, Mark. I already ate."

"Oh. Well, is it okay if I eat still?"

"Go right ahead." She grinned.

I dug in with gusto, eating the chicken with my fingers and spooning the cottage cheese right out of the tub. Between mouthfuls I asked, "So . . . Joan . . . what do you want to do with your life?"

•   •   •

Eight months later, Joan agreed to marry me.

Except the next day she told me she had changed her mind—not to a refusal, but to a maybe. "I just need a little time to think about it and make sure, Mark."

I could certainly understand that.

But when I asked her again several weeks later, she said yes. "Yes!" with an exclamation point and laughter and the tightest hug I had ever felt. Absolutely, completely yes.

Joan kept working in the schools, I kept up my duties on the base, and the wedding date rushed toward us. Joan rented a house where we would live together after the wedding, and in mid-December the guests began to arrive. Her parents, along with all five siblings and their spouses, flew in from Wisconsin. My side would be next, with Dad and Ann flying in from Michigan, as well as Mom and Sheri, and Jerry would arrive from

Greece, where he was stationed in the Air Force. For the first time since the divorce, all of us Boumans would be together in the same room.

I was a wreck. For a bachelor like me, thinking about getting married was stressful enough. Every stereotype about clueless single guys fit me perfectly. But now the actual event was barreling toward me, and the thought of so many eyes watching us made my stomach clench. I had no idea what would happen when Joan finally met my parents. She had heard plenty of "tank stories," as we called them, but what would happen when she met Dad?

Pastor Mike from our church would be officiating, but we had to rent a larger church for the ceremony and reception. Between our families and the fact that our entire congregation wanted to attend, the guest list swelled to nearly three hundred. The older women at church were especially keen to witness the union, given that most had believed such a thing to be impossible. My hunting trophies outnumbered my dates a hundred to one. The joke around church was that I was so awkward with women that I'd named my dog Buck—and Buck was a female.

Everyone gathered together for the evening rehearsal at the church. Dad and Ann arrived, arm in arm. He was dressed in a fedora and a long overcoat, and when he removed his hat, I could see the top of his head shining. Pastor Mike knew a great deal of my story, so he moved the rehearsal along briskly, interjecting jokes whenever he could to keep the atmosphere light.

"Dad, stand over here," he ordered my father, pretending to have a military air. He pointed, and Dad dutifully followed and came to stand next to me. We looked at each other for a quick second, and what I saw in his eyes surprised me. It was pride. That wasn't a feeling I was used to, but I liked it.

"And Mark, when I tell you that you can kiss the bride tomorrow . . . no sloppy stuff, okay?"

That earned a laugh from everyone.

The rehearsal finished, and everyone caravanned to our house for dinner. Friends had set out a buffet of tacos with all the trimmings, and as people began to line up with their plates, Mom and Dad and Ann met in the living room.

"Hello," Mom began.

"Hello, good to see you," Dad tried.

"And Ann, how are you?"

"Fine, thank you."

"Well . . ."

"Yes, we should probably get our food."

It was cordial but forced. Once the inevitable greeting was out of the way, Mom and Dad were able to stay apart for the rest of the evening. Even as I chatted with what felt like an endless stream of well-wishers, I observed my family. Mom was visibly nervous whenever she had to pass near Dad. Her head pulled back slightly, as if in slow-motion recoil from a fly buzzing near her nose. Jerry was practically a Ping-Pong ball, bouncing back and forth between our two parents, anxious to catch up with both of them. Sheri seemed glued to Mom's side. I saw Dad and Joan in line together at the taco bar, chatting as they piled food on their plates. Joan was everywhere, able to enter and leave conversations in a graceful way that I couldn't.

Mom and Sheri were sitting together when I drifted over to chat. "Mark, how did you find Joan?" Sheri asked.

"At church," I said simply.

"She seems *great*," Sheri said, pulling a face. "*Much* better than I expected from you!"

"Sheri!" Mom commented, but with no real anger. "But I *am* so impressed with Joan, Mark. She'll be a wonderful wife. You made a wise choice."

"I'm so thankful," I agreed.

"I mean, she's educated and articulate and pretty and . . ."

"Okay, Mom! Mark's gonna get a big head!"

Jerry joined us. "Hey, Mark! Finally getting married, huh?" Jerry joked. "Seriously, though, Joan sure seems like a nice girl. Does she know what she's getting into?"

"She's got a pretty good idea, but yeah."

"Well, you got lucky, that's for sure."

Later I found myself near Dad and Ann in the kitchen. I hugged Ann, who smiled at me and said, "We're so happy for you—the Lord bless you, dear."

Then I chose to hug Dad. He seemed quieter, but not because he was weaker. More that he was *calmer*, somehow, on the inside, and I could see it on the outside.

"Congratulations, Son."

"Thanks, Dad."

And that was that. Normal words spoken between father and son. A normal hug to mark the eve of a wedding and the start of a new chapter in life. Dad left with Ann, and I wondered if I was seeing a father so changed as to nearly be a new man.

The night wore on, and one by one everyone headed back to houses and hotel rooms. After the last guest had gone, I helped Joan finish cleaning up. We were putting away the vacuum when Joan told me, "I'm so surprised by your dad."

"In what way?"

"He just seems so soft spoken and mild mannered."

"He didn't use to be."

She smiled but didn't say anything else. When the house—*our* house!—was tidied up, I joked, "See you tomorrow?"

We laughed, shared a quick good-night kiss, and I walked out into the night. The steering wheel in my truck felt like ice. As I drove back to my apartment along dark, silent roads, I shook my head several times. I was getting married, with my family there to witness. Me! It was a strange thing to believe, but the evidence was overwhelming.

•   •   •

My hunting buddy and roommate, Jerry, was my best man, and my brother was my groomsman. The two of them made sure that I looked presentable and that I was standing at the front of the church, all in plenty of time for the ceremony: black tuxedo, white shirt, black bow tie adjusted and readjusted. A friend from church played a classical piece on the piano as Joan came up the aisle on her father's arm, with the bridesmaids and groomsmen following. Joan's best friend, Valerie, was her maid of honor, and her youngest sister, Lucy, was the bridesmaid. The women wore royal blue dresses and matching shoes.

Hands behind my back, I pinched myself. This was really about to happen: Joan was going to marry me. I tried to keep breathing.

Another friend from church sang a song while Joan and I knelt, side by side, to light a unity candle. I held a small taper, as did she, and we touched the two flames together on the wick of a wide, white candle. Once the candle in the middle was glowing brightly, we blew out our own candles.

And then Joan fainted.

I didn't notice until it was too late to catch her. She leaned a little, kept on leaning, and then she appeared to be resting gently on the carpeted floor. Someone raced back with a glass of water, her bridesmaids helped her sit up, and before two minutes had passed, Joan was back on her feet and smiling.

"Let's get to the *greatly shortened* message," quipped the pastor.

After the message, we took communion together, while yet another friend provided special music. She was meant to sing along to a taped instrumental track, but the tape began to play in the middle of the song. Recovering without a hitch, she belted out a shortened version.

Then it was time for our vows. I have no idea what either of us said. All I remember is Joan's smiling face, her eyes shining through the veil, and the taste of her sweet, soft lips when I lifted that veil and kissed, for the first time, my wife.

When the pastor introduced us as Mr. and Mrs. Bouman, Joan gave me a quick grin and a minuscule shrug that seemed to mean, "Oh well, it is what it is—and it's good!"

• • •

The next day we took leave of our families. I hugged Mom and Sheri and Jerry.

"Love you, Mom. Thanks for making the trip. I know it was a long way for you," I said.

"I sure like Joan—she's wonderful. I'm so sorry she fainted," Mom sighed.

"She'll be fine," I assured her.

"Well, we had a wonderful time," she said, before adding, "I'm glad for you, Mark, really glad."

"Good luck, Mark," Sheri said. "We're so glad we could make it."

"I'm glad too. Travel safe."

"Joan's a keeper!" Jerry added.

"I know. I *know!*"

When they left, I said good-bye to Ann and Dad. I hugged Ann, and with tears in her eyes, she hugged me back with the biggest hug her tiny frame could muster. I realized how similar my body was to my father's when he was my age: strong arms, large hands, a barrel chest. I was starting my life as a married man, just as Dad had twenty-five years earlier. He'd screwed that up about as thoroughly as possible, along the way fathering and raising—if you could call it that—me and my siblings. When I was a child, nearly every day had been slow-motion agony of one variety or another.

Now I was married, I had a good job and a nurturing church, and perhaps strangest of all, I woke up feeling hopeful most days. There was no way to slice it and make my life sound like that of Mark Bouman, the weirdo kid from Belmont. *I must have myself confused with someone else. Aren't I the Tank Man's son?*

Dad was standing behind Ann, dressed once again in his overcoat and fedora.

"Seems like you got a good one, Son." He put a hand on Ann's shoulder, and she looked sideways at him and smiled.

Dad nodded at me. I nodded back. I was my own man, and I knew that fear would never again rule my relationship with my father.

Soon Joan and I were alone. Together in our bedroom, we packed suitcases for our honeymoon. The next morning we would drive to Alberta, Canada, after which we'd drive to Wisconsin to celebrate Christmas with Joan's family.

I closed the lid of my suitcase and latched it with a click. It was a far cry from the broken suitcase I'd taken to Bible camp so many years before, the one I'd held together with one of Dad's whipping belts. It was a family suitcase, and Dad had used it too. One Friday, as we were preparing to leave for the Grand River to spend the weekend on the ship, Dad had barked at me, "Take my suitcase to the car. Hurry up!"

I obeyed, lugging it awkwardly through the door and trying to hurry toward Mom's car. Before I reached the car, however, the suitcase burst open, scattering Dad's clothing across the sand. Panic filled my throat. If Dad came outside, he would beat me, but if I went back in and told him what had happened, he'd still beat me. Without much conscious thought, I knelt and quickly stuffed everything back into the suitcase, sand included.

Dad never said a word about his dirty, disheveled clothes. Hadn't that been the reality of my childhood? Punishment could arrive at any moment, yet just as easily never arrive. That uncertainty, that continually possible violence, was what had nearly destroyed me. How had I not simply died on those eleven acres of Michigan sand and scrub, the gradual victim of my father's commands?

It was a mystery, but one I celebrated gratefully. I was about to leave on my *honeymoon*, for goodness' sake, with a woman so far out of my league it was comical. When I was a boy, I never had any inkling of what my future might hold. The only thing that seemed certain was that it would involve suffering.

Now that I was in the Air Force and married to Joan, I had even less of a clue about my future. We were a new family, but how long would it be only the two of us? We were optimistic and free, and we could go anywhere and do anything. Anything! I savored the feeling that there were adventures waiting to be seized and lessons waiting to be learned without an abusive teacher.

Terror, after being my constant companion for most of my life, had vanished. In its place was a new and wonderful sensation—hope—and I knew that *whatever* was waiting around the bend, it would be less like another slap and more like a sunrise.

PART SIX
A MISSION

39

Soon after Joan and I were married, I chose to leave the Air Force and go back to school. I earned a degree in electrical engineering, and we moved to Wisconsin. We had a son, and despite my upbringing, I discovered that I already knew how to love him like crazy.

Then, as soon as I got comfortable, God threw me a curveball. Joan and I were sitting in our small church in central Wisconsin, and our son was downstairs in the nursery. That morning a visiting missionary talked about Cambodia, and he wasn't one to beat around the bush.

"We have an orphanage there that cares for more than one hundred children, and sometimes we need people to come and help out. Maybe some of you will come!"

While I recrossed my legs and continued to listen politely, Joan leaned into me and whispered, "Oh, I would *love* to do that!"

You've gotta be kidding me—you'd *go to Cambodia?* I wondered.

As we stood to sing the closing hymn, Joan whispered again, "We need to talk to that missionary right after the service, since we're interested!"

"We *are*?" I blurted.

But I hadn't ended up with Joan by overthinking things. After the service ended, we chased down the missionary, and our conversation stretched to an hour. One step led to the next, and each step felt right, and less than four months later I was looking out an airplane window at the humid sprawl of Phnom Penh, Cambodia's capital.

We had committed to serve for twelve months, and we spent most of that year working in the capital as well as visiting the orphanage the missionary had spoken about. It was every bit the adventure I'd anticipated, especially when I heard that quiet voice again—the one I'd heard hunting with Zeke—telling me we'd be back after our year was up. Back for good.

. . .

When we returned more than a year later, after our second son was born, we were given shocking news: we were being put in charge of the entire orphanage!

Learning to run the orphanage was incredibly difficult. Our Cambodian staff saved us from countless errors, but we still made plenty. We adjusted to the heat and humidity and rain. We picked up bits and pieces of the language. We got to know the kids. And then, somewhere along the way, we realized we were actually *in charge*. We were responsible for the well-being—spiritual, physical, emotional—of all the kids and our staff of several dozen.

So we put our heads down and went to work. But what surprised me more than anything was how often my childhood kept coming to mind—not to curse me but to bless me.

The entire orphanage used water that came from a single, shallow, hand-dug well. The procedure had always been to fill large plastic canisters with the well water and then insert ceramic filters into the canisters until the water was clean enough to drink and cook with. The filters always needed changing, and the water was never very clean, not to mention the odd frog I'd find perched on a filter and goggling up at me.

The solution was obvious: drill a deep well. Dad's well was two hundred feet deep and hadn't run short of water once during all our years in Belmont. I hired a local guy to drill a well on the orphanage property, and even though it took him and his rickety gasoline engine three weeks to drill sixty feet, that was plenty for our needs. We slapped in a pump, installed water lines to each main building, and never bought another filter.

I had to put out fires—literal fires—in both the dorms and the yard. I didn't have a tank to help me, but I did have Dad's kind of attitude: just get the flames out and get back to more important things.

I had to stare down the barrels of guns. Cambodia was rife with attempted carjackings, robberies, and shakedowns, and we simply had to deal with it. Some part of me understood that God had a way of taking care of us, even in this chaotic mess. I didn't fight back, but I did manage to turn the tables more than once, intimidating the would-be thief into stunned silence as I drove off.

I witnessed every kind of injury and health crisis imaginable, from broken bones and lice to gaping cuts and wasting diseases I didn't even know existed. In Cambodia, knowing the difference between a minor medical situation and something serious enough to warrant a trip to the clinic could mean the difference between life and death.

Sometimes, though, despite all our efforts, we couldn't save a child's life. No one from the Cambodian government ever asked what happened to that boy or girl, and there was never a death certificate or a coroner's report. We simply wrapped the body in a blanket and carried it to a hill nearby, where we would bury the child. We did what we had to do, and then we kept going—the de facto motto of my childhood.

Joan and I were there for the kids, present with them, when no one else was. They weren't just marginalized in that society; they were nothing.

Less than nothing. But trying to meet the needs of 130 kids in a war zone was like trying to keep the sand out of my childhood home. Joan and I joked that on a scale of one to ten, with ten the most difficult, running the orphanage was a twelve. Yet in spite of such difficulty—or perhaps because we stuck by the children in the midst of the difficulty, even to death—a bond formed between all of us. Joan was affectionately called *Mommy*, and I was given a new name as well. One that would have made precisely zero sense to me when I was a child, even as I began to wonder if my childhood was what had made the new name possible.

They called me *Papa*.

40

"MARK, WHAT ARE YOU doing right now?" The voice on the phone was Bill, a missionary living in Phnom Penh. Joan and I and our two boys were hours away at the orphanage in Sihanoukville, by the Gulf of Thailand.

"Whatever you do, Mark, do *not* come to Phnom Penh." Bill's voice was shaky. "There's scattered fighting here. We've got a curfew in place. Tanks are rolling in the streets, and the fighting is moving from the outskirts toward the city center. We think they're heading for the airport. This might escalate into something big."

"Something big" was code for civil war.

Bill's warning didn't worry me much, however. Joan and I had only been in charge at the orphanage for a year, but we had made it through plenty of tense situations already, and I didn't think a few tanks up in the capital would be of any concern to us.

What *did* worry me were the kids and staff I was responsible for. No matter what happened, I needed to keep them safe. And the best way to do that was to stay put. So it was easy to reassure Bill. "No problem, we're not going *anywhere*."

Bill's call confirmed local gossip, but we'd heard similar things before. The Cambodian people had just endured twenty years of bloodshed and upheaval. Mistrust was a way of life, and violence was, for many, the natural response to conflict. Even in peaceful situations, like during the New Year celebration, we'd stand outside and watch tracer bullets light the sky from all directions. It seemed as if owning an automatic weapon—indestructible AK-47s, mostly—was a requirement for being a citizen.

Occupied as I was with the orphanage, I didn't give Bill's warning any more thought.

•   •   •

"Mark, this thing is escalating." It was Bill again, less than a day later. "The airport was destroyed by the tank battle that took place here yesterday. The markets and banks are all shut down. Food is disappearing, and if you have any money in the bank, you can forget that—whatever cash you've got, make sure you hang on to it. All commercial flights in and out of Cambodia have stopped. We've been declared a war zone. There are a few thousand foreigners trapped right now with no way to get out. I heard Thailand and other nearby countries are going to evacuate their embassy personnel tomorrow. They're bringing in military transport aircraft to get them out."

"What about our embassy?" I asked.

"They're saying you have to find your own way out. They don't want to make a big scene by evacuating all the Americans. The embassy rented the large ballroom at the Cambodiana hotel here in the city. We've sent some of our people to the evacuation center there—might be safer. One of our missionaries got caught in a firefight. She couldn't get out of her house, the fighting was so bad. She's a wreck and wants to go home right now, but I don't know how that's going to happen. Most of the others want to stay. You might want to look into some other means to get out of the country just in case. Do *not* try to drive to Phnom Penh. The road's been cut, and soldiers are robbing people in broad daylight—shooting drivers and stealing the cars. There's looting everywhere."

"Don't worry! I have no intention of moving."

"It's crazy here, man—fighting's spreading around the city, and fires are burning from the artillery and even *tank* blasts. You should have heard the shells screaming overhead last night."

I couldn't help picturing the tanks—probably Soviet-era T-55s. "We'll stay here at the orphanage until this thing blows over," I managed.

"Mark, this might blow *into* Sihanoukville before this is over."

I hung up in disbelief and drove along my usual route to the orphanage.

I heard the news as soon as I pulled into the orphanage: troops were on their way from the capital. I fought the temptation to panic, gulping air through pursed lips. If the fighting came to us, no part of the country would be safe. Our only chance was to leave, or risk getting caught in the cross fire.

But how could I run at the first sign of trouble? And what was the best way to protect my family and staff?

This can't be happening, I thought over and over, as if on the thousandth repetition the chaos would magically resolve itself. A feeling of helplessness swept over me, something I had not experienced so powerfully since my youth. It was that all-too-familiar burst of hysteria I felt when I saw Dad bearing down on me, belt in hand. My mouth was cotton.

It was somewhere inside that terror that I found comfort. I had spent my entire childhood living with fear. Uncertainty was my air and water. And here I was, still alive. Even happy, at least most days. *I've been through this before,* I told myself. And it was that truth that removed the paralysis from my mind and muscles. I knew I was capable of doing *something,* even if I didn't yet know what. Like Dad had done too many times to count, I'd find a way to make this work.

• • •

I received another phone call, this time from Ron, the regional director of our mission organization. We had some American college students helping at the orphanage for the summer, and Ron made it clear that we needed to get them out of Cambodia.

"Like, *yesterday*," he emphasized.

I stood, frozen, in the quad between our buildings at the orphanage. I'd worked on all the structures surrounding me—painting, plumbing, and wiring, not to mention counseling, praying, and crying—from the chicken coop all the way to the dormitory. What was I about to do?

The children knew something was happening. They came outside quietly, looking at me and waiting. None of the older kids wanted to approach me to ask the question that was on all their minds, and none of the younger kids could form the question—except one small girl, who approached me and tugged on the side of my pants. "Papa," she asked, "are you leaving us?"

What could I say? I loved her—truly, I did—but would she have any reason to believe that when I fled?

"I have to take our helpers to Thailand," I said, "but I'll come back as soon as I drop them off."

She walked away, and I couldn't tell whether she believed me. Part of my heart went with her.

Just then Joan drove through the orphanage gates, braked to a stop, and waved me over to the driver's window. "Mark, no American can stay behind."

"I know; I'm working on it."

"But Mark . . . we all have to leave—and stay out. Even you."

• • •

This news was devastating. Yet despite the rip in my heart, I had to focus on the task at hand: we Americans needed to leave—immediately.

I collected the college students and my family. "Let's go!" I yelled.

"But what are we going to *do*?" someone asked.

"I don't know," I replied. "But we're getting out of here. Now!"

It was just like Dad had often said: "There are leaders, and there are followers. Most people can't think for themselves—they're just followers, waiting to be told what to do."

What Dad hadn't mentioned was that there was a good chance the leader everyone was following would be scared witless and have absolutely no idea what to do next.

We piled into the van, I floored it, and despite Bill's warning, we took the road to the capital. An hour out of town we reached the first roadblock. About a dozen soldiers were covering the road, some standing directly on the asphalt and some in flanking positions along the shoulders. All were heavily armed and staring at our van as we approached. I slowed down and prepared to stop. I had no idea what was about to happen or what we should do.

The lead soldier stepped forward and pulled a pistol from his belt, which he cocked and pointed at me. The knots in my stomach suddenly became unsolvable tangles.

The van bounced to a stop. I rolled down the window. Everyone inside was quiet. I could see the soldier walking toward me, still pointing his pistol at my head. It was a cheap Chinese Type 54, but I knew it could still shoot me plenty dead.

A thought flew into my mind: *I'm going to act like a clueless tourist.* Crazy. Stupid. Maybe even suicidal. I can't explain why I chose to do what I did. Maybe it had something to do with the chaos of my childhood—with Dad's modus operandi of *it doesn't have to be pretty as long as it works.*

I hoped against hope that *this* would work. My heart was pounding so hard I thought it was going to break out of my chest. The soldier reached my window and stopped. I could see down the barrel of his pistol, and behind that I could see his eyes, hostile and stony.

I smiled a cheeky smile, waved, chirped out a singsong "Hello," put the van in gear, and pulled away.

The other soldiers who had been on the road had already moved to the side, expecting their leader's pistol would be a sufficient roadblock. The leader realized we were leaving, but he stood rooted in the road, immobile and still clutching his pistol. He had an expression on his face that seemed to say, "Wait! You haven't paid me yet!"

In seconds we were clear. I looked back over my shoulder, and I could clearly see the soldier, still standing in the middle of the road, still holding his pistol extended. *He must be as confused as I am*, I thought. Neither of us knew what had just happened. All I knew was we were driving away, safe for the moment and closer to our goal.

• • •

That scene repeated itself twice more on the road to Phnom Penh. Both times I played the part of the clueless tourist, smiling, waving, and driving away despite the gun pointed at my head. Both times stunned soldiers simply watched us leave.

When we finally entered the capital, the scene was straight out of a disaster movie. Streams of people were becoming rivers, all flowing out of the city as fast as their legs could carry them. Women hugged children to their chests, and men carried baskets and satchels and pushed carts. Children lugged whatever their small arms could hold. Kitchen utensils, pots and pans, and bundles of food were balanced precariously atop heads. Bikes were loaded down with makeshift saddlebags. The river of humanity was flowing away from the fighting, away from the smoke and shelling, like water flowing downhill.

And we were headed upstream as fast as we could drive, desperate to reach the airport.

The stench from dozens of fires burned our nostrils. Occasionally we cringed as an armored personnel carrier or a tank rumbled past, driving toward Sihanoukville. Some looked ready for battle while others moved slowly, piled high with loot. Televisions, motorcycles, refrigerators, sewing machines, and other stolen goods were stacked to overflowing on top of instruments of destruction, and a sudden memory flashed in my mind of Dad driving his tank away from the wrecked farmhouse, the tank's deck and turret absolutely buried in bricks. Smoldering cars and tanks clogged the road, and we had to steer around them like a skier avoiding trees. Every few blocks we passed bodies sprawled on the pavement, gruesome reminders of what was taking place.

The roadside trees had been stripped of their foliage by tank and mortar blasts. Gas stations were in shambles, having long since been robbed and left in ruins. Even the pumps had been stolen. The main hospital had a hole in its side that looked as if a tank had simply driven through. If we passed a single intact window, I never saw it. Here was the real-life version of Dad's war games, and it was anything but a game.

The international airport was just as bad. A hole the size of a Volkswagen Beetle had been blown in one terminal wall from a tank round, and many other walls had been reduced to rubble. A dozen Cambodian police officers stood guard in front of the entrance, brandishing batons and sporting machine guns slung over their shoulders. Locals were threatened or beaten if they dared approach the airport entrance.

Behind the police line, hundreds of foreigners milled about in the parking lot, since the inside of the terminal building was almost completely destroyed. The airport was inoperative, and the foreigners were stuck between their hope of flying away and the utter chaos surrounding them in the city. The tarmac was deserted. No parked planes. No takeoffs or landings. Just glass, rubble, and the acrid stink—so familiar, so common from my childhood—of smoke and gunpowder.

Now what?

A van full of Americans pulling up didn't go unnoticed. The police lines parted, and we drove into what was left of the main terminal.

After the eerie approach through the city streets leading to the airport, things began to happen quickly. The word was that someone had chartered a jet from Thailand, and it was landing in twenty minutes.

Bill emerged from the crowd. "Mark, you're going to pay to get our personnel out of the country," he said sternly. "Oh, and you're paying to get a few other people out of here too. Hope you don't mind." Bill nodded toward a group of anxious Westerners, folks I'd never seen before. I tried to smile at them.

"Pay that official over there," Bill commanded. "They aren't taking credit cards, traveler's checks, or even Cambodian money—it's American greenbacks or nothing, and you've got what they want, right?"

Surprisingly, I did. I had taken money out of the bank the previous week to pay for structural repairs at the orphanage, but Joan convinced me to hold on to the cash for a few days, since the repairs were not urgent. Now, in a desperate situation at the airport, I was glad for my wife's foresight.

Sitting at a folding table on the side of the tarmac, in plastic lawn chairs, were two Cambodian airport officials. I approached and unfolded a thick wad of hundreds. The men smiled. Amazingly, the customs officer still demanded that I pay a seven-dollar "airport usage fee" for each person planning to leave. I glanced at the ruins all around me and thought, *What airport?*

Thirty minutes later we heard the whine of a descending jet. The L-1011 dropped out of the sky, and the minute it taxied to a stop in a cloud of tire rubber, the crew dropped the door. The engines were still racing as we jogged across the runway. Joan led our boys, each by one hand, toward the plane. I was near the back of the pack, trying to count heads and make sure all the people I was responsible for were in front of me. Not that they'd be anywhere else.

The engines were deafening. Everyone tossed their bags into a pile below plane as they leaped up the stairs. I scanned the tarmac, found it clear, and sprinted up the stairs as well. No seat assignments, claim tickets, safety checks—this was barely contained panic. The crew slammed the door closed behind me, and minutes later the pilot goosed the throttles and we leaped down the runway. The moment the tires left the runway, the entire plane erupted in cheers. "Yes!" "We're outta here!" "All right!" "Hallelujah!" We had made it. Against all odds, we had made it, and exuberant shouts filled the airplane.

But I felt sick. I stared out the window as we climbed into the sky. I could see columns of smoke rising from the capital. I couldn't see Sihanoukville with my eyes, but I could picture it in my mind. *What have I done, God? I just left an entire orphanage full of children in a war zone. Kids I promised to take care of.*

I closed my eyes. *What have I done?*

41

AFTER WE LANDED safely in Thailand, everyone who was not a career missionary was sent home to the States on the next available flight.

The rest of us found a hotel in Bangkok, and our leadership team flew in from the States, along with several trauma counselors. I hoped the counselors were getting overtime pay.

Most of us wanted to get back into Cambodia right away, but that was impossible. No airline was willing to risk flying into Cambodia. The airlines honestly didn't know if they would be able to refuel or take off again, and in any case no insurance company would insure a plane in a war zone. We could have taken a boat, but if the airlines weren't going to risk landing, it probably wasn't safe enough for us to return a different way either. Every day we tried to get news about what was happening in Cambodia, and every day we were frustrated. Thai television, international newspapers, people we chatted with at cafés—no one seemed to know what was going on. CNN did little more than loop the same footage of fires burning throughout the city.

I second-guessed myself constantly. What would have happened if I had stayed? What was going on at the orphanage? Were the children safe? Phrases I had read about the Khmer Rouge kept surfacing in my mind. No foreigners had been allowed back into Cambodia for thirteen years after that regime had taken over. Nearly a quarter of the population had been starved or murdered.

The counselors sat us in a circle, and then one of them began.

"Who would like to share what happened to you?" he asked.

We waited for someone to start. And waited. Finally, one young woman raised her hand and began to tearfully recall what she had experienced. I listened halfheartedly. The only thing that haunted me was leaving the kids back in Cambodia, and that wasn't anything the counselor could help me with.

My mind wandered. Was there anything I could have done differently? Our escape had been pure chaos—nothing could have prepared me for it. I had done the best I could, but had it been enough?

The woman's account was still unfolding. "And *then* I saw a man with a gun. Some kind of long gun. He was shooting as he was running down the road, right in front of me."

"What were you thinking?" the counselor asked.

"I was so scared. I've never seen anything like that in my life! The gun would have terrified me anyway, but then there were tanks going by, and soldiers sitting on top of them, and more and more guns." She brought her hands up to her face, her chin quivering, then buried her face in her hands and sobbed. "I just can't go back there! I wasn't made for this!"

The counselor thanked the woman for sharing, and two other women went over to the crying woman and placed their arms around her shaking shoulders.

I tried to be sympathetic, but it was difficult. *What's so scary about a bunch of guys with guns? I've seen that since I was a kid. And tanks aren't scary—my dad had one.*

As the next missionary shared, my mind cataloged my childhood.

Pistols, rifles, antitank guns, simulated knife fights, the tank, the ship, the dynamite—all united by a near-constant sense of chaos and fear. I still had shrapnel in my ankle!

That's when the blinders fell from my eyes. Maybe the other missionaries hadn't been prepared for what happened to them, but God *had* prepared me. Specifically, for that time and that place. Words from the biblical story of Joseph sprang into my mind.

"You intended to harm me, but God intended it for good."

Suddenly I saw it. God had used the evil of my youth to prepare me for my time in Cambodia.

42

Two weeks later I got a call from San, my right-hand man at the orphanage.

"Papa, soldiers came to the orphanage today. They spoke very rough to me. They told me they're going to come back. They told me if there is a foreigner here taking care of this place, they will leave us alone, but if not, they will take away every valuable thing. Papa, can you please come back? Just to show your face and let them know you are still looking out for us? If you do, they will leave us alone. If you do not come back, they are going to take everything from us. I'm afraid something bad will happen."

The pause stabbed my soul.

"Can you please come back?"

I *had* to get back. My friend was right. I wasn't my father, but I was Papa, and the kids needed me.

I called our regional director, Ron, and explained the situation.

I couldn't wait for things to "get better" inside Cambodia. "Ron, I have to go back. Now."

"You can go back," he relented, "but you have to go alone. It's still too dangerous for anyone else to go with you."

My earlier epiphany returned: *I have been prepared specifically for this time in Cambodia. This is going to work. Somehow it is going to work.*

The next day I said good-bye to my family, then went to the airport in Bangkok. A few Thai airlines had reopened flights into Cambodia the day before. Foreign journalists lined up to fly there and report on what was happening, and they were willing to pay a premium.

When I arrived at the airport, I found myself caught in a small mob of people who were pleading with an airline attendant for a seat on the next available flight into Cambodia. I stood there for a minute, listening. Person after person asked, "When will a seat be available?" The attendant seemed flustered. She told them she was sorry, that no seats would be available until later. Without waiting to hear her finish, I wandered over to another desk that had no one waiting in front of it. I politely asked if there were any seats available on the next flight into Cambodia.

"Let me check," the attendant said. After a couple of minutes she looked up at me. "Yes, there is a seat available. May I have your passport?"

I handed her my passport, hardly able to believe what I was hearing. I glanced back at the crowd still surrounding the adjacent counter, wondering by what miracle I got a seat while others were being turned away. As soon as I had my ticket in hand, I slipped past the mob.

Less than two hours later, the wheels of my plane smacked the tarmac at Phnom Penh.

•   •   •

The road south to the orphanage was nearly deserted. All that remained of the wrecked tanks and vehicles were charred spots on the pavement. Dark stains I knew to be blood were still visible. Gas stations were silent, and only the regularly spaced bolts testified to the pumps that had once been mounted there. Whole blocks of factories in what used to be a thriving garment industry were empty. House after house was destroyed, with bricks strewn about from shattered walls, a testament to the errant tank rounds that had blown fragments in every direction. Shards of glass gleamed across the dirt. The houses looked exactly like my childhood house after the tornado leveled it.

One thought filled my mind. *Get to the orphanage before the soldiers do.* I repeated it at every mile, as if saying it enough times would make it come true. *Get there before the soldiers. Get there before the soldiers.*

Three hours later I pulled up to the orphanage gate. Everything on the grounds seemed silent and deserted. A wave of fear swept over me. Normally the orphanage was bustling with life as kids ran across the grass or lined up to choose sides for soccer.

The gates were bolted. Something terrible must have happened. I climbed out and walked along the sidewalk that led to the main building. My mind was reeling. *Where is everyone? What happened? Am I too late?*

I stood in the middle of the compound, motionless. There wasn't a single sign of life.

A piercing scream set my spine tingling.

"Papa!"

Then longer. "Paaapaaa!"

Suddenly a great chorus of shouts rose up around me, coming from everywhere at once.

"Papa, Papa, Papa!"

The kids had been hiding inside the buildings, cowering in fear. Now their shouts of disbelief and relief announced them as they streamed out from all sides, streaking toward me across the grass like fireworks.

Boys and girls leaped and cavorted, shouting as they ran and spun in circles, as if words were insufficient and only their small bodies could express their overflowing happiness. Some ran so fast they slammed into me while trying to hug me, and soon they were in my arms, too many to count, surrounding me, and we clung to each other in a tangle of happiness.

A father to the fatherless, prepared to care for these children by the apathy and evil of my own childhood. I was my dad, but changed— turned inside out by grace and granted a chance to redeem the past. I was Papa.

"You're back! You came back!"

"Papa, you're back, like you promised!"

"We didn't think you'd come back, Papa, but you did!"

Joy was in flood, and I was drowning in it. Every word healed me. Every word left me wanting more.

EPILOGUE

As an orphanage director in Cambodia, speaking at churches back in the States was part of my job description. It was a good way to raise funds for everything the orphans needed, from job training to English classes to hot meals to hospital and funeral services. I never needed notes: after living side by side with the staff and kids for years, I had seen God do so many amazing things that I could fill an entire book. I would simply speak from my heart, telling the congregation first about my own childhood and then about the orphanage.

Telling my story with Dad in the audience was never part of the plan.

When it came to choosing churches, I avoided my old neighborhood. Speaking to strangers in Ohio or North Carolina, I could almost pretend I was talking about someone else, but I knew that wouldn't be possible if I ever spoke near where I'd grown up.

Yet on one fund-raising trip to the States, for some unfathomable reason, I felt compelled to call a church that had been started a few years earlier just down the road from Blakely Drive. When I told the pastor over the phone about what God had done in my life, he agreed to let me speak. And then he asked, "Why don't you invite your dad to the service?"

Sure, why not? Dad and Ann lived nearby, and he had never heard me speak at a church before. This time I would simply stick to stories about what God had done in Cambodia. There was no need to bring my childhood into the picture.

As soon as I hung up with the pastor, I dialed my father's number. "Hey, Dad, I'm going to be speaking about Cambodia at a church near you. Would you like to come?"

"Sure, Son. Which church?"

•　　•　　•

Two days after I invited Dad to the service, the pastor called me back. "Mark, I know you said you would speak about Cambodia. And that's great! But Mark, I believe God wants you to share your *testimony* at that service."

My heart sank. I knew exactly what he meant by that word. *Testimony.* The things I had witnessed. My story. My *entire* story.

"Mark? Mark, are you there?"

"How can I do that?" I managed. "My *dad* is going to be there."

"I really believe that's what God wants you to do, Mark. There's a reason for this."

"I don't know," I said, stalling. "I already invited my father to the service, and he said he was looking forward to hearing me speak. I can't undo that, can I?"

"Don't undo anything—just have him come like you've already planned, and then plan on sharing your testimony."

I hung up the phone with a shaking hand. *How am I going to get myself out of* this *mess?* I was trapped. The pastor's words continued to race through my mind. There was simply no way I could describe my childhood with my father in the same room. And there was no way I could share my testimony without describing my childhood. Hardest of all, something in my heart told me the pastor was right: I *did* need to share the whole story.

I tried to look on the bright side. Maybe I would get violently sick on Sunday morning.

•　•　•

The next few days were agony. I searched every corner of my brain for a way to uninvite Dad, but every idea was worse than the last. Finally, desperate for help, I reached out to a friend.

"Why don't you call your dad?"

That thought had never occurred to me. I screwed up my courage and dialed Dad's number.

"Dad, the service you're coming to . . . well, I was going to talk all about Cambodia. Look, I don't really know how to say this, but the pastor wants me to share my life story at that service."

There was a pause on the other end. I took a breath and kept talking. "I would never do it to make you look bad—I just want to tell people what God has done. But I won't do it without your permission."

The pause stretched.

"That's okay, Son. Go ahead. You can do it."

I was scarcely able to believe his words. Never in my memory had my father put himself in my hands. I had always been the one who was powerless, but now he had chosen to turn the tables.

I knew it was largely a testament to Ann. She had kept me posted on how Dad was doing over the years, since he wasn't one to speak much about himself anymore. The shape of their relationship had surprised both of them, from start to finish. One time she recalled, with equal parts surprise and laughter in her voice, one of their first dates, just after Dad emerged from his mother's basement.

"I pointed out a full moon to him, Mark, rising above the trees, and he stared at it for a minute. And do you know what he said?"

"I could probably guess," I joked.

"He said, 'Yep, that's a great bomber's moon for sure!'"

Dad had always spent whatever money he had. Whether it was ten dollars or a thousand dollars, he would come across something he needed to buy, right then, before some other guy got it first. Ann, to whom every nickel was absolutely precious, put a stop to that right away.

But there had been deeper issues. Ann believed she had made it this far because of God's continued provision, and she wasn't about to turn her back on that, so she laid down the law to Dad: "If we're going to be together, you will start serving the Lord!"

At first she thought it was her job to make sure that happened. It took many long and painful years for Ann to admit that she couldn't transform Dad by herself. But since she still loved him and still believed he could change, she looked to her one remaining hope: God.

God answered by starting to wear down my once-dauntless father. He had no kids around on whom to focus his authoritarian tendencies, and Ann refused to be controlled by him. She didn't scream back at him or hit him. She didn't curse him or attack him in quieter ways. She simply went on living her life—canning, working, praying, sewing, and believing that Dad was headed in a direction he couldn't yet see. He began to suffer through various health problems, from back pain to failing eyesight to the early stages of Parkinson's, and consequently he was forced to do something he had never done before: rely on someone who loved him for everyday help.

It wasn't easy. It wasn't immediate. It wasn't without regression and tears. But everything good that happened to Dad after his divorce happened through Ann.

Once, years before, Joan and I had gone to a flea market with Ann and Dad. It was a bright, sunny day, and Dad wanted to protect himself from getting sunburned, so he donned one of those caps with an umbrella stuck to the top. He brought along his video camera, too, which was just slightly different from the average model. Since changing dead batteries annoyed him—he could take hours of footage of engines and parts and vehicles—he'd yanked out the original battery and soldered in some long wires that he ran down to a fanny pack. Inside the fanny pack was an entire motorcycle battery.

"He's all function and no form," Ann griped to Joan and me when Dad shuffled off to take more video. But there wasn't any venom in her voice. And the second she saw him turning to walk back toward us, a smile wrinkled the corners of her eyes.

•   •   •

The sound of the three-part *amen* faded, and in the silence that followed I glanced again at the program in my hands. Nothing else was listed that would shield me from what was about to happen. I tried to swallow. I tried to pray, but all I could manage was a kind of wordless, terrified sigh.

The pastor, a neat-looking man in a dark suit, stepped to the pulpit and began his introduction. "Friends, it's my great honor and privilege to introduce our speaker today. Mark Bouman grew up in these parts, and some of you may remember him. He's been living somewhere very different from Michigan for quite a while, though."

The pastor paused, touching each pew with his gaze.

"For the last decade-plus, Mark and his lovely wife, Joan—" he smiled and inclined his head toward Joan, who sat beside me—"have made a home for themselves far, far from here, all the way across the world in the city of—let's see—See-han-ook-ville, Cambodia. Did I pronounce that right, Mark?"

I managed a nod. It was one of the better pronunciations I had heard.

"Just think of that, friends—Cam*bo*dia! That's a long way from here, but Mark went there for a very good reason: to be a father to more than a hundred orphans and to share the love of Jesus with each and every one of them. Mark's going to speak to us about the ministry he directs, and I'm sure his words are going to bless you."

I stood, thinking the pastor was finished, but he wasn't. Not quite.

"Oh, and I'd also like to mention that Mark's father was able to join us today." The pastor gestured toward Dad, who was sitting next to Ann at the back of the church. I heard more than a few murmurs of recognition in the audience behind me—some of the members remembered his exploits, no doubt—and another small sigh escaped my lips. The pastor was beaming at my father from the pulpit, and all across the sanctuary pews creaked and groaned as people turned to look at him. I turned as well.

Dad was in his late fifties but looked ten years older. What little remained of his white hair was combed neatly across the top of his head. He seemed uncomfortable in his gray polyester suit. His hands were folded in his lap, out of sight, but I knew that his palms would be rough and marked with grease, his fingernails each ending in an arc of dirt. His face was expressionless.

"Mark," the pastor said to me, "thank you for sharing with us this morning." With that he sat down in a chair behind the pulpit.

The congregation applauded. Each person there assumed the obvious narrative: a proud father watching his son preach.

Except that for the next hour, I told them a different story.

I tried to tell everyone sitting in that church as much of the truth as I could. I spoke about firing guns, driving the tank, living on the ship, and Dad blowing up a stump with dynamite. I recalled the feeling of Dad's hand and Dad's belt. I stalked again through the Grand River in search of turtles and heard Zeke's eager barking. I revisited Cambodia, witnessing orphans surprised by hope and finding a future they had never dared to dream of. With my father sitting not fifty feet from me, I spoke my way inside my own past. I lived each event as it emerged from my lips and relived it as I watched the crowd absorb what I was sharing.

Finally, I realized my stories were finished. No one moved. I searched inside for what to say next, and I found the words already waiting for me.

"I'm not telling you these things to make someone in my family look bad. I just want you to know what God can do. If God can use me, then God can use anyone."

You intended to harm me, but God intended it for good.

Our ramshackle home, our poverty, our good-enough-if-it-works existence, our injuries, our fights, our familiarity with chaos—even our abject fear and shame and the seemingly bottomless well of pain from which Dad constantly supplied us—hadn't *all* of that been used for good? Those things weren't good in and of themselves. Many *were* evil. Rather, my childhood had *become* good. It had been intended for evil but *transformed* into good. Transformed by God, whose reservoir of grace made my father's well look like a child's bucket.

I had become who I needed to become for the saving of many lives—not the least of which was my own. Dad had been the unwitting agent of my remaking, from the boy I was into a father with his own two sons and into Papa for the children at the orphanage.

I looked at Dad. He seemed frozen in the back row. He was too far away for me to read any nuances in his expression. The silence felt like it wanted to stretch forever, and part of me wanted to let it. But I had more to say. I raised my arm and pointed directly at him.

"I want you to know something, Dad. For all that happened, you're still my dad, and I still love you."

I didn't say that because I was speaking in a church or because I was trying to create a fairy-tale ending to my life. I said it because it was true. In a way that made no sense apart from grace, it was true. I loved my father.

I still couldn't read his expression, but I could see the overhead lights glinting off the tears on his cheeks, as I knew they were from mine.

I sensed the pastor was at my side. When had he arrived? How long had I been standing there looking at my father? I stepped away from the microphone, spent.

Then the pastor stepped forward and called my father to the front.

The only sound in the sanctuary came from crying parishioners and perhaps from the hammering of my own heart beating in my temples. Dad stood and began to walk toward me. He moved slowly, pressed down perhaps by the weight of his life. I knew the feeling, and I had walked a similar aisle back in Montana—an aisle that introduced me to Jesus.

When Dad reached the front, the pastor motioned for him to stand beside me.

"I'm going to pray that God brings healing to both your lives."

Dad and I both nodded, unable to speak. The pastor put his hands on us and prayed. I can't remember what he said. No words could break through the emotions overpowering me. I had trouble listening. I couldn't open my eyes. But one sentence punched through my heart like a slug through steel.

"God, restore their relationship."

Those four words changed me.

I had forgiven my father privately, or I thought I had. My father had shamed me publicly, however, more times than could be counted. And there was something about standing beside him in public now that rebuilt our relationship. The pastor's prayer showed me that on the other side of forgiveness, friendship was possible.

It was as if my father and I had been sitting across a table from each other, civil but distant. Between us was a box, and inside the box was something of which we both were terrified. Our fear of what was in the box prevented us from reconciling. Both of us were guarding a part of ourselves. The pastor's words opened the lid on the box, and I discovered what was inside.

Nothing. The box was empty.

It *had* held things in the past. But now, as I looked into it, I found that each one had disappeared.

When the pastor said, "Amen," Dad turned and looked at me. He was still crying.

"Mark," he said, leaning his head toward mine, "I'm so proud of you. I pray for you every day. And I love you."

A boy, even when he is a man, longs for his father's approval and love. Those were the greatest words I had ever heard my dad speak, and I will hear them in my heart until I die.

• • •

A few months later, I visited Dad at his home. He sat on the edge of his bed, staring at the floor.

"How's it going, Dad?" I asked, sitting beside him.

"Mark, I think every day about the things I've done and the people I've hurt."

"Dad, I've forgiven you. You know, we'll have all of eternity to remember the good things God has done."

Dad buried his face in his hands and sobbed like a boy. I wrapped my arms around him, and together we cried, father and son.

While he wept, I told him, "Dad, for all that's happened, you're still my hero."

It was okay. Everything had become okay. I loved my dad. And no matter what had happened to me, I was—and always will be—the Tank Man's son.

ACKNOWLEDGMENTS

THANK YOU TO the many people from the small church in Great Falls, Montana, who invested in me when I was a young believer. You took me in, gave me hope, and allowed me to grow, despite my many character flaws. You treated me like a son.

Thank you, Joan. You took a risk and married me while I was still a little rough around the edges. You are God's gift to me and a fulfillment of his promise.

To Bob Houlihan, you encouraged and mentored me. Thank you for seeing in me what could be rather than what was.

To my brother, Jerry, thank you. We share a bond that is only understood by those who have experienced what we have. I love you, bro.

In memory of Sheri, my sister and friend. There is no cancer in heaven, and I look forward to our reunion there. I miss you, sis.

Thank you to Don Jacobson for being a terrific agent and a godly example. You believed in me and my story, and you helped this book become a reality.

To David Jacobsen, thank you. Your incredible, God-given talent made this book possible. Your insight and gift of writing made it seem as if you had experienced my life with me.

Thank you to Carol Traver for your wisdom and patience in sorting through my endless crazy stories. It was a joy working with you. And thank you to Jonathan Schindler and the entire Tyndale team for your expert guidance and confidence in me.

Most of all, thank you to Jesus Christ, my Lord and Savior. This book is your story in me.